For Jill

Prologue

Patna in the Bengal Presidency, India 1769.

THE small woman, her head covered with a black calico scarf made from scraps collected at the nearby mill, timidly approached the two sepoys guarding the military encampment on the bank of the river Ganga. She politely asked to speak with the white sahib known as Baker. They smiled at her request but did not respond, so she spoke to them again, now begging to see the European.

"He has taken my boy," she cried. "He is too young to fight. He is needed at home. His father is dead and his elder brother has gone. Who is to support me when I get older? Please sahib, I beg you let me see the Baker."

The two men looked again and this time took sympathy. To lose the only man in your family, no matter how young, was a serious matter.

"Who are you woman?" one of the sepoys asked.

"I am the wife of Mahomet, who served as subadar to the Raja Shitab Rai. My husband was cruelly murdered a short while ago when collecting taxes from the brothers Boudmal and Corexin. Yet he was a courageous man, and would not see his wife distressed so. My son must respect his father and stay with his mother. I must tell the Baker this."

The strength of her pleading played on the minds of the sepoys, and finally one agreed to take the woman before the man she requested: Godfrey Evan Baker, the twenty-year-old Irishman who was the quartermaster of the 3rd European Regiment of the Bengal Army. As they walked through the camp the fragile woman cowered from the bright military uniforms and fierce horses, drawing her scarf across her face to form a protective veil from the swirling dust and eyes of the men. The sepoy halted before a large tent, indicated for the woman to stay where she was, and went inside. She kept her eyes firmly on the ground, fearful of looking to either the left or right, and waited an uncomfortable ten minutes for the sepoy to re-appear and summon her inside.

She was confronted with the smell of sweat and spices. She saw scores of wooden boxes piled high to one side of the tent while to the other was a small wooden desk behind which sat a young white man with sandy blonde hair and wearing a red tunic. His black hat sat on the desk next to some papers and behind him stood another sepoy. He looked up at the woman who immediately cast her eyes down. Then he spoke and the sepoy behind him translated his words.

"You are the boy Mahomet's mother?" the sepoy asked and she nodded. "What is it that you want?"

Again she told her story, pleading now with the young white sahib while the sepoy translated into English. Baker listened then spoke once more, and the woman looked up expectantly at the translator.

"Your son is under the protection of the sahib," he began, "just as his brother is under the protection of Captain Adams. Both sahibs act in gratitude of the memory of their honoured father. You are entitled to live on the property of your late husband, why then do you need your son for support?"

When she heard these words she realised the officer was not going to release her son from his service so began to cry, and then to wail, beating her chest and causing a great commotion within the confines of the tent, to the evident embarrassment of Quartermaster Baker. Calming herself, from the confines of her dress she took out 400 rupees and placed it on the table, much to the surprise of the Irishman. It was a handsome gift from a desperate woman, and it swayed him to agree to speak with her son. She was instructed to depart and wait at home. He left the money untouched on the table.

It took some time to find the boy and bring him before his master. In the months since he had first been brought to the attention of Mr Baker, young Mahomet had learnt the basics of the English language and had impressed with his willingness to work. After the shock of losing his father, the boy felt comfortable and secure within the confines of the army camp, and looked to the sahib as more than just a master but also as a teacher. So he was shocked to learn of his mother's attendance earlier in the day, and more so when Mr Baker made it clear that he was prepared to return him to his mother if that was her wish.

"No sahib, please do not say so," the boy implored, but Baker was unsure. He gave the 400 rupees to the boy and told him to return them to his mother, and to make peace with her if he could. Only if the boy could ease her distress could he return to the camp.

Riding in Baker's personal palanquin, which was borne by four domestic staff along the sun-baked road from the camp to the town, the boy seethed at his mother's actions. How could she do this to him, when she had allowed his brother to leave so easily? The intricately carved boxed litter made its way towards the palace of the Raja Sataproy, behind which Mahomet's mother lived in a small house. When she saw him enter the house her heart leapt with joy – the bribe had worked and the sahib had sent him back. She was confused, therefore, when as she stood to embrace her younger son he held out the money in his hand, his face frozen with anger.

"What is this?" she asked, feigning any knowledge of the money.

"Sahib Baker returns your money and says I am not for sale," he coldly replied.

She gasped and placed her hands to her heart.

"No!" she cried, "no! You are my son."

She went to embrace him again but her eleven-year-old stood back.

"Take your money mother and let me go."

Tears began to roll down her cheeks as she saw all her efforts to keep her remaining child falter. But she was not yet prepared for a life of loneliness.

"No my son, return it to the sahib. He shall not take you from me. Your father would not wish it so. Would you disrespect him?"

This angered the boy more, who still held out the rupees. "I am going because I honour my father. My brother and I are serving his name faithfully. It is you who show disrespect by being so selfish." Yet seeing his mother in such anguish brought tears to his own eyes. "I will not stay mother. Take the money."

Again she shook her head and held out her arms to him in despair.

"If you will not take the money then you shall never see me again," he declared, stopping the woman's cries with the shock of his statement.

Mother and son remained in that house for some time. Slowly he worked on her fears in a manner far beyond his years, assuring her at length that so long as she took back the money and accepted his decision to join with the British then he would take every opportunity to call on her. And finally, reluctantly, she acquiesced. As he sat back in the wooden palanquin and looked through the latticed side at his tearful mother standing on the step of the house watching him depart, he knew he was leaving the family home for the last time. His heart broke, and his tears joined with hers to mark the parting of two lives.

Chapter 1

To The Reader.
I believe I have attempted a branch of Cookery, which nobody has yet thought worth their while to write upon: but as I have both seen, and found, by experience, that the generality of servants are greatly wanting in that point, therefore I have taken upon me to instruct them in the best manner I am capable; and, I dare say, that every servant who can but read will be capable of making a tolerable good cook, and those who have the least notion of Cookery cannot miss of being very good ones.

The Art of Cookery Made Plain and Easy
By a LADY.
LONDON 1774

London in the late summer of 1811.

THE small, dark-skinned man stood in the gardens to the centre of London's fashionable Portman Square watching the traffic of carts, gigs, whiskies, buggies, dog carts, sociables and dennets, all pass in quick succession as they came to and from the busy Oxford Street nearby. A casual observer might assume this man, given his Occidental look, was consumed with awe at the orderly business of the British capital. And perhaps he did present the demeanour of a foreign traveller, as his head slowly turned to observe the elegant façades of some of London's finest houses. From a distance his clothing also displayed an appropriate sense of affluence associated with a better class of visitor – a smart, black, Bath-cloth morning coat contrasting with freshly pressed cream pantaloons; a pair of highly buffed black boots in the style made fashionable by the Marquis of Wellington some years previously; and a deep yellow silken waistcoat set-off by a neatly tied white cravat and shirt. All in the very best European taste.

Yet if the same casual observer came closer, taking care in crossing the cobbled roadway to approach the formal gardens, they would note other, far more revealing signs about the man. While he was of mature years, possibly fifty or more, he still had a fine head of wavy black hair, albeit now receding from the forehead and flecked with grey. And if he smiled in acknowledgement as the observer approached then he would present a passable smile of fairly even, and even fairly clean, teeth which he had nurtured through the years with the use of Indian tooth powders. Yet the observer would also note the frayed cuffs of his shirt and coat, the small light brown stains on his yellow silk waistcoat and the ever widening cracks in the leather of his boots which even the application of copious amounts of polish now failed to mask. And his eyes, which usually sparkled brightly with curiosity and interest, today looked at but did not see the grandness of the surroundings. For his mind was taken with cares, which transported him to another place, one in which he was mired in worry, distress and anxiety.

The cause of this melancholy was money, and his fading fashions were an indicator that all was not well. Two years ago he had alighted on a fine business prospect, one, which he knew, would secure the future for him, his wife and their children. Drawing on his Indian heritage, and his experience of managing households both in London and Ireland, he had been encouraged by no other than his patron, the Honourable Basil Cochrane, to open a coffee house purveying the finest curries India had to offer. The Hindostanee Coffee House was, quite simply, unique in London and therefore all Europe. His recent advertisement in *The Times* had announced that his Indian dishes had been "allowed by the greatest epicures to be unequalled to any curries ever made in England." And with quality English beers and spirits – and, of course, the finest Turkish coffee – the Hindostanee Coffee House had opened at 34 George Street, just behind the very Portman Square in which he now stood, to great fanfare.

Mahomet had also been fascinated by a portrait of the Emperor Shah Jahan at the home of his patron the Honourable Basil Cochrane. In his travels through India, he had seen for himself the glorious mausoleum the

Shah had built for his favourite wife, Mumtaz Mahal, some miles from the city of Delhi. In the portrait, which the artist must have imagined as it was painted in the Western style a hundred years after the Shah's death, he was dressed in a beautiful cream silk brocade quilted coat overlaid with a finely embroidered red velvet waistcoat and matching turban. Mahomet thought recreating this uniform to be an ideal way of promoting his coffee house, and had spoken to a seamstress of some note who had recreated this ensemble and also added a red and cream striped silk cummerbund for added effect – as if any were needed. This costume he described his "curry uniform", and considered it to be every inch as fine as those he wore for the East India Company. He also justified the cost to a sceptical wife by saying that as he was descended from a Mughul prince himself he had every right to wear such an outfit.

At first business had gone well. Portman Square was known to house many wealthy colonial adventurers like his patron. Britons who travelled to India for fame and fortune were disparagingly called Nabobs in polite society. Frowned on for their acquisition of wealth by dubious means, on their return they had settled in some numbers in the newer developments to the west end of London and away from the traditional centres of power. These men had been flattered when the Hindostanee Coffee House opened in their honour, and they enjoyed eating the spicy food and smoking the ornate hookahs, especially in the dark, dank days of winter. Yet their interest soon waned. Fickle tastes, and the fact that business to the Orient continued to be conducted exclusively at the Jerusalem Coffee House near to the Royal Exchange, meant custom slowly fell away. Moreover, when the Nabobs did yearn for a taste of their glory days, then most had brought back with them a goodly complement of Indian servants for that special curry.

So the Hindostanee Coffee House had been left to rely on a loyal but ever diminishing clientele, and the man who owned the coffee house, now standing in the centre of Portman Square, did not have deep pockets – indeed his left one had a hole which his wife had yet to sew. In his mind he could see the walls of the Fleet prison, or worse still the Marshalsea, with his family struggling through the gates weighed down by their debts. And needless to say, the Mughul costume was now resigned to a box deep within the bedroom wardrobe.

So deep in thought was the small dark man that he failed to notice the youth – barely more than a boy and just in his thirteenth year – approach.

"Papa?" the boy whispered as he came near, as if not recognising his own father. "Papa, I've come to bring you home."

The boy's skin was lighter by several shades than that of the man, but his dark, wavy hair and large distinctive nose attested to a familial likeness. The youthful voice brought the man back from the darkness, and he turned to look at the boy and smiled.

"William my boy?" he questioned, "why are you here?"

The lad repeated his statement.

"Mama has sent me to collect you papa. You had been sighted, standing here," he explained. "She needs your help in the kitchen."

The man looked at his child, his eldest, earnestly in the eye – as the father was just, and the son nearing, five feet in height this was not too difficult a task. He was a good boy, honest and hard working and, given the chance, would make a fine man. This chance his father knew he must provide, but it seemed further away than ever. The man breathed deeply and looked around him once more at the activity in the square.

"Come my son, and let us to your mother, given she is in such need. We would not wish the curries to burn for want of watching." They smiled.

THE Harding family liked to put it around that the baronetcy had been granted by Charles II for some great service – and at least in one sense this was true. Oliver Harding had provided the Merry Monarch with something he could not be without: female company. In return he had been appointed Procurator General or, as the more unkind courtiers put it, the Great Pimp.

Still, Oliver did not go unrewarded and, one hundred and forty years later, his progeny enjoyed all the trappings of squirearchal England: a large estate in Warwickshire and a substantial house and land to the north of

London abutting the Crown land of Mary-le-Bone Park. The current incumbent of the family escutcheon, the fifth baronet Sir Josiah Harding, was now approaching his fiftieth year and fitted his role as county landowner like an old pair of breeches. He embraced hunting, shooting and fishing with vigour, and had more recently become a convert to the country's latest sporting passion: cricket. In this he had been encouraged by his younger son, named William, who was becoming quite a young master at the game. Sir Josiah had granted the sporting impresario Mr Thomas Lord the lease of a tract of land on his London estate on which to lay out a ground, after Mr Lord and his cricketing crowd had been removed from their established ground for the building of Dorset Square in Mary-le-Bone. William repaid his father's support handsomely, and at a recent match had hit 73 runs for the gentlemen of Paddington against a side from the St John's Wood Cricket Club. William's score was by far the greater part of a total of 92 achieved by the Paddington men, and he was undefeated at the end. Needless to say, Mr Lord was very grateful for Sir Josiah's kind condescension and for providing the match umpires that day.

A few days following this match Sir Josiah was to be found at his favoured dining place of the Hindostanee Coffee House in the company of his two sons: William the cricketing prodigy and George, the elder liability. Or this is how Sir Josiah had become to view his heir apparent. Unlike William, George took to country sports not for character building or social relaxation, but for the gambling opportunities they provided. This became a running sore between father and son – not so much that George gambled, but that he lost. Constantly. And expected his father to bail him out time and again. George's losses were such that they now placed an uncomfortable burden on the family estate.

This burden could have been lifted by a recent opportunity when Sir Josiah had been approached by the directors of a newly proposed canal company to sell his London estate for a most attractive sum. Attractive, that was, to the indebted George. Yet Sir Josiah foresaw the sale of land as the beginning of the end of the Harding dynasty, and William knew the sale could end his budding cricketing career, as the proposed canal was to pass through the centre of Thomas Lord's new cricketing square!

The three Hardings – Lady Harding was now safely at rest in the crypt of St-Mary-le-Bone church – had argued incessantly since George first became aware of the offer. This he discovered one evening at Gentleman Jackson's boxing academy in Bond Street. It was the only good news to be had that day; one which had seen George's three favoured boxers end up in close proximity to Gentleman Jackson's parquet flooring, together with the best part of 100 guineas. The teller collecting the wagers had casually mentioned that George might soon be able to match his royal boxing patrons in the size of wagers, given rumours of the canal company approach. George had sallied forth to his father's mansion a few minutes later.

SAKE Dean Mahomet listened attentively as his wife issued her regular list of instructions prior to the opening of business. At five-foot nine inches, Jane Mahomet was considered very tall for a woman and held a physical dominance over her husband. As usual she was dressed in a dark blue, three-quarter sleeve muslin dress protected by a brilliant white and crisply starched apron. Her mousy coloured hair was tied back into a tight bun and hidden beneath a slightly old-fashioned ruffled mobcap, and her overall appearance belied the fact that she was twenty years her husband's junior.

"And it would help," she caustically concluded, "if you did not occupy your time speaking to guests, Mr Mahomet. Yesterday one gentleman waited for over half an hour because you were busy relating some bogus tale or other."

Mahomet sighed. "The guests like to hear tales of India, my pearl."

"I wouldn't mind if there were more than just a smidgeon of truth to them," she continued, ignoring the plaintive look, which she knew only too well. Those dark, doleful eyes had enchanted her fifteen years previously and she was still unable to completely break their spell.

Jane Mahomet's family, the Dalys, were important members of the Irish Protestant Ascendancy in Cork, and at sixteen Jane had been sent to Mrs Murray's Finishing School for Young Ladies in Grattan Street. Next door was Mr Murray's College for the Education of Gentlemen, and it was from the window of her classroom that Jane first caught sight of the handsome and decidedly dark man entering the next door college. Jane discovered all she could about the exotic student. She established that Sake Dean Mahomet was either a servant or companion, depending to whom she spoke, of a Captain Baker who returned from India ten years previously. He was called Sake, or a sheikh of Araby, because his family had accompanied the great Mughul emperors in their conquest of India from Persia. He was also an accomplished author, having recently published an account of his travels in India to great acclaim within polite Cork society. Even the nuns of the local Catholic convent had purchased a copy. Jane was entranced from afar, and engineered an introduction to her quarry – the exact details of which she was now too embarrassed to recall. If she had, she would have surely blushed at the coquettishness and feminine guile, though this could be excused in a sixteen-year-old girl. As it was she was completely smitten with his good looks, his tales of the Orient, his impeccable manners and the correctness of his English. And although Mahomet was considerably older than the local Irish men with whom she was acquainted, by comparison they were uncouth and ungentlemanly. He was a man amongst boys.

As they grew closer they decided to meet clandestinely; Jane's father, William Daly, was a prominent merchant and she knew instinctively he would not be impressed by her association with the Indian, not simply because of his race but also, and probably more importantly, the fact he was a Mahommedan. In Ireland the concept of a Protestant girl marrying a Catholic boy was unthinkable, but for Jane to marry someone who did not follow the word of Christ was simply impossible. So they eloped to Dublin. There Mahomet converted to Christianity and found a Church of Ireland padre prepared to marry them. For Mahomet the change of religion was not as important as his commitment to Jane. An all-seeing God – Allah – would understand this.

Still, on their return to Cork Mahomet had prepared himself to be strung up and thrown into the river Lee, and so was pleasantly surprised when Jane's father quickly accepted his new son-in-law. While William Daly may have simply resigned himself to a *fait accomplit*, more cynical members of the Daly clan suggested the fact he saved paying a substantial dowry for a daughter to whom the soubriquet "plain" was all too apt also played its part in his acceptance. She could, after all, have cost him a small fortune!

Fifteen years on and the Mahomets, with their four children, were now the proud owners of the Hindostanee Coffee House. Sake Dean Mahomet had chosen the interiors for the terraced property in George Street carefully, with bamboo and wicker furniture tastefully arranged beneath large ceiling fans and between exotic palms to imbue a decidedly Oriental atmosphere in west London. On two walls he had commissioned fine murals, one of a large Buddha with prostrate followers and the other a jungle scene with tygers and elephants.

Jane Mahomet ran the kitchen, using curry recipes concocted by Mahomet himself and also from descriptions she found in newspaper cuttings. She also possessed a well-thumbed copy of *The Art of Cookery Made Plain and Easy*. This book, first published fifty years ago, was her prop, and included a recipe for curry made the Indian way. The recipe explained how to prepare a chicken curry, from cutting the chicken to adding tumerick, a large spoonful of ginger and beaten pepper, salt, cream and lemon. From this recipe she had experimented using beef and mutton, and was particularly proud of her special recipe for a vegetable curry, to which she added ground horseradish to give that extra – and quintessentially English – bite. The book, it seems, was written by "A Lady", although her husband had suggested that such a comprehensive guide to cookery – there were over 150 recipes – must have been written by a man. Yet Jane Mahomet, to the contrary, decided that a book which displayed such common sense could only have been written by a woman.

IT was no surprise to find the canal company proposition once more the subject of heated conversation at the Harding table in the coffee house. Sir Josiah sat to the centre, his large, rotund presence dominating the table. William, as willowy as a cricket bat, sat on his left while George, a younger and only slightly slimmer version of his father, was to the right.

"I will not prostitute this family's fortunes for your debts sir," Sir Josiah raged at his elder son, barely keeping his voice from polite company while they waited for their food.

"If I might say so sir, that is contrary given our family history," hissed George, emboldened by his frustration.

"Papa is right George, it is never wise to sell off land," William added in support of his father in a hushed tone.

"And what is this to you sir?" spat Sir Josiah at his younger son. "I have told you before, you have no interest in the estate. It is George's inheritance of which we speak. It is about time you made your own way in life. India calls you."

Sir Josiah, of course, was speaking the truth, if indelicately. The Hardings adhered closely to the laws of primogeniture: to the eldest everything and to everyone else – nothing. William would not be the first junior Harding to learn to his to cost that filial love was skin deep when it came to money. Still, Sir Josiah had done everything he could to secure William's future by gaining for his younger son a position in the East India Company, an effort for which the boy was less than truly thankful and had still to take up. Sir Josiah considered his younger son to be wilful, and had been unable to knock any sense in to him no matter how much hard correction he had administered. But in the end it was George who would be responsible for the Harding estate, and this mere thought made Sir Josiah shudder.

"You would be well advised to take the position I have secured for you boy," continued Sir Josiah at William before turning to George. "And the fact remains, sir, that while I live the canal will have to find another course. Hopefully I will live long enough to frustrate both it and you," he concluded, looking around.

"You can keep the manor house father, and just sell the tract of land they need for the canal," George now pleaded.

William coughed. "But that runs right through the cricket ground! You have given Mr Lord your solemn undertaking papa."

"Cricket!" exclaimed George disdainfully.

"Yes cricket, brother. You may not be sporting, but I value it greatly. It has brought me great pleasure, and papa was willing to grant Mr Lord the land when the Mary-le-Bone club were turned out of their old home. We must not allow this misfortune to happen to them again."

"Must we not? A band of ragger-muffin cricketers cannot stand in the way of men of progress. Why, even the Prince Regent supports the canal."

"Does he now," interrupted the father, "well then that is another good reason to oppose it. If I have spoken once on this I have spoken a thousand times. I will not sell the land! If they seek the approval of Parliament to rob me of my land then I am not without friends in that bawdy house to frustrate them. I tire of this George so you will put it from your mind. While I live the canal will have to find another course. Now where is that damned curry ... ah, at last, here is Mahomet and his man. I warn you George, no more of this nonsense."

The three gentlemen fell into a seething silence as they waited to be served by the small Indian owner of the coffee house, who had appeared together with a kitchen porter carrying a large tray on which sat three silver domes covering hot food beneath. With the tray placed on a nearby sideboard, Mahomet set about carefully and correctly presenting the endeavours of his celebrated kitchen, starting with Sir Josiah. The Harding men greeted the uncovered plates of curry with grunts of appreciation. While Sir Josiah had opted for his favourite, a spicily flavoured curry made with fresh vegetables from a kitchen garden in Camden, the Harding brothers opted for lamb (or perhaps more correctly mutton curried as).

They fell upon their feasts as if attending the last supper – table manners were not a Harding speciality – and it was not long before George, yet again, returned to the canal. "If only you would see sense papa," he began once more.

Sir Josiah, who had been distracted by an unusually bitter taste in the vegetable curry, reached for his glass of claret to wash away a slight thrilling in his mouth and a prickling of his tongue. "George! I will hear no more of this non ..."

He failed to complete the sentence as a number of things happened to his body at the same time. Painful spasms in his stomach accompanied a paling of his face and a blurring of his vision. He reached out towards his younger son for support but could not feel any sensation in his hand. His eyes widened as he looked at his two anxious offspring sitting either side of him. His body fidgeted and shook uncontrollably, then his head jerked forward and he vomited greatly, returning partly digested vegetable curry to his dish. He cried out in great agony and fell forward, his head joining Mrs Mahomet's creation on the pewter plate. Then he convulsed once more and slipped from his chair to the floor. And with that the body of the fifth baronet twitched some more before becoming stilled, and the dining room at the Hindostanee Coffee House became as silent as a morgue.

Chapter 2

London, the same time.

DECIMUS Doyle was quite the beau and, as a young man of twenty-four with handsome looks and an income of over £2,000 a year, he had every right to be so. Yet parading around London in the latest outfit from Schweitzer & Davidson, his fashionable tailors in Cork Street who were by appointment to the Prince Regent and, even more importantly, to Mr Brummell himself, was not sufficient for Decimus. On leaving Trinity College Dublin two years previously he had crossed the Irish Sea to study at the renowned Hunterian Medical School. London was also home to his favoured cousin Jane and her exotic husband Sake Mahomet. Both had spoken on his behalf to his father, who had not considered medicine as seemly for a gentleman, and they had prevailed with Decimus' thanks.

Doyle's mother, Frances May Daly, had married Squire John Doyle to much celebration within her Cork family. Frances May was the only daughter of the wealthy patriarch Harry Daly, while Squire Doyle was the owner of considerable estates throughout Ireland, including coalmines in County Tyrone which brought him great wealth. Yet while he was able to occupy his time improving his estate at Mount Doyle, some fifteen miles from Dublin, what the squire really desired was a family. When the pretty Frances May Daly said yes, therefore, the squire thought his life complete.

Even though there was a considerable age difference between them, they were blessed with an all-embracing love. Children, however, were another matter. Frances May suffered a series of miscarriages and stillbirths, the last nearly taking her life. Doctors warned she would not survive another pregnancy, but because of her love for her husband and an overwhelming desire to bear him a child she kept this advice to herself and fell pregnant once more. When she had carried the child for six months they dared to hope that this time they would be blessed. And the early stages of her accouchement went well, but then the child moved and it became impossible for a natural delivery to take place. When it looked like both mother and child would die, Squire Doyle was forced to agree to a Caesarean. In the early hours of a bitter winter morning a live male child was delivered but Frances May, the light of her husband's eyes, faded away. The squire named the son Decimus Solus, in remembrance of the miscarriages, stillbirths and his beautiful wife for whom he would now forever mourn.

It was another sad day for Squire Doyle when he saw the child he loved so much set sail for England. To the very last he had hoped the boy would change his mind and stay at Mount Doyle, growing into his rightful position as a country gentleman. Yet the squire would later admit that the Hunterian seemed to be the making of young Decimus. Situated on Great Windmill Street in Soho, Doyle tasted as much vice and virtue in two years as his father had in a lifetime. Moreover he showed promise in his studies, and his tutors were beginning to predict great things of the young Irishman. He lodged with one of those tutors, Dr Simon Bunton, a large man with a personality to match. Bunton constantly teased his young protégé, calling him "Brummell Minor" and a "Bond Street Beau", but it was all given and received with good heart and affection. Indeed, by the end of Doyle's second year at the school Bunton considered himself to be *in loco parentis* to the young man, though had Doyle heard this he might have raised a sharp eyebrow and recalled the scrapes and dubious establishments into which he had been led by his self-proclaimed guardian.

It was while both Bunton and Doyle were at dinner early in the evening that Bunton's housekeeper, the ever dependable Mrs Mac, entered to announce that Doyle had an urgent message – brought by a young black boy. The messenger was shown in, and Doyle was taken aback to see his cousin's eldest son standing before him.

"William!" he exclaimed.

"You know the lad?" asked Bunton, suspecting a connection.

"Yes, he is my second cousin."

Mrs Mac gasped in amazement but Bunton nodded, already aware of Jane Daly's unusual marriage having previously met with Sake Mahomet.

"William, what is it?" asked Doyle anxiously.

Young William Mahomet first glanced at the fearful looking – to young eyes – Dr Bunton before turning and stepping towards his cousin.

"I've come from papa, cousin Decimus. He has asked that I bring you immediately."

"Immediately? Why?"

William hesitated, as if under instruction not to disclose a family secret among a room of strangers.

"You can speak freely William. Dr Bunton is my friend and tutor."

The boy swallowed hard. "Papa says you must come. There has been an accident at the coffee house."

"Accident? Is one of the family hurt?"

William shook his head but did not reply, instead stealing another quick glance at both Bunton and Mrs Mac.

"Then who? A diner?"

The boy turned back to his handsome cousin and nodded.

"I am not a physician yet. Sake Mahomet knows this. How can I help?" This last question was directed towards Bunton.

"We will both go," the tutor replied. "An urgent house call will give you good experience." Bunton then addressed the lad. "Has the patient been made comfortable?"

It was a perfunctory question which elicited an unlooked for response.

"Not really sir ..." the lad said very quietly. "Papa thinks mama may have poisoned him."

MAHOMET had rushed into the kitchen calling for a pitcher of boiled water; one of the guests had taken gravely ill. From the dining room his wife Jane could hear a great commotion, although she knew there were only three tables occupied. She sent Sarah, their maid, to see what she could through the latticed screen which hid the kitchen door from the diners. When the girl returned, less than two minutes later, she was in great distress, and all Jane Mahomet could ascertain from her was that a gentleman had been laid out on the floor of the dining room and that the master was shaking his head gravely. Jane decided to venture into the dining room herself, but as she reached the door her husband re-appeared.

"There has been a terrible happening" he told his wife before calling to their son William, who was scraping potatoes in the pantry, and speaking so quietly to him that Jane could not hear what was said. William looked anxiously towards his mother before running out of the rear door of the kitchen, sent on an urgent errand by his father. Mahomet explained to his wife that one of the diners, Sir Josiah Harding, had been taken gravely ill while eating and now lay unconscious on the floor of the coffee house. He called to the kitchen porter, Walker, to accompany him into the dining room to help make the gentleman more comfortable, and advised his wife he would have close the coffee house and escort the other diners from the premises. He also told her that a physician had been summoned from further along George Street – she assumed this was where William had gone.

Being at a loss to know what to do for the best, Jane sat herself at the kitchen table with Sarah and, anxiously watching the door, waited for further news from the dining room. It was at such stressful times that she appreciated Mahomet the most: he was always so calm. She looked to Sarah, who seemed in great shock, and reached for her hand, stroking it gently as they waited. Sarah for her part smiled wanly at her mistress. She so loved working for the Mahomets, even though her mistress had a sharp tongue and would chide her for the smallest of mistakes. They had taken her into their family during the past year, and apart from her household duties she often looked after the three youngest children – Amelia, Henry and Horatio – to allow her mistress the time to work in the coffee house kitchen.

The two women sat in silence in that kitchen, their ears pricked for any sounds they could hear from the dining room, before the porter returned carrying plates and shaking his head. "Dead I reckon," was all Walker would say with a curious smile on his lips, to gasps from Sarah and tuts from Jane. Fifteen more minutes passed, and Jane had tired of watching Walker clean up in the kitchen. She once more considered going into the dining room herself when Mahomet returned, this time accompanied by a stout gentleman wearing a dark morning coat and trousers and even darker expression on his face.

"My dear," Mahomet began, "this is Dr Phillips from further along the street. He has attended to Sir Josiah ... I am afraid it is not good news ..." Mahomet's voice trailed off as his wife instinctively put her hand to her mouth to stifle a cry.

"Mrs Mahomet," said Dr Phillips in a deep baritone voice imbued with both authority and foreboding, "I am afraid Sir Josiah Harding has died, after suffering a violent expulsion from his stomach which I can only assume was brought on after partly consuming one of your dishes. Unfortunately all this took place before I arrived." He looked accusingly at Mahomet, as if the Indian were responsible in some part for this delay.

Sarah gasped and squeezed Jane Mahomet's hand tightly.

"But how? ..." Jane asked, hardly understanding the doctor's words.

"That I do not know," the doctor continued. "From appearances it would seem Sir Josiah was substantially built and no stranger to the dinner table. I will have to make a full report to the coroner in Bow Street, so could you please tell me the exact contents of the meal he was consuming when he died."

Jane only partly heard what the doctor said as her mind was concentrated on the body laid out in the dining room of their coffee house. She looked to her husband.

"Is the body? ..." she nodded towards the door.

Mahomet shook his head. "He was dining with his two sons. They have called for their carriage and taken him back to ..." Mahomet did not know exactly where the Harding boys had taken their father.

"Mrs Mahomet," interjected Dr Phillips, annoyed he was not being given her full attention. "The contents of the food served to Sir Josiah?"

Jane Mahomet turned her head back. "I am sorry doctor, this is such difficult news. Yes, the contents. Sir Josiah had my vegetable curry ... which is made of the freshest ingredients," she hastily added.

"Which are?"

"Err ... onions, potatoes, cabbage, egg plant, salt, olive oil, kidney beans, dried chilli, a pinch of tumerick, some cumin and coriander, curry powders and horseradish."

"Egg plant?" questioned the doctor, "isn't that unusual."

Jane Mahomet shook her head. "The kitchen garden we use in Camden grows it under glass cloches. It needs a lot of sun, but in a warm year such as this they are quite successful. It is very expensive."

The doctor grunted. "And the curry powder?"

"We have it delivered from one of the Company warehouses," Mahomet interrupted. "It is imported from India and is of the finest quality ... it is widely used."

Dr Phillips, not used to and wary of such an exotic diet, was far from convinced.

"But I still do not understand," said Jane Mahomet forcefully. "Even if Sir Josiah experienced a strong reaction to the food, how can it kill him ... and so quickly?"

Dr Phillips conceded the point.

"I managed to question the sons before they left," he advised, "and one of them told me he had not been in good health for some time. I suspect had it not been your curry, Mrs Mahomet, then he would have succumbed to something else. Though I have no doubt the spicy ingredients you used did not help," he added caustically.

The Mahomets were used to such prejudices, and were usually able to brush them off. This however, was a much more serious matter.

"And what," asked Mahomet gently, "is your conclusion doctor?"

Phillips looked around the kitchen. After Walker's efforts it was very clean and tidy, with just one copper pan simmering on the range. Then he looked in turn at the Mahomets and their staff.

"My conclusion," Phillips sighed, "is that Sir Josiah Harding died of natural causes. The description of his death does suggest a most violent reaction to something he had eaten, but as he had digested nothing ... out of the ordinary ... I conclude that the problem lay within the constitution of Sir Josiah himself. This is what I will report to the coroner."

The relief on Mahomet's face was palpable. Slowly he escorted Dr Phillips back into the dining room and to the front of the coffee house, where he promised to settle the doctor's bill promptly, then firmly shut and bolted the door. It was when he returned to the kitchen that he found his wife weeping; Sarah and Walker had vanished.

"I sent them away," Jane said through her tears. "Sarah has gone to attend to the children upstairs and Walker will return tomorrow morning. I suppose we will have to pay him for today as he has cleaned up."

Mahomet smiled and walked over to his wife, placing his hands on her shoulders as he stood behind her.

"Hush now, my pearl," he whispered as he leaned forward to kiss the top of her head, covered as it was with a white linen cap.

She reached up with her right hand to touch his on her left shoulder.

"You know what people will say," she croaked, "that he died because of our curries."

"No," he countered softly spoken, "no my pearl, no-one will think that."

"Yes they will," sniffed Jane, now bringing her emotions under control, "and you know it."

Mahomet sighed and held his wife's shoulders tighter. Yes, she was right, people would say that. The gossips who seemed to take delight at mocking his family would have a field day. Trade at the coffee house was already poor; this could finish it off. As these black thoughts descended on both husband and wife, there a sharp rapping on the kitchen windowpane. Both Mahomets turned to look and through the window they saw the concerned face of Jane's cousin. She gave a startled cry. "Decimus! What on earth ...?"

"I sent William to fetch him, my pearl," Mahomet said quickly as he let go of his wife's shoulders and made his way to the kitchen door. "I think we need all the help we can call on."

Jane struggled to compose herself as Mahomet let in Doyle, Dr Bunton and William. Mahomet had met Simon Bunton on two occasions when he had called on Doyle at the Hunterian, but this was the first time Jane Mahomet had the pleasure, and Bunton was suitably fulsome in his greeting. William was quickly sent upstairs by his mother while the two physicians, tutor and pupil, put down their bags and seated themselves around the kitchen table with the Mahomets.

"So cousin," began Doyle earnestly, "William has spoken of an illness."

Jane Mahomet could not suppress a sob as his words brought back all her dark thoughts.

Mahomet nodded. "A good customer, Sir Josiah Harding, died while at dinner."

He then explained the circumstances of the death and the attendance of Dr Phillips. Doyle looked to Bunton.

"Of Phillips I am aware," advised Bunton, "and in so far as I can speak, then I think he has a good reputation. If he says the death was from natural causes then none will gainsay him."

Doyle nodded and Mahomet looked relieved.

"But it is not right," said Jane Mahomet, to the surprise of the three men.

"You are distressed cousin," said Doyle gently.

"Of course I'm distressed!" she retorted, and then realising she was speaking harshly softened her voice. "I know you mean well Decimus, but I stand by what I say: it does not seem right. How can a man die so violently and with such speed?"

Her question seemed to fall on deaf ears.

"Well Decimus? Dr Bunton? Is this usual, for a man to be taken ill with some stomach malady and then die within the instant?!" her voice became shrill once more.

"Shhhh my pearl, or the children will hear," cautioned Mahomet.

Jane Mahomet turned to her husband at the table and sobbed. He, in turn, reached towards her with his arms and drew her to him. While Bunton looked embarrassed, Doyle seemed perplexed. After a moment of thought he turned to Bunton.

"What my dear cousin says is true Bunton. Death did seem to come quickly."

Bunton sighed. "It could have been brought about by an existing malady Doyle, as Phillips seemed to suggest."

Doyle nodded then turned to Mahomet, who was still consoling his wife.

"Perhaps cousin Jane would benefit from some rest Sake Mahomet. And a cup of Roman Chamomile tea ...?"

Jane pulled away from her husband and looked to her younger cousin. Her eyes had reddened and puffed slightly.

"How could I rest at a time like this?" she chided.

Doyle held out his hand across the table. "I have only your best interests in mind, as you know. Perhaps Dr Bunton could provide you with a relaxing infusion to help you. You will feel all the better for it, and there is little now for you to do since the coffee house is closed."

Mahomet reached for his wife's hand. "Decimus is right, my pearl. We will not open again today. Why don't you go upstairs and I will be along presently."

With little further cajoling Jane Mahomet retired, though declined to take anything Dr Bunton was willing to provide. When the three men were alone in the kitchen Doyle addressed Mahomet.

"When William brought his message earlier Sake Mahomet, he suggested you thought the poor man had been poisoned."

Mahomet looked down sheepishly. "I was mistaken," he said quietly, glancing over to the staircase, which led to the family rooms.

"Still," pressed Doyle, "it was quite a conclusion to make. Why was this?"

Mahomet continued to look down. "I was mistaken Decimus," he repeated, " ... though ..."

"Yes?"

" ... I have witnessed a similar death before," he finally stated. "In India," he quickly added.

Bunton and Doyle looked at each other and then back at Mahomet, who felt obliged to continue by their attention.

"Poison is an acceptable form of killing in the Orient," he explained. "It is said that long ago beautiful young girls, the Vish-Kanya, would be fed drops of a serpent's venom so their kiss would be deadly to any man. King Chandragupta sent such a maiden to Alexander the Great when he invaded India. And poisoned robes, or killer killats, have been supposedly used by Mughal emperors and Rajas even to this day. You may have heard rumour of officials of the East India Company refusing gifts of elaborate golden robes for fear they may be poisoned. Well, just before I left India for Ireland twenty-five years ago, I witnessed a man poisoned by his wife. I was dining near him and he was eating a curry prepared by his wife. The European doctor who attended suggested he had been killed by the "Queen of Poisons", and later the wife confessed. The poison had been brought into India from the Nepal kingdom of the Himalaya mountains. The death was very similar to that experienced by Sir Josiah Harding – a twitching and flaying of the arms and legs, a loss of vision and the senses and then the slow loss of the pulse. I estimate it took Sir Josiah less than fifteen minutes to die."

Both Doyle and Bunton sat back in surprise as Mahomet spoke.

"The Queen of Poisons?" repeated Bunton slowly. "By that I assume you mean *Acontium napellus* ... wolfsbane or monkshood as it is commonly called, or aconite. It is widely available throughout Europe, but it is relatively benign in its solid form. It has to be ground into a powder and dissolved in alcohol or a weak acid to have any real effect. We do not use it regularly in this country, but I have heard American doctors use very mild doses for certain treatments, such as fever, headaches, inflammations or neuralgia, though even this is uncommon as it is known to be very toxic."

"And would a strong dose kill?" asked Doyle eagerly.

Bunton sighed. "Yes, undoubtedly! It is a very effective killer, as Mr Mahomet witnessed in India all those years ago. But it has a very bitter taste and is difficult to take."

Doyle looked around the kitchen. "Unless the taste was masked by a very spicy curry ... Sake Mahomet, is there any curry left of that which was eaten by Sir Josiah?"

Mahomet looked at the young Irishman horrified. "You are not suggesting Decimus ..."

"No sir," injected Doyle, "but I think we ought to consider all possibilities."

Mahomet sighed. He was ready to object strongly and suggest that Doyle and Bunton should leave as he needed to attend to his wife, but curiosity got the better of him. The three men stood and made a thorough search of the kitchen, but it seemed that Walker had cleaned all the pots and plates before leaving and taken the slops out to the cesspit. Nor were their any signs of Sir Josiah's regurgitated remains in the dining room: the table and floor had been cleaned and scrubbed.

Frustrated, the three men sat down in the kitchen once more.

"Well, we will never know I suppose ..." Doyle began, before being interrupted by Bunton standing quickly and walking over to a basket in the corner where Jane Mahomet kept her vegetables. He bent down and picked up a root.

"What is this?" he asked and Mahomet turned.

"Horseradish, I think," replied Mahomet, not used to being questioned on the contents of the kitchen. "Mrs Mahomet uses it in her curries to give them an extra kick."

Bunton whispered to himself before asking aloud, "And how does she do that?"

"By making it into a paste before stirring it ..."

Mahomet was now perplexed by Bunton's questioning and stood, as did Doyle. They watched as Bunton slowly brought the root to his face, sniffed it and then licked it with the tip of his tongue. A few seconds later he spat onto the earthen floor.

"This is not horseradish, Mr Mahomet. This is monkshood ... wolfsbane ... the Queen of Poisons!"

Chapter 3

London, the same time.

THE brothers sat opposite each other in the great hall of the mansion coming to terms with the events of the day. Their father's body lay at rest in his bedchamber, and undertakers from Pall-mall had been summoned and were at work making him presentable for his last journey – to join his wife at St Mary-le-Bone church. The funeral was already set and a curate had come and gone, mumbling the usual platitudes. George, now the sixth baronet, had performed his first task as head of the family by briskly escorting the curate to both his hat and the front door.

In the hours since the Harding brothers had witnessed the sudden demise of their father, they had undergone at first similar, and then diverging, emotions. The coffee house proprietor had summoned a local doctor who pronounced their father dead. Their coach had been summoned and they accompanied the fifth baronet home, William watching over the ever-stiffening body on the floor of the carriage while George sat beside the coachman, a grim smile establishing itself on his face as he realised the consequences of the death. The goddess Fortuna had finally smiled on him, showering him with the bounty of his inheritance some fifteen or twenty years before he could have reasonably expected it. By the time the coach had journeyed up Edgware Row, through the village of Paddington and turned into the entrance of the Harding estate, George had already sold the property – in his own mind at least – to the canal company.

Thoughts such as these continued to cross his mind as he sat facing William. The brothers had also been joined by the youngest member of the Harding clan, their seventeen-year-old sister Charlotte, or Lottie. A willowy young lady, Lottie was named after her mother Lady Harding who had died in giving her birth. And like her mother, Lottie suffered from a general malaise which continued undiagnosed, despite the best efforts of physicians. One doctor even had the temerity to suggest to Sir Josiah that his daughter was simply seeking attention. This, Sir Josiah knew, could not have been the case as he doted on his daughter and constantly attended to her, sometimes to the obvious discomfort of others who thought such close signs of affection to be inappropriate. Lottie, to the contrary, had seemed oblivious to his holding and stroking. For her, the witnessing of Sir Josiah's constant chastisement of her brothers was far more distressing, and she had come to despise this aspect of his character. It was the sister who first broke the silence which had fallen on the house: the head footman had stopped the clocks on Sir Josiah's arrival.

"Does it seem right?" she asked, though her words were not truly directed at either brother.

"What?" questioned George, awakened from his scheming, "what did you say Lottie? What does not seem right?"

"Father's death," continued the young lady. "To die so suddenly and in such a manner. Do you think it was something he ate?"

"What do you mean? That the Indian poisoned him?"

"No!" cried a shocked young lady. "Why would you say that George? ... Well yes, I suppose I do mean that in a way. Perhaps he ate something so disagreeable that it killed him. Papa did like the spicy food ... perhaps it did for him? He was in perfectly good health, after all."

Both brothers looked to their sister, George with mouth agape and William with flushed cheeks.

"Poppycock!" snapped George. "You were not there and did not hear what the doctor said ... papa died of natural causes. That is what he said. My dear Lottie, do not seek out fanciful reasons. We know you were his special one, but papa was sick and now he is dead."

The sharpness of her brother's tongue caused her to well up, which soon broke into a steady stream of tears accompanied by a plaintive weeping.

"George!" exclaimed William. "Do not speak to Lottie like that! Now look what you've done. Come Lottie, control yourself. You know I hate to see you crying. Ignore George, he is just being his brutish self."

Through her tears Lottie managed to reply: "You have no feelings George!"

"And what would you have me do little sister?" replied George, not prepared to let matters rest. "Should I order that they cut open father's body just because you think his death to be strange? Are you mad? What would that establish? For the Lord's sake, Lottie, stop that infernal noise."

His chastisement did not make matters any better, and he also had William in his sights. "And what about your brother? Should we take a knife to our father's body? I am sure you would like that!"

"George!" cried Lottie. "Do not say such things George, please! Oh William, what are we to do?!"

"You heard Lottie, George. You are causing her unnecessary distress. Father was a good churchman so we cannot request any desecration of his body, Lottie my sweet. I also heard the doctor as clearly as George … father did die of natural causes. Though I am not surprised that George is prepared to accept that conclusion so readily. After all it is you George who benefits from his passing."

George did not like the way this conversation was progressing. The doctor had quickly established that their father had died naturally and advised he would report this conclusion to the coroner. To place doubt on his death now would be to complicate matters unnecessarily and, most importantly, it might delay his inheritance. George had too many creditors, some with very aggressive means of collecting debts, to allow this to happen. Both Lottie and William would have to be silenced.

"You are wrong, both of you, and I will not allow you to repeat these baseless suspicions in public," he chided. "Papa died of natural causes … and you are also wrong if you say he never complained about his health. Why, I clearly recall him mentioning to me only recently of pains in his chest and stomach. Perhaps he held matters from you Lottie … given you were his especial favourite. In any case, I am now head of the family and I will not brook such talk … and you will not continue in such a manner, if you both know what's good for you. And William, if anyone were to welcome father's death, I would have thought it to be you."

William's jaw dropped at this oblique threat. "And what does that mean, pray?"

George, now in his stride, smiled maliciously. "Come now brother. You felt the sting of his horse-whip more than I, and we all know that papa was preparing to pack you off to India. So, if you wish to receive any benefit of his passing from the estate, then you will not provoke me," he replied, so demonstrating to his younger brother the quality of his Harding genes.

Lottie squealed. "George! You are utterly beastly! How can you speak to William in such a way?"

But the newly ennobled Sir George Harding was far from finished.

"This house and land will be sold. So both of you must look to your future. While I cannot force you to India, William, I should remind you that I am now Lottie's guardian. We have some cousins in Warwickshire, I recall, and it is about time you were acquainted with your family, Lottie. I would start packing for a journey if I were you."

Another shriek from Lottie was accompanied by her rushing from the room.

DECIMUS Doyle sat opposite Sake Dean Mahomet in the dining room of the Hindostanee Coffee House. It was gone midnight and Dr Simon Bunton had left some time ago to attend to a delivery of medical supplies at the Hunterian. Yet the discovery he left behind now sat in the centre of the table. Bunton had promised to make no further mention of what he had found, leaving it to Mahomet and Doyle to consider the consequences.

"You will have to speak to cousin Jane," Doyle said softly.

Mahomet first nodded then shook his head. "How on earth could such a root find its way into our kitchen?"

Doyle shrugged. "Bunton said it is a rare find, even for apothecaries. He does not know of a supplier in London but believes some herbalists still grow the plant, though he does not know any physician prescribing it."

Mahomet looked around the dining room, as if searching for an answer in the dark recesses. He clutched at possibilities. "Perhaps it was delivered by mistake by our market gardener?"

Doyle sighed. "We can surely ask, but I think you already doubt this possibility as much as I Sake Mahomet."

The Indian nodded reluctantly. Then another realisation came upon him. "But Decimus, this means Sir Josiah was poisoned ... we did poison him!" his voice rising with the horror of the statement.

Doyle put his finger to his lips to hush his cousin's husband. "Quietly, Sake Mahomet."

Mahomet looked hard at Doyle and then put his head in hands, hardly able to comprehend the enormity of the situation. Doyle was pained to see him so.

"Let us consider this," the young man whispered, anxious that no one else in the house should hear their conversation. "It now seems Sir Josiah's curry contained ... the Queen of Poisons ... of sufficient amount to kill him expeditiously. This was administered by accident or design ..."

He stopped, realising the accusation he had made. So did Mahomet, who looked up from his hands.

"You are saying my wife deliberately poisoned this man ..." he hissed.

"No, Sake Mahomet, no ... she could not possibly ..." but even Doyle was unsure of his cousin Jane's actions. "We have to speak to her," he repeated.

They stared at each other for some time before Mahomet nodded.

"I will ask her to describe exactly the way in which she prepared the vegetable curry, without telling her the reason ... for the moment. That is, if she had not retired for the evening."

As it happened, sleep was the last thing on Jane Mahomet's mind, and she was soon standing in the kitchen with her husband and cousin. Doyle had returned the monkshood root to the vegetable basket. Reliving the events of earlier in the day seemed to give them all a purpose, and the men watched carefully as Jane described how she made the curry, pointing with a finger to various points around the kitchen where she had gathered, prepared and cooked the ingredients. When she came to the part at which she added the horseradish, she did not indicate the vegetable basket but instead pointed towards the adjoining pantry.

"You keep the horseradish in the pantry?" Doyle queried, now confused.

Jane tutted. "Of course. Once we've made a new paste it keeps for quite a few days in the cool."

Doyle looked despairingly towards Mahomet.

"And when did you last make a paste, my pearl?" Mahomet asked.

Jane looked affronted. "It was fresh, husband," she emphasised. "Walker made some up only today."

Doyle walked over to the vegetable basket. "From this root cousin?" he asked, holding up the monkshood.

"Of course!" she replied, before paying attention to what he was holding. It was now her turn to be confused. "What is that?"

"The horseradish?" Doyle volunteered.

"Nonsense!" she retorted. "I agree it looks vaguely like horseradish but ..." her voice trailed off. She looked hard at Doyle and then at her husband. "What is going on?" she demanded.

Mahomet guided his wife to a chair at the kitchen table then seated himself next to her. Doyle joined them, bring with him the offending root, which they all now looked at with suspicion.

"That, my pearl, is monkshood."

Jane Mahomet looked at her husband quizzically, not recognising the name.

"It is called the Queen of Poisons and was responsible, we believe, for the death of Sir Josiah Harding earlier today."

His wife sat open mouthed as she listened to Mahomet explain the similarities between the death earlier in the day and the one he witnessed in India many years ago. The connection between the two was the root now taking centre stage on the kitchen table which Dr Bunton had recognised earlier. Jane could hardly believe her ears.

"But how ...?" she pleaded and the two men shrugged their shoulders.

"Cast you mind back, cousin," Doyle urged. "You said Walker had prepared the horseradish paste. Did you watch him do so?"

Jane Mahomet sat back in her chair, her eyes closed as if communing with the past. The two men waited patiently for her response.

"No," she recalled, "I was busy at the range and he was working in the pantry." She pointed once more to the door off the kitchen. "I remember calling to him to bring the horseradish and him replying that he would made some fresh. He has done so once or twice and knows what to do, although his is usually quite weak as he uses too much vinegar." She paused. "It should be strong, as it is the heat of the horseradish that gives the curry its distinctive taste," she added by way of explanation ... or excuse. They all looked down at the monkshood, and in particular to that part of the root which had been freshly cut.

"Did you taste the curry before it was served?" asked Doyle, curious to know why his cousin still seemed in good health. She nodded but then paused. "But before the horseradish was added. Walker was very slow in making the paste, so I told him to pour it over the curry on the plate and stir it in. If you remember, husband, you were waiting for the dishes."

Mahomet nodded. He now recalled his wife shouting at Walker to hurry up.

Doyle picked up the root. "Bunton said that in its current state it is perfectly benign, and the poison only takes on a potency when the root is ground and added to an acid."

"Vinegar!" exclaimed Jane Mahomet quickly.

"Yes cousin, I am sure that would suffice. But the question still remains; how did this root find itself in this kitchen?"

Neither Mahomet could answer the question.

"I wonder if Walker tasted the paste?" mooted Doyle.

"Perhaps Sarah could tell you," replied Jane Mahomet. "Since he started two weeks ago she has watched him like a hawk. I don't think she trusts him ... and she counts the spoons regularly."

The maid was duly summoned even though she had long retired for the evening, and it took the comfort of Jane Mahomet's hand to calm her when they began to recall, once more, the events of the day.

"There is no need to take on so," her mistress said softly. "We just want to know what you saw."

No mention had made of the monkshood, though Sarah soon noticed it on the table.

"I made him put it back," she said forcefully. "I did right, didn't I ma'am?"

The others looked at her curiously.

"Put what back, Sarah?" asked Mahomet.

"The horseradish, sir," she replied, nodding to the root. "I saw him put it in his pocket and told him I would call you if he didn't put it back. He'd no right to take it ... that's stealing. It's not as if he's hungry. The mistress feeds him enough for two."

The matter seemed to becoming more confusing by the minute.

"When did you see Walker take it, Sarah," asked Doyle, reaching out tentatively for the root as if it were a suspect medical specimen.

"Just before he left sir. I saw him pick it up from the pantry where he'd left it. I made him put it down. After all, it costs, doesn't it? And he'd already used enough of it in that paste. I saw him shave off a great amount and grind it down in the pestle. He could hardly fit it all in, it was spilling so over the side." She gestured with her hands. "No wonder it took him so long to make. And it must have been really spicy, because when he was cleaning up after ..." and here she paused, not willing to mention Sir Josiah's demise, "he threw it away and washed out the bowl. I thought what a waste! The mistress could have watered it down and used it in tomorrow's ... ohhh!"

A sudden realisation dawned on Sarah. "It was in the curry wasn't it? The paste. He'd made it far too strong. It probably choked the gentleman!"

Sarah looked around the table for support.

"Ssshhh now Sarah," Mahomet cautioned. "Horseradish didn't harm the gentlemen," he stated truthfully. It took a minute for Sarah to regain her composure and shortly afterwards she was dismissed back to her bed.

When they were alone once more Doyle asked his relatives: "What do you know of Walker?"

Mahomet looked to his wife who sighed. "Not too much, Decimus," he explained. "He appeared one morning with a letter of introduction written by our previous porter, who explained that he had enlisted in the Royal Navy but recommended Walker to us in his stead. It was quite a shock. He lives along Oxford Street, near to the market in Little Cattle Street. It is quite poor a dwelling, I think, though I am not certain. He said he used to be a butcher or such like; in the meat trade anyway. I agreed to take him on trial. He's clean and tidy enough although quite rough at the edges. Still, he works hard, is here at ten every morning and the kitchen is always clean."

"And now from Sarah we know he prepared the monkshood and cleared it up afterwards," Doyle added.

Jane Mahomet gasped. "Decimus! You don't think ..."

"I think it is our first real fact. What did Sarah say? That he had shaved off a great mass of the root. Why did he do that if, as you have said cousin Jane, his horseradish paste was usually weak? Had you told him to make it stronger?"

Jane Mahomet shook her head.

"And then he clears up the evidence and tries to walk out with the remainder of the root," Doyle continued. "What if he brought it into the kitchen for this very purpose?"

"Thank God you didn't try the sauce first!" exclaimed Mahomet as he reached across the table for his wife's hand.

"It's possible she would never have been allowed to," countered Doyle. "You also said he was slow preparing the paste, cousin. This might have been deliberate. Who knows how much he put into the curry ... obviously enough to kill Sir Josiah. Then tried to take the root away with him and cleaned away the remainder of the sauce. May I stay the night? I think you and I, Sake Mahomet, need to have a talk with Mr Walker as soon as he appears tomorrow morning."

THE three men looked up together at the sound of rustling bushes nearby. They stared into the deep night, stopping their breath as their ears strained to hear what they could not see. The man with the wooden spade gripped the handle tightly, turning it from a tool into a weapon, while the one with the lantern held it up against the darkness in a desperate attempt to cast a light. On seeing this, the third man reached out his hand and forced the lantern back towards the ground, shaking his head vigorously. The bushes moved again and a small shape, blacker against the black, could just be made out moving along the ground following the line of a hedgerow.

"Fox," whispered the man with the spade and all three let out their breath before turning back to the task in hand. The spade man resumed his digging while the other two watched first him and then for signs of movement elsewhere, a difficult task in the darkness which surrounded them, masking their presence but also any possible danger.

The land on which they stood had been purchased by the worthies of Westminster three years previously. The demand for, and price of, land in the city was now so great that this place was the nearest, and cheapest, that could be found. While there had been plans to build great mausoleums for the wealthy, in the end it was being used as a place of repose for the labouring poor and county – that is pauper – burials. The city fathers had built a high wall to enclose the burial ground, but this did not deter real men of business such as the three who now plied their trade in the middle of the night.

The spade man had been digging for less than five minutes when he hit wood. "Shallow," said the lantern man smiling.

Quickly all three joined together to clear the soil from the lid of the box, which lay a foot or so below ground. Clearing a space for himself, the spade man jumped into the pit and, with his feet on either side, prized open with his bare hands the wooden lid, which quickly splintered and gave as he pulled.

"Don't make 'em like they used to," quipped the lantern man, who lowered his light to inspect the contents of the box. "E's in a good state," he said approvingly.

"Good innuf fer Barts?" asked the third man.

"Better the 'unterian," advised the spade man, "e's 'ardly started to go off."

Indeed in life young Robert had been a fine specimen of a man – a farmer's boy who had left the bosom of a loving family and ventured to London seeking his fortune. His destiny lay, however, beneath an overturned wagon in Oxford Street, and by the time they removed the weight from his crushed leg he had bled to death. Unknown and uncared for in the great city, his body had been quickly dispatched to the burial ground to the north east of the village of Paddington. Now his only possessions were a dirty muslin shroud in which his body had been wrapped, and a thin silvered ring on his left digitus minimus mánus – his pinkie – a family heirloom which had been passed from father to son over the years before finding its way into this shallow grave. Why those who had prepared, conveyed and buried young Robert had not acquired it was a mystery, but the lantern man, when his sight caught the glint of the metal in the light he was holding, was less reticent. He quickly grasped the hand and pulled the ring from the finger, dislocating the bone in the process.

The spade man, who had been lifting the body to the side of the grave with the third companion, snarled. "Leave it!" he hissed, his voice breaking into the silence of the night.

"But ..."

"Leave it I said. It could be a trick. No takin'. I'll not be 'anged for you."

The lantern man, now clenching tightly the treasure trove in his hand, drew breath and readied himself to make an argument, but the spade man grasped his arm.

"It'll go back in the 'ole and you wiv it. Now drop it!" he barked.

For a moment there was a tense atmosphere as, standing over the body of the young farmer, they faced each other. Then the lantern man dropped his shoulders and, smiling ruefully, threw the small ring into the grave. I can always come back for it, he consoled himself, though even as he thought this he knew he wouldn't. In any case, he had just successfully completed a special commission for a gentleman who had paid him very well, and he had already decided that this would be his last dig. He needed neither the company of these two ruffians nor money from digging up the dead. Now he wanted to catch-up on some sleep so would leave these two idiots to sell the body and collect his share later. Albeit he had worked much harder in his time, the stresses of the day had taken their toll.

His erstwhile companions, seeing him relent, quickly stripped Robert of his muslin shroud and threw that into the grave as well, at which the spade man began filling in the hole. The others wrapped the body tightly in hessian cloth and tied it up securely. Within ten minutes they were gone, and only a sharp-eyed gravedigger or undertaker would ever suspect that young Robert was no longer at rest. And even if someone did spot the telltale signs of disturbed earth, would they really care?

WHEN the young Scottish physician William Hunter first arrived in London in the 1740s, he studied under the great William Smellie, known as the father of British midwifery. Hunter soon made his mark, and his courtly manners and common sense led him to become physician to Queen Charlotte. By 1768 he was so established as to be able to build his own medical theatre and school in Great Windmill Street – modestly named the Hunterian. Dr Simon Bunton had first attended classes given by the august William Hunter some ten years later, and the good doctor was later able to use this association to his advantage, claiming that Hunter often remarked how able he, Bunton, was as a student. The fact there were no longer any colleagues at the school able to gainsay this claim also weighed in Bunton's favour.

It also helped that the Hunterian was in receipt of a steady flow of newly deceased bodies. The only legal supply of bodies for medical research came from the gallows after those condemned to death by the courts received the ultimate judgment. Unfortunately for medical schools judges were increasingly partial to transporting criminals to the new colony of New South Wales at the other end of the world for heinous crimes such as stealing bread. Less than one hundred bodies were legally available each year, even though the medical schools required nearer five hundred to conduct their work. And as the number of medical schools in London increased, they were not averse to using the services of resurrection men, who would secretly disinter bodies from graves for medical research.

For a country so squeamish about interfering with the dead, stealing a corpse was simply classed as a misdemeanour, and so subject to a small fine. It was only if the body snatcher took possessions from the grave along with the body that it became a felony and punishable by prison or even, ironically, the noose, so they were very careful to stay on the right side of the law. Resurrectionists flourished, and relatives would stand guard over a body and keep watch after the burial, to ensure their loved ones had a chance of true resurrection on Judgment Day. Wealthier families even commissioned iron railings around the graves called mort safes.

Midnight had come and gone on the day in which Dr Bunton had attended the drama at the Hindostanee Coffee House, and he was now to be found waiting patiently at the rear doors to the Hunterian's surgical theatre, with two assistants in attendance. There was rhythmic knock: the signal. Bunton nodded to the assistants and they opened the double fronted door. In stole two men, wheeling between them a covered costermonger's cart. Both wore hats drawn low over their eyes and were enveloped in over large black coachmen's coats. Bunton thought they could not be more suspicious if they tried.

"Gentlemen," the doctor said in a low voice as the doors were closed behind them. "Quickly now ... you are late. So, what have we here?"

"See fer yerself guvnor," said the taller of the two men, drawing back the cloth in the cart. Bunton stepped forward and, gingerly, began to pull at the thin cloth. He exposed the remains of a young man, possibly no more than twenty years old. He must have been quite tall, because in order to squeeze him into the cart the resurrection men had broken his spine to force the top of the body backwards. There was also very serious damage to the right leg, the bones of which were crushed.

"He is in a contrary condition," said Bunton, more to himself than the men., "and has a badly damaged leg I see."

"He's young guvnor, and 'ardly gone off," replied the taller man, who was obviously the negotiator. "You'll find 'is innards all there, and 'e's very 'ealthy, so to speak."

Bunton directed his assistants to lift the body partly out of the cart to continue his inspection. The poor boy, he thought, is probably of a similar age to the gentlemen who would get to dissect him later that next day. And the resurrectionists knew their business: apart from the leg he had been in good physical condition – a fine specimen, in fact. He signalled to the assistants to take the body into the theatre and turned to the men of the night.

"How much?"

"Fifty guv'nor," came the sharp reply.

"Shillings?"

"Guineas!"

Bunton laughed quietly. "I'll call him back and you can take him away."

"He's the best you'll see fer some time," replied the tall man sharply, now pushing his hat back so Bunton could see his entire face. It was hard, the face of a man who had seen too much too quickly. A large scar down his right cheek was displayed like a badge of authority. The doctor knew this was going to be a challenge.

"I'm only authorised to go to ten guineas," he replied in a neutral voice.

"Then giv us 'im back," came the tart reply.

Bunton sighed. "I cannot give you what you ask," he pleaded. "If you take him from here, what are the chances of you making it all the way to the London?" He also knew that Sir William Blizard of the London Medical School at Barts was a tight fisted old curmudgeon who would never pay more than twenty guineas – and the resurrectionists probably knew this as well. The two men looked at each other for some time.

"Forty," the resurrection man finally relented.

"Fifteen."

"Thirty five."

Bunton tutted. "Look man, this could go on all night. You'll take twenty or take the body. Which is it?"

The force of Bunton's voice brought the two Hunterian assistants back from where they had placed the body. Whether it was the fact the two body snatchers were facing superior numbers or that Bunton's last statement had an air of finality, the tall man nodded to Bunton.

"Good," sighed the doctor, and began counting the coinage into the proffered hand. As they were about to leave Bunton asked curiously: "Where is the third man who is usually with you?"

The tall man looked back at the doctor and smiled. "Disappeared 'e 'as! So we're cuttin' 'im out. Anyways, 'e's a pain in the neck and would 'ave us swinging from the rope if 'e could. Good riddance to Walker, I says."

Chapter 4

London in the late summer of 1811. The following afternoon ...

THE London home of the Honourable Basil Cochrane was reputed to be the largest mansion in Portman Square, and quite befitting the sixth son of the eighth Earl of Dundonald. Yet this might not have been the case, since as a younger son Cochrane was born with limited prospects. In 1769 young Basil was placed as a clerk in the East India Company based in Madras, and when he returned to England forty years later was fabulously wealthy. This was due to contracts he negotiated to supply the Royal Navy in the Eastern Oceans, and the size of these contracts raised more than an eyebrow in Parliament. So Cochrane's first task on returning to England had been to defend his wealth from charges of embezzlement – something of an occupational hazard for East India Company men.

Cochrane's mansion housed not only the noble Nabob but also the Ambassador of Mahmud II, Sultan of Sultans, Khan of Khans, Caliph of the Faithful, Servant of the Cities of Mecca, Medina and Jerusalem etc. etc. etc. to George the Third, by the Grace of God, of the United Kingdom of Great Britain and Ireland King, Defender of the Faith ... and so forth. Not that Farmer George would have been aware of such an illustrious visitor coming to call. In February 1811 Parliament had passed the Regency Act, setting up the King's vainglorious son the Prince of Wales as British Regent in his father's stead. Throughout his life King George had suffered from illness, which sometimes displayed itself in the most bizarre behaviour such as his rumoured talking to trees, and this latest bout had left the ailing and aging monarch confined to a small suite of rooms in Windsor Castle watched over by surgeons whom his ever devoted Queen referred to as gaolers. By contrast the Ottoman Ambassador, Ramadani Efendi, occupied a suite of rooms within Cochrane's palatial house which included a private prayer room facing Mecca, grandly referred to as a mosque.

Nor was this the only Oriental flavour to the Cochrane household. On the ground floor, accessed by a side entrance off Portman Square, was a vapour bath which the altruistic Cochrane had established for use by London's lower classes – or in any case for those of a lower rank than the sixth son of an eighth earl. He had patented his own Indian water cure, which included a complicated process of sitting in a flannelled tent while a spray of heated water was applied by an attendant who also used soapy pads on those parts of the patient's body which could be accessed with modesty. Sadly, the baths had not been deemed very popular among Londoners, who balked at the idea of paying money to cleanse themselves.

For the main part, though, the Cochrane mansion reflected others around the square; imposing front doors opened onto a marbled main hall, from which a delicate staircase swept majestically upwards towards the reception rooms on the first floor. The decoration of the house was an eclectic mix of classical and Oriental, as championed by the late Robert Adam in other properties around the square, including the house originally commissioned by Elizabeth, Countess of Home and which was now occupied by Cochrane's good friend John Murray, the 4th Duke of Atholl. And it was while he was entertaining his noble friend that Cochrane was disturbed by one of his Indian servants, a distinguished looking man in flowing white robes and neatly trimmed grey beard called Manjai, who had silently entered the library on the first floor where the two men were seated discussing the latest political affairs. Bowing low and speaking in an even lower voice, the servant begged his master's forgiveness.

"My apologies, sahibs," he said, bowing again to the two men. "I have been asked to request that my master grant an urgent audience to Sake Dean Mahomet, who has presented himself together with a young gentleman by the name of Doyle. I advised you were in conference with the noble lord, but the Sake asked that you be made aware of the pressing nature of his call."

Cochrane raised an eyebrow as he looked first at his servant and then at the duke. He had known Mahomet from his time in Madras and had readily accepted his re-acquaintance when the man had come looking for work some years ago. The Indian had impressed in running the London household, and especially in handling Cochrane's Indian servants, who seemed to look on Mahomet as a visiting member of Mughul royalty. So when Mahomet had outlined his plans last year to open a coffee house, Cochrane had offered his fulsome support. It was unlike the man to call unannounced, especially when he knew his patron was entertaining someone of the stature of the Duke of Atholl. He paused to consider the request.

"Very well Manjai, if his grace will pardon my leave to attend to this interruption ..?"

The duke nodded. "If you think it important Cochrane, then I am sure I can keep myself amused ..." and waved his hand airily towards the library's groaning bookshelves, while his head nodded towards the decanter of port wine and glasses that sat on the small table between them. Both men had several physical similarities. They were roughly of the same height of five foot nine, wore traditional, and now very old fashioned, short powdered wigs in public to shroud their thinning grey hair, and both displayed all the necessary attributes of a comfortable life – including ruddy cheeks and a generous girth.

There was also another, more secretive, association between the men. Both were members of the Ancient Grand Lodge of England, which in Free Masonry rivalled the Premier Grand Lodge in importance. Atholl was now serving his second term as Grand Master, and indeed the Ancients were often referred to as the Atholl Grand Lodge since the 4th Duke's father, the 3rd Duke, had been Grand Master before him.

Cochrane followed his servant from the library to a small audience chamber at the side of the grand staircase on the ground floor. On entering, he was faced by Mahomet and Doyle standing to the centre of the room, the Indian's face displaying great anxiety. All three men bowed and Mahomet quickly introduced his companion to Cochrane.

"So you are an Irish cousin of Mrs Mahomet?" Cochrane asked curiously.

"Doyle is studying at the Hunterian Medical School," explained Mahomet before the young man could reply, "and is close to the matter on which I have come urgently seeking your advice sir."

Cochrane nodded. "Well, Mahomet, you had better out with it," and he gestured for them to sit.

Quietly and succinctly Mahomet explained the events of the previous evening, eliciting murmurs of commiseration from Cochrane, followed by genuine shock at the news of the demise of Harding, and then great concern as the Indian went on to explain the existence of the Queen of Poisons in his kitchen.

"Doyle and I waited for Walker to appear this morning, but he did not arrive. We ventured to his supposed address along Oxford Street but could not find anyone who knew of him. He had told us he worked in the cattle market but, if so, no one was willing to acknowledge his existence. He seems to have disappeared."

Cochrane tutted as he considered the story Mahomet had related.

"This is a to-do, Mahomet, and no doubt about it. I know – knew – Sir Josiah personally and, while I have no great favour for him, would not wish to have seen him suffer so. You say a stranger comes to work in your kitchens and within two weeks has poisoned one of your patrons. A careless happening I would say," he added unhelpfully. Then he shook his head. "It is certainly a nefarious tale, but I fail to understand why you have come to relate it to me."

Mahomet coughed, clearing his throat, and glanced quickly to Doyle before looking earnestly at Cochrane.

"I ... we ... are in a quandary, your honour, which is why we seek your opinion as a gentleman of great wisdom and understanding. The authorities consider that Sir Josiah died of natural causes, yet we now suspect this might not be the case. What should I do?" he pleaded. "This Walker has disappeared, and we have no physical evidence of the poisoning apart from the remains of the root, my own observations on the nature of Sir Josiah's death, and my housemaid's recollections. Do I report these and, if so, do I stand by and watch my business disappear – which it surely will. And even if I do report it, sir, who will investigate? The magistrates or the coroner or the Runners? And who will pay them? I am not a wealthy man, especially if my business is closed while such an investigation takes place."

Mahomet sat back in his chair overwhelmed by the consequences of such thoughts, and Cochrane looked at Doyle, who simply shrugged and shook his head. Reaching for a delicate porcelain snuffbox from his waistcoat pocket, Cochrane offered a pinch which neither man took.

"I comprehend your difficulty Mahomet," he said after a substantial sneeze. "Who knows of all this?"

"Ourselves, Mrs Mahomet and Dr Bunton sir," replied Doyle, speaking for the first time.

Cochrane paused, turning matters over in his mind.

"Well," he adjudged at last, "my advice is to make sure no more is said. Can this Dr Bunton be trusted to hold his tongue?"

"I think so sir," advised Doyle.

"Make sure he does," retorted Cochrane sternly, before turning to Mahomet. "There is little you can do, sir, to remedy the situation. It is conceivable that you have been as much a victim of an evil act as poor Harding, but how are you to find out if that is the case and what good would it do? No doubt this Walker, if he conducted matters as you fear, was planning to walk away without you ever knowing the truth. And I strongly advise this remains the case. Had you been none the wiser, you may have considered his subsequent non-appearance as simply an understandable fear of being so closely associated with death. I also doubt whether any magistrate or coroner would welcome a wild goose chase. Nor, as you have already said, would the Runners."

The system of law enforcement in London had changed little since medieval times. In 1748 the author of Tom Jones, Henry Fielding, was appointed chief magistrate at London's Bow Street Court. He reported to the government that too many people were coming to London for an easy life; government corruption was rife; people were choosing crime rather than hard work; and London's constables were useless. He sacked all but six of London's 80 constables and set up his Bow Street Runners. Similar to "thief-takers", men who would solve petty crime for a fee, the Runners were mostly paid by the court. Fielding's brother, John, took over from him as chief magistrate in 1754 when Henry died, and continued to mould the

Runners into an effective police force. Being blind, John became known as the "Blind Beak of Bow Street", and was said to recognise over 3,000 criminals by their speech alone. Yet Cochrane was right that it was unlikely that the Fielding brothers' successors would have been unduly interested in Mahomet's suspicions.

"In the meantime," continued Cochrane, "we must take steps to protect what trade your coffee house has, sir. To this end I will make every effort to attend and will encourage other fellows to do so as well. I appreciate your efforts to present Indian delicacies, Mahomet, but perhaps this is the time to offer simpler fare, such as beef-steaks and pies. After all, as news circulates about this death of yours, I doubt you will find many takers for curries and the like, even for those not prepared with poison."

SAKE Dean Mahomet and Decimus Doyle sat in the small family drawing room above the dining room of the Hindostanee Coffee House considering the events of the day. They had both come away from their meeting with the Honourable Basil Cochrane with a feeling of discomfort, yet neither was entirely convinced why. It was late afternoon on another fine summer's day. The children were playing in the small gardens of Montague Square further along George Street, and Jane Mahomet was preparing for their re-opening. She had already turned away a couple of patrons who had knocked fiercely at the door demanding entrance. She suspected these as being no more than ghoulish interlopers, so she had placed a sign on the door saying the coffee house would re-open from six o'clock that evening.

"I will caution Bunton when I return to his house this evening," Doyle advised, and Mahomet nodded but did not speak. "You seem distracted Sake Mahomet," he added cautiously.

Mahomet stood and began pacing around the small room.

"It makes no sense Decimus, no sense at all. Why kill this man in my coffee house? I do not know much about the Hardings, but they seem to be a very reputable family. What possible connection can they have to this man Walker? And what of Walker? Unless he was hiding a considerable light under a bushel, I would not have said him capable of planning such a thing."

Steam seemed to rise from Mahomet's brow and he took out a handkerchief to wipe it away.

"You are right that there are so many questions, but how can we answer them?"

Mahomet looked at the young man.

"Well Decimus, by my reckoning only we can. I have to agree with Cochrane's advice and say no more publicly on this matter, if only for my own family's sake, but I cannot stand by and witness a man poison one of my customers. We must do something about it."

Mahomet's determination took Doyle by surprise.

"I repeat my question, Sake Mahomet. What can we do?"

Mahomet stopped pacing and sat down in his chair.

"We know the poison, the poisoned and the poisoner, that is a start. So we must find Walker and find out why he killed Sir Josiah. If only for my own peace of mind, I must know why this wicked thing has happened."

Doyle sat back in his chair, considering their options, which did not look promising. "Walker has disappeared without a trace ..."

"But we might be able to find out more about him," Mahomet interrupted, not prepared to be gainsaid. "He might have spoken with Jane and Sarah about his life, and perhaps there was some truth in what he said. I will sit with them tonight and make them remember. Jane says Sarah was suspicious of him from the beginning. Perhaps she saw or heard more than she has yet to recall."

Doyle was encouraged. "And I will find out more about Sir Josiah."

"Jane said there was a death notice in today's *Times*. He is being buried at St Mary-le-Bone tomorrow."

"Then I will start by attending the funeral," nodded Doyle. "Surely there must be some connection between him and Walker. I cannot believe it was simply co-incidence that Walker prepared the horseradish paste for Sir Josiah's curry. How often did the dead man visit your coffee house, Sake Mahomet?"

The Indian considered this. "I would say at least twice a week. At first he was mostly alone, but for the past few months he was accompanied regularly by his younger son. I think he was educating him in Indian tastes. Yet he always ate the same dish, Jane's vegetable curry. Walker would have seen him a few times before yesterday, as I often require help in carrying dishes through to the dining room. If he were observing Sir Josiah, he would have known for whom the vegetable curry was ordered."

Both men sat in silence for some minutes. "Poison?" said Doyle questioningly. "I have not seen Walker, but from what you and cousin Jane have said, it does not seem ... natural. I mean, a cosh over the head in a dark alley would sound his sort of thing."

Mahomet thought about this and nodded. "You are right, Decimus. It was a very sophisticated way to kill someone. Far too clever for Walker. But then, if so, he must have been working for someone."

"He was a hired killer?"

Mahomet nodded. "An assassin."

"Was Sir Josiah that important?"

Mahomet shrugged. "You will have to find that out."

THE lady looked intently, firstly at her dress and then to her face in the silvered glass peering back at her in the darkened room.

"Out, damned spot! Out, I say!" she exclaimed, staring maniacally at her reflection. "One; two; why, then, 'tis time to do 't. Hell is murky! Fie, my lord, fie! A soldier, and afeard? What need we fear who knows it, when none can call our power to account? Yet who would have thought the old man to have had so much blood in him?"

She paused, her ample bosom heaving beneath the brocade dress with the intensity of her words. Her cheeks had flushed, though it was difficult to tell beneath the powdered mask that was her face. She drew in air, filling her lungs in preparation for another declamation when a petite, young woman appeared in the mirror behind her, and curtsied. The woman expelled her breath.

"Yes, Melissa, what is it?" she asked irritably.

"Begging your pardon ma'am but it's nearly time to go."

"Time?"

"The rehearsal ma'am. We must leave shortly."

The lady sighed. "Confounded nuisance!" she exclaimed. "I was distracted by the notice in the paper concerning poor Josiah. Why did he have to go and die now?" She paused. "Oh well. He was good to us and deserves a hero's send off. We will go to the funeral. For now I will have to show mourning, so the black crepe dress I think, Melissa."

The young woman bobbed and left her mistress alone once more staring into the mirror.

"To-morrow and to-morrow and to-morrow creeps in this petty pace from day to day," she recited. "To the last syllable of recorded time, and all our yesterdays have lighted fools the way to dusty death."

She smiled into the mirror, which was lit to one side by a large candle in a silver holder.

"The men always get the best lines," she told herself, and in her mind an image passed of a youthful actress playing the lead in *Hamlet* to great acclaim and much controversy. Then she exclaimed: "Poor Josiah! ... Your suitors are beginning to fall off at a pace Sarah. You will have to find another comfort now for your retirement."

She put a hand to her face, gently smoothing the powder, before reaching up and slightly adjusting her hair, which she wore parted at the front and tied into a loose bun on top. It had also been dyed black by means of a boiled concoction supplied by her apothecary and made from the rind of the fig tree, galls, dates, brambles and cypress. She sighed. It was at times like this, at news of death or infirmity, that she felt all her years. She had recently decided the time had come to step down from the stage, and news such as the death of her friend only reassured her of that decision. If she was to enjoy her remaining years and bask in the plaudits – and the money – she had earned, now was the time, before God took it all away from her. This latest death had disturbed her. She had always considered Josiah to be hearty. It had been some time since they had entertained each other in intimate liaison, but surely his ample size was testimony to his rude health?

The return of her young dresser carrying an elaborately embroidered black silk dress broke her train of thought. Standing up, she felt a twinge in her hip, a reminder of a bad fall on stage last year and another reason for her decision to retire.

"Come Melissa, help me out of this and into that. Then I need the silver button shoes and the grey pelisse with the fur trim. Let the others be in full mourning should they so wish. In any case, I doubt I would be welcome by the family if I were to turn up at the funeral."

The next few minutes were taken in making madam presentable, the final act being the drawing on a pair fine black kid gloves. The lady looked in the mirror.

"A bit of a mish-mash perhaps but it makes the appropriate gesture, I think."

She paused once more, looking first at the young woman next to her, then at her own reflection in the mirror and then finally at the candle. She touched the large jet necklace at her neck and reached for the silver snuffer.

"Out, out, brief candle!" she cried theatrically. "Life's but a walking shadow, a poor player, that struts and frets his hour upon the stage and then is heard no more."

And with that she extinguished the light and swept from the room, her dresser following in her wake.

Chapter 5

A good crust for great pies.
To a peck of flour add the yolks of three eggs; then boil some water,
and put in half a pound of fried suet, and a pound and a half of
butter. Skim off the butter and suet, and as much of the liquor as will
make it a light crust: work it up well, and roll it out.
The Art of Cookery Made Plain and Easy

London in the late summer of 1811. The following day …

DECIMUS Doyle had returned to his lodgings at Dr Bunton's house in
Soho late the previous evening, after leaving his cousin and her husband
still in some state of anxiety. He had walked slowly along Oxford Street and
then down Swallow Street, before cutting through Golden Square and
home. The house was quiet and Bunton not at home. The housekeeper Mrs
Mac rustled up a wholesome pottage and bread, which he downed with a
glass of claret before retiring. Yet tired though he was, he could not sleep.
It was after midnight when he heard Bunton return, and mooted whether
he should rise and discuss matters with him. However, on hearing his tutor's
profanities as he tripped over something in the darkened hallway, he
realised that a late night conference was not advisable. Dr Bunton, it
seemed, was in his cups. So Doyle turned over in bed and tried to sleep
once more, but when he finally rose at seven the next morning he felt just
as agitated and uneasy as he had the night before.

The death notice in *The Times* had said Sir Josiah was being interred at
St Mary-le-Bone parish church at eleven that morning. He wanted to be
early so he could study the mourners as they arrived, and was correct in
guessing that he would probably leave the house before Bunton rose. He
was determined to have a word with him at the first opportunity following
the funeral, if only to impress on him Cochrane's counsel in keeping silent
about events at the coffee house, so asked Mrs Mac to detain her master at

home for as long as she could. To her credit the housekeeper, used to Bunton's often-erratic behaviour, suggested it was unlikely the good doctor would venture forth at all that day.

"As you know, he always ... take solace ... after cutting up a body, sir," she cautioned as Doyle left for the funeral. "It affects him, especially if it is a healthy specimen. A porter at the college told me they had a young man in yesterday, and the master was quite melancholy during the examination. I suspect the White Horse made a tidy profit last night."

The current parish church of St Mary-le-Bone was the third dedicated to St Mary the Virgin by the Ty bourne (now no more than a covered sewer), and was constructed in 1740. It was small and intimate – indeed too intimate for the recently arrived and wealthy residents of west London, and the Duke of Portland had commissioned the construction a new church further along the High Street. As this had yet to materialise, the place in which Charles Wesley was buried and where Lord Nelson had once worshipped – and his daughter Horatia baptized – still ministered to the needs of the parishioners of Mary-le-Bone village. Among its worshippers the late Sir Josiah Harding had been a benefactor, and for his efforts had been able to purchase a place of rest for his wife and himself in the crypt below the altar.

When Doyle arrived at quarter past the hour of ten the cramped oak panelled church was still empty. After walking around, where he came across a brass plate bearing the name of Elizabeth, Lady Harding, dearly beloved wife of Josiah and mother to George and William and her infant child Charlotte, he settled himself in a boxed pew to the rear and near to the door; an ideal vantage point. Slowly the mourners arrived, though not as many that might have been expected for a Knight of the Realm. At a quarter to the hour he was surprised to see a lady of some bearing enter the church, her face obscured by a large black felt hat with veil and accompanied by a pretty, if petite, young woman. The lady looked around and was observed by some of the mourners, most of whom were seated towards the front. Her presence caused an immediate stir, with rapid whispers and furtive glances among the thirty or so who had gathered. The lady, who was standing close to Doyle's pew, nodded at him and presented herself, indicating he should move along so she could be seated. Doyle, now flustered, shuffled along rather than standing. The power of her scent as she sat down next to him was overwhelming, and reminded him of the smell of incense on his occasional visits to the Catholic church of his father's tenants back in Ireland. He was about to introduce himself when the organ started playing funereal music and the church doors opened. A small procession made up of the vicar, bearers carrying a large oak coffin and followed by two gentlemen mourners and a lady shrouded in black made their way up the aisle.

Doyle had only attended three funerals in his life, and this was his first in England. To him it was as formal as the dancing assemblies he had attended. There was little emotion, apart from the occasional sob from the lady sitting next to him, and the word he would later use to describe it to Mahomet was perfunctory. He strained to catch sight of the principal mourners, whom he identified as the sons from Mahomet's description of them. But with their backs turned he could guess little of their emotional state from the partial facial expressions he observed.

At the end of the service the coffin was taken to one side, he assumed for later interment in the crypt, and the mourners were led from the church by the Harding brothers. As they passed the pew in which Doyle, the lady and her maid were now standing both George and William gave them hard, accusing stares, while the veiled lady nodded slightly. Most of the mourners, especially the women, scurried past. The church was now empty apart from one or two stragglers, and Doyle waited for the lady and her maid to leave the pew before he, too, could depart, as he was keen to question some of the disappearing mourners. But instead the lady turned and, with a piercing look, said; "Funerals are always difficult, don't you think?"

Her voice had great resonance which temporarily captured the student doctor's tongue, yet he was able to say; "It was a moving service."

She looked at him surprised. "Really? You think so? Then you have not experienced much in life, young man."

He was taken aback but before he could respond the lady spoke again.

"Poor Josiah deserved more than this ..." she began but then caught herself. "But perhaps not. He really did not contribute much, for all his worldly advantage. No, on reflection this was probably all he could expect – indolent children and indifferent mourners. But for all that, he was a good friend."

The lady looked at Doyle for a few moments, as if calculating his worth.

"And you, young man ... you are Irish from the sound if it ... what are you to the deceased?"

Doyle had rehearsed what he would say if asked this question while walking to Mary-le-Bone village, but now had to grasp at words in his mind.

"I ... I am a representative of the establishment where Sir Josiah died," he said.

The lady raised an eyebrow above one of her dark eyes.

"You were present at his death?"

Doyle shook his head. "Shortly afterwards ma'am."

She hesitated, and then turned to her maid.

"Wait at the door Melissa," she commanded, before turning back to Doyle.

"Come young man, and accompany me around this pretty little church. There is a plaque on the wall yonder I would wish to examine."

She left the pew and walked up the aisle of the church, now deserted except for the organist looking down from his gantry in the loft. Doyle followed close behind. Who was this lady, he wondered, and what did she want? He tried to estimate her age; forty, possibly, but not much more. She paused to the left of the altar and looked upwards, as if to read the inscriptions on remembrance plaques. Doyle stood to her side and also looked upwards.

"My name is Decimus Doyle, ma'am," he began but she held up a gloved finger.

"Names are of no importance sir," she countered in a stage whisper. "What I would like to hear is a true account of poor Josiah's final moments. ... Please Mr Doyle."

He then recounted as accurately as he could the description of the death he had been given by Sake Mahomet. He half considered omitting the part where Sir Josiah's body shook and then slowly expired, but had a feeling this lady would keep her own counsel. He did not, however, mention any suspicion that the dead man had been poisoned. The lady shook her head when he finished.

"Poor Josiah," she whispered, and reached for a lace handkerchief from the folds of her grey coat. They stood in silence for some moments, before Doyle asked, "You were closely acquainted with Sir Josiah, ma'am?"

The lady turned to look at him and smiled wanly. "Not any more, Mr Doyle, but we once shared a brief moment in our lives. I had hoped to renew our acquaintance next year when I expect to have more time. We ... shall we say parted ... a few years ago, strangely just after his wife died, though he still called on me occasionally, you understand."

Doyle thought he did and nodded, but was not quite sure.

"Sir Josiah's sons did not take too kindly to our presence I fear," he prompted, hoping she would continue. She duly obliged.

"My presence, I think you mean. His sons never appreciated my friendship with their father. I supposed they saw me as a replacement for their mother. Charlotte Harding died in giving birth to Lottie, you see, hence the young girl's name. Later I realised the boys were simply jealous of the attention Josiah lavished on me. William was especially spiteful as a child and was a problem for Josiah, who in turn would never spare the rod. His chastisement of William concerned me, and I suppose placed some distance between us, as did his close attachment to Lottie which I suppose could be seen as indelicate ... well, no matter now. It must have been quite a shock for them both to see me here today. I thought at one time I could be a mother for little Lottie, but it wasn't to be. Poor child. Josiah protected her jealously, and the boys followed his lead. She knows little of life, and is hidden away in that ramshackle house of theirs. She must be, what, seventeen. Who will bring her out into Society now? Not fat George, the eldest, that's for sure ... Sir George now, I suppose. I wouldn't be surprised if he hadn't contributed to putting his father into an early grave."

Doyle's ears pricked up. "In what way ma'am?" he asked eagerly.

She waved her hand airily towards the remembrance plaques as if bringing them into their conversation.

"Oh!" she declaimed, "every one knows he's a gambler, and a bad one at that. If it moves, George will bet on it ... and lose. He is good for nothing except for tending to his blessed plants and making bad wagers. It's a shame he doesn't apply himself more. Poor Josiah was at his wit's end ... at least that is what he told me last time we met ... what, two months ago? Perhaps all that shaking your friend witnessed at the end was Josiah's heart giving up. You did say the boys were with him. No doubt their mere presence was enough to finish him off. Thank you for giving of your time sir. You have been a most attentive gentleman. Good-day Mr Doyle."

The lady's opinion of the Harding brothers was far from complimentary, but Doyle was unsure whether this was grounded in truth or grief at the passing of her dear friend. She sniffed and drew in a great gulp of air, as if inflating her lungs for a final denouement. But instead she turned and began to walk towards her maid at the rear of the church, the student doctor following meekly. At the door she turned to Doyle and nodded.

"Thank you young man for your time," she said and turned to leave before Doyle could make any further comment. He watched her stride off along Mary-le-Bone High Street, her maid scurrying behind.

"Amazing woman," said a voice from behind, which startled him. It was the organist who had come down from his lofty eyrie.

"You know her sir?" Doyle asked.

"Of course sir, as should you."

Doyle was at a loss and the quizzical look on his face invited the organist to continue.

"Have you never been to the theatre sir? You have just been talking to Mrs Siddons ... Sarah Siddons the renowned actress."

AT the Hindostanee Coffee House things were returning to normal – or as near to normality as circumstances would allow. In the kitchen Jane Mahomet was being excessively careful, constantly locking and then opening the large oak dresser in which much of the food had now been consigned, to check that none had been tampered with. And at her husband's suggestion she was elbow deep in beef dripping and flour, making a crust for the steak pies they were now to offer. Both the horseradish and ginger roots had been unceremoniously disposed of and Sarah was under strict instructions to scrub all surfaces over and over again. With Walker's disappearance, William Mahomet had been from his schooling to help his mother in the kitchen until another pair of hands could be engaged.

That morning Sake Dean Mahomet had once more spoken to his wife and their maid about Walker, hoping to shed some light on the mysterious man they had allowed into the kitchen with such tragic consequences.

"I'd rather not recall anything more about the wretched man," Jane Mahomet had initially declared, and it took some effort to calm her down in the privacy of their upstairs sitting room.

"I need to know what you can recall about him, my pearl, even the most innocuous details," he implored and, understanding the seriousness of the situation, she finally agreed to concentrate on Walker's time at the coffee house. Yet there was little she could add.

"He seemed to talk and talk but, you know husband, I cannot recall what he talked about. It was just nonsense and I didn't often respond except to ask him to be quiet."

"How did we know that he worked as a butcher?"

She closed her eyes. "If you recall, husband, he told us where he lived when he first arrived looking for work. You liked that he lived so close." Then she furrowed her brow. "Did he tell us he had been a butcher? I don't now recall. Perhaps because he lived near the market we assumed he was a butcher. He could have been a drover or delivery boy!"

This isn't helping, thought Mahomet, then a curious thought crossed his mind. "Do you recall how he knew we were looking for help, my pearl?"

Walker had presented himself at the kitchen door with a letter from the Mahomets' previous help, Samuel. It was a shock when they read that Samuel had been recruited into the Royal Navy while visiting his family in Deptford. The Mahomets had often heard Samuel, who was in his late twenties, talk of going to sea like many others in his family, but they had considered this to be no more than bravado, and on hearing the news were unsure whether he had been pressed into service or otherwise compelled. However, Samuel was by now far out on the High Seas. His letter had strongly recommended Walker for the position and was in Samuel's rough hand.

Jane Mahomet shook her head. "It was such a shock to receive that news. Samuel was so good with the younger gentlemen, if you recall, and took after you in talking to them. Remember, husband, that I had to chastise him for being so familiar, especially with the son of the gentleman who died."

"Sir Josiah's son? Yes, I recall now. Sam was such a good boy."

"We were simply grateful that Samuel had sent us Walker in his stead. He seemed capable, so you asked him to start straight away. With so many men in arms, we both know how difficult it can be to get good strong help. I remember you saying not to look a gift horse in the mouth. Now, let me return to the kitchen if you will."

For her part the housemaid Sarah was very suspicious of her master's request that she tell him everything she could about Walker, and she again spoke of her anxiety that the gentleman diner had, in fact, died through too much horseradish in the curry. Yet Mahomet was insistent.

"Please, Sarah, think carefully and tell me everything you can of what Walker said while he was here. Did he mention family or friends, what he had done in the past or where he went to late at night?"

As the master sounded so earnest in his plea, she stared down a the floor for some time deep in thought, though she could not think for the life of her what help she could be.

"I really don't know sir," she said at last. "He would speak all sorts of nonsense which I did not rightly understand, but I cannot recall that we ever had a sensible conversation."

Mahomet sighed so she tried hard to think once more of something, anything, which might help.

"Well," she continued, "I do recall him mentioning some night work he had to attend to that day, though what that was I could not say. And I remember him being vexed when you kept the coffee house open after ten o'clock one night last week. He kept mumbling that he would be late but when I asked what for he just tapped his nose."

"A woman?" asked Mahomet and Sarah blushed. "I don't think so, sir. He wasn't the most ... wholesome ... of characters. He said he acted as an escort to protect gentlemen on the town or such like. I do recall him telling me of fighting off the fallen women of Covent Garden who had alighted on a party of cricketers, and of the respect those gentlemen showed towards him. Walker took delight in trying to shock me."

Walker's seedy nature, in her opinion, prompted in Sarah another memory. "He also mentioned a tavern he liked to frequent in Soho, but the name of it ..." her voice trailed off.

"Please Sarah, try hard to remember, was it in Soho Square?" Mahomet implored, grasping at any straw.

She paused. "No sir, not Soho Square ... Golden Square perhaps ... but not in it ... near to it. It must be next to a brewery, as he boasted that the ale did not have to travel far."

Mahomet knew there to be a brewery in Soho, situated appropriately in Brewer Street. Yet try as she might, Sarah could not expand on this chink of light into the life of the erstwhile Walker.

"I'm sorry master, but that's all I can recall about the man. A know-it-all he was, always going on about his specialist knowledge of herbs and the like. I suppose that's why the mistress trusted him to make the horseradish sauce." At which point, with the terrible memories of the fateful evening coming back to her, she gurgled and held her hand to her mouth. Bobbing quickly, she exited the room.

DR Simon Bunton was fascinated to hear Doyle's recollection of his encounter with Mrs Siddons earlier in the day. Before he returned to his lodgings Doyle had walked from the church in St Mary-le-Bone to the Hindostanee Coffee House where, seated with Mahomet once more, they had poured over the few scraps of information they had gleaned. It was agreed they would visit the taverns around Brewer Street the following evening to make enquiries or, even better, run Walker to ground, and Mahomet was particularly interested in the news of George Harding's considerable debts. Doyle had agreed to call on Mrs Siddons to see if she would take him further into her confidence.

"So you are intending to call on your *femme fatale*!" smiled Bunton, when Doyle outlined his plan for the following day after one of Mrs Mac's more filling dinners, laid on specially to replace the hole left in Bunton's stomach from the previous night's alcohol.

"I do not think it would be appropriate for you to accompany me ..." Doyle began to explain, but Bunton waved his excuses away.

"Of course not! It would be highly inappropriate to join with a Bond Street beau to an assignation with an actress." Still, as a cognoscente of London theatre he was also somewhat envious of the young Irishman.

Doyle winced at his suggestion. "I was hoping you would know where I might approach her, Bunton, giving your particular knowledge of actresses."

Bunton continued to smile. "It has been a long time since I have been tempted by such dalliances, young man, but I think you could do worse than to start at the Covent Garden theatre. I believe she opens in *Macbeth* later this month. You might have to fight the other beaus hanging around the stage door, though, to gain entrance."

Doyle paused at Bunton's remark. "No doubt she was a beauty in her time, sir, but I should think her attractions are now somewhat limited. She is a fine, but mature, woman."

"Love looks not with the eyes but with the mind, young man," responded Bunton, using one of his favourite quotes. "Do not belittle the power Mrs Siddons holds over men. Her fame is as intoxicating for many as more fleshly conceits, so I give you a word of caution. Do not enter the temptress's lair with an unprotected heart, or she will devour it. But do not take my word for it. Ask Mrs Galindo. She published a pamphlet – before you enrolled here some three years ago but not long enough for it to fade from memory – accusing our temptress of seducing her husband. Galindo was Mrs Siddon's Dublin fencing master it seems, and taught her more than just how to thrust and parry ... and the lady did not deny it!"

Bunton winked at his young protégé but Doyle thought the venerable doctor's mind was still suffering the effects of last night's excesses so decided to change the subject.

"Would you accompany us tomorrow evening in our search for Mahomet's missing servant?"

Bunton smiled once more, this time at his student's obvious deceit, but found the offer of a night frequenting inns of ill repute tempting.

"Of course, and perhaps we should take one of the college porters for protection. There's no need to take any chances if we find your man."

Doyle nodded. "A strange co-incidence," he said. "Mahomet mentioned that his maid thought Walker was also working similarly for young bucks and the like."

"Is that his name ... Walker?" asked Bunton.

Doyle nodded.

"I would swear I've heard that name mentioned to me quite recently." He paused. "Oh well, it'll come to me no doubt."

Chapter 6

London in the late summer of 1811. Some days later ...

SAKE Dean Mahomet sat in the family room above the Hindostanee Coffee House staring at the piece of paper before him. It was the bill from Dr Phillips for attending on Sir Josiah Harding – five guineas, a princely sum for such a brief visit and an amount Mahomet knew they could ill afford. He turned the paper over in his hands time and again, as if the movement of his fingers would magick it away. The business was already heavily indebted to the bank – Drummonds, courtesy of an introduction by the Honourable Basil Cochrane – and he did not possess anything else to present them with as surety. They has taken his hard earned deposits accumulated over the past twenty years, together with the small mining investments bequeathed to him by his first patron, Godfrey Evan Baker. The family had been reduced to making do and mending, and to eating entirely from foodstuffs which should have been prepared and sold in the coffee house – not that this affected the little trade they now had. And the quarter day rent was due next month. He had already missed the June payment and knew the landlord would not be understanding for much longer. They needed more money, and quickly.

He sighed, stood and, clutching the paper, walked over to a small mahogany bureau in front of the window, unlocking it and pushing the doctor's account into a draw already full with similar bills of trade. He looked down at the evidence of a failing business; the first time he had addressed the issue for some time. As fewer diners came through the doors of the coffee house the bills had mounted, and in turn Mahomet had pushed these problems into the drawer of this bureau, where they could be safely locked away. How different everything had been just a year earlier, when people had been falling over each other to lavish praise on the coffee house and to offer Mahomet generous lines of credit to decorate the property in George Street he and Jane had chosen with such care.

When she entered the room some moments later, Jane Mahomet saw the silhouette of her husband against the morning light coming through the window, his head bowed towards the bureau in which he kept all the business papers. His did not react to her entry, but instead remained still, as if the bureau was exerting a power over his body. And she knew what this power was – fear.

It troubled her to see him like this: he was ever the optimist who was confident better times lay just ahead of them. It was usually her Irish melancholy which pressed down on their problems. She crossed the room and gently touched his arm, stroking it as if consoling a grieving widow. He did not look up.

"There was a letter for you ..." she said softly in an enquiring tone.

Mahomet nodded. "The doctor's bill ... for Sir Josiah ..."

He saw no need to continue and a silence fell on the room, broken only by the rhythmic ticking of the mantel clock – a mahogany and brass-mounted chimer made by Thwaites & Reed of Clerkenwell and a present from Decimus for some kindness or other.

"Was ... was it much?" she hardly dared ask.

He smiled, finally turning his head towards her.

"Five guineas, my pearl. Not so great a sum for the proprietor of a famous coffee house ..." He paused. "But perhaps an unwelcome strain at just the moment."

Jane Mahomet looked into her husband's chocolate brown eyes, which were trying – unsuccessfully – to hide the anguish behind them. She bit her lip, before speaking again.

"Let us write to papa, Mr Mahomet," she whispered, though as she spoke she knew the trouble her words might cause. The last time she mentioned asking her father for help was a few weeks ago, and it had created an argument between them the like of which she could not recall having before. She now hoped that the passage of time, and their pressing need, would encourage her husband to be more amenable to the idea. Such hope was short lived, however, as she saw his face harden.

"You know my position, wife," he replied sharply. "Do not vex me!"

While he meant this to conclude any further discussion, Jane Mahomet was made of sterner stuff.

"I do not understand, Mr Mahomet, I truly do not. What hurt can such a letter do? I know papa will be only too happy to provide a small investment until we can establish more custom. This is my birthright, husband, the dowry I never ..."

She was cut short. "I will not countenance it woman, I will not!" he retorted in a raised voice. "I will provide for my family and I will make sure the coffee house endures. I will not beg the support of others, however willing. For once, Mrs Mahomet, you will do as I instruct and cease this chatter. I will not write to your father."

The tone of his voice, and that he had called her "woman", had taken her breath away. After Mahomet had excused himself and left the room – glancing at the bureau on the way out to make sure it was locked – she sat down at the table and took a small linen handkerchief from the sleeve of her dress, lightly dabbing her flushed cheeks with it. Jane Mahomet knew her husband's reaction was caused by worry and she could excuse it, but at times he was insufferable. Why had he set himself so adamantly against her suggestion? She knew her father would be willing to help and he had already said as much the previous year when they were starting out – he was in business and understood these matters.

Mahomet was a proud man, she reasoned, but now he was simply being stubborn. She could only imagine what would happen if the coffee house failed, but she had heard terrible stories of men incarcerated in debtors prison while their wives and children were left on the streets, or worse in the poor house. Jane Mahomet was determined such a thing would not happen to her family. She had fully supported her husband in this enterprise but would do what she thought was sensible. He might not be able to write to her father, but a daughter could – and would. Quickly glancing up to the door he had forcibly closed behind him, she stood and took from a bookcase the elegant rosewood writing box she had cherished since first being presented with it at her confirmation. If I am quick, she thought, I will still make today's Irish Mail.

THE second Theatre Royal in Covent Garden had opened two years ago. The first burned down in December 1808 and London had lost the building in which George Frederick Handel conducted many of his operas and royal command performances of his great oratorio Messiah, as well as the organ he bequeathed. A new theatre was built by public subscription, and opened in September 1809. However money was tight, so the theatre's actor-manager, Mr John Philip Kemble, increased seat prices considerably, which led to the so-called "Old Price Riots". At the opening performance of *Macbeth*, with Sarah Siddons playing the Lady herself, protests about the price increases broke out and hissing and hooting continued through the play. The great actress was even jostled by the mob when leaving and vowed never to return: "Nothing shall induce me to place myself again in so painful and degrading a situation." Mr Kemble, however, who just happened to be Sarah Siddons' younger brother, was able to talk her around, and in the end she decided once more to suffer the slings and arrows of outrageous fortune. Now she was rehearsing her most famous role for what she had privately determined was to be her last London season; next year she would finally retire from the stage.

Standing before the portico of the theatre in Bow Street, Decimus Doyle was also rehearsing – the lines he had prepared should he be granted an audience with the great actress. Bunton had kindly – eagerly – told Doyle all he could about her. Sarah Kemble came from a theatrical family and had married an actor, William Siddons, when young. Many moons ago she had made a great impression on old King George and Queen Charlotte, and had been appointed Reader in English to the royal children. But it was a non-theatrical role, as the subject of Sir Joshua Reynold's painting *Sarah Siddons as a Tragic Muse*, which really made her famous. Bunton had gone to see the painting several times when it had been exhibited at the Royal Academy and proclaimed it a masterpiece, as had others with far more standing in the arts world than the good doctor. Since then it was her acting in the role of Lady Macbeth which brought her to prominence. Dr Bunton recalled seeing her at the Drury Lane theatre in the 90s: "When she came on stage for the sleep-walking scene, Decimus, you could have heard a pin drop. She captured the whole audience, wrapping you up in her madness and sending a chill down the spine."

It was late morning and the sun was high: it was becoming an unusually hot summer. Doyle's gaze followed the four Doric columns up to the triangular cornice they supported, and then to the Classical friezes that ran along the top of the building to either side of the portico – the building was indeed impressive in a suitably theatrical way. Lowering his eyes, he noticed a small sentry box at the top of the brief flight of steps which led to the theatre's main doors, in which an elderly gentlemen, dressed in a red tunic and white powdered short wig, was sitting. Doyle climbed the steps towards him. The attendant studiously avoided Doyle's approach, keeping his eyes cast down looking at the palms of his hands which lay on his knees as if supporting an imaginary book he was reading. The young doctor gave his most diplomatic cough.

"Good day sir," he began politely, " I am in need of some assistance."

The attendant did not move, so engrossed was he with his "book". Doyle persevered.

"I wish to present a message to Mrs Siddons ..." still no response "... and would greatly value your advice."

From the pocket of his green silk waistcoat Doyle took a shiny crown piece and gently placed in one of the man's open palms. This action had the desired effect of distracting the attendant from his "reading" and he looked up.

"Mrs Siddons, you say?" he said in a voice that whistled the "s" through a large toothy gap. "And what message, young man?" he enquired.

From his coat Doyle took a folded and sealed envelope in which, early that morning, he had placed his calling card, on the back of which he had written: *We met yesterday in the church. I must speak with you most urgently. Sincerely, DD.*

He handed it over. "I will wait for a reply," Doyle advised, but the old man shook his head.

"Madam's rehearsing and naught gets in her way," he fretted. "I will pass it on." He slipped the envelope within his red tunic.

"I will wait a reply, sir," said Doyle firmly. "The lady will wish to know I attend on her."

Whether it was because the young man before him looked such a beau, or the fact he was now looming over him, or simply because it was a chance to get out of the heat, the old attendant snorted, rose shakily from his seat in the sentry box and shuffled over to the main door, rapping on it until it partially opened and he slid inside.

Several minutes passed and Doyle paced to and fro, glancing occasionally at the door and then at the busy noonday traffic passing along Bow Street. Opposite the Theatre Royal stood the London Magistrates Court, and he observed lawyers and Runners going in and out of the building, together with several shadier characters. Their presence brought to his mind the death of Sir Josiah Harding and made a meeting with Mrs Siddons all the more pressing. He was beginning to wonder what to do if she refused to see him when the theatre door opened and out stepped the old man together with the small pretty girl who accompanied Mrs Siddons the previous day. She recognised Doyle immediately and bobbed.

"Madam is engaged, sir, but has instructed that I escort you into the house to wait on her until the end of the rehearsal," she said and Doyle nodded, palpable relief showing on his face. He followed her back through the theatre doors that closed behind them. The foyer was very dark, lit only by occasional shafts of light coming from small windows high in the walls. He instinctively kept close to the small shadowy figure guiding him through the darkened labyrinth of the theatre until she stopped and, reaching right, opened a door, whispering to him "this way". They were in a box to the left hand side of the stage. The theatre was lit with candles along the stage front and two large chandeliers protruding either side of the proscenium arch. There was very little light otherwise but Doyle soon made out they were in the lower tier of the auditorium. The maid gestured for him to sit in an ornate chair before turning and leaving.

Sitting back Doyle noticed three people on stage in deep discussion – two men and a woman – and it was some moments before he recognised Sarah Siddons. Presently one of the men exited the stage to the right while the other moved over to the far left, leaving Mrs Siddons centre stage. Doyle then saw the man on the left signal to the leading lady, who began to speak:

"That which hath made them drunk hath made me bold;
What hath quench'd them hath given me fire.
Hark! Peace!
It was the owl that shriek'd, the fatal bellman,
Which gives the stern'st good-night. He is about it:
The doors are open; and the surfeited grooms
Do mock their charge with snores: I have drugg'd their possets,
That death and nature do contend about them,
Whether they live or die."

Her voice was strong, and Doyle recognised elements of the force of nature he had encountered in the church the previous day. Off stage a man's voice was heard: *"Who's there? what, ho!"* and Mrs Siddons looked towards the voice.

"Alack, I am afraid they have awaked,
And 'tis not done. The attempt and not the deed
Confounds us. Hark! I laid their daggers ready;
He could not miss 'em. Had he not resembled
My father as he slept, I had done't."

The man who had recently left the stage re-entered. *"My husband!"* cried Mrs Siddons.

The next hour was one of the most enthralling Decimus Doyle had experienced in his young life, as he watched Britain's greatest actress hone her craft in the role she had come to call her own. Again and again she rehearsed the scene, each time adding just that bit more emotion, and he did not miss the irony of Lady Macbeth's murderous intent. When she took the knives from Macbeth and cleaned up after his deadly deed, Doyle thought back to how clean Walker had left the Mahomets' kitchen once Sir Josiah had been poisoned. Did murderers usually clean up after themselves, he wondered?

Time in the theatre stood still and it seemed only a few minutes after she had left that Mrs Siddons' maid re-appeared in the box and indicated to

Doyle that he should follow her. They ventured once more into the stygian gloom of the darkened corridors before finally entering a room bathed in natural light from a large window.

"This is Mr Kemble's chamber," the maid explained. "Madam will be along presently."

Doyle was left alone in the large office and strolled over to the window. The sun was beating down. He could see two men slowly making their way along Bow Street shovelling horse dung into a handcart, working around the occasional carriage passing by and in between those vehicles waiting in front of the court opposite. They were making a great play of their work, both for their own amusement and for that of passers by, and Doyle became so engrossed that he failed to hear the door open behind him.

"You seem somewhat distracted, sir."

Responding to the voice Doyle turned quickly and beheld a vision in a brown brocade dress, which was tightly cut and with a low neckline to accentuate an ample bosom. The lady's hair seemed less dark than the previous day – more brown than black, and around her neck a pearl creation cascaded down like a vine full of ripe grapes. Doyle now questioned Bunton's estimation of the lady's age as being mid fifties. His own close observation of mature women was somewhat limited to an aunt in Dublin, his cousin Jane and Bunton's housekeeper Mrs Mac, and none of these ladies looked anything like the statuesque Aphrodite now standing before him. For her part, Sarah Siddons quickly approved of the young, handsome and very well attired gentleman waiting on her. She also found his smile quite disarming.

"Mrs Siddons, ma'am. Thank you for agreeing to see me with such little introduction."

The lady nodded. "Your note seemed curious, Mr Doyle. How did you find our rehearsals?"

"Most engaging, ma'am. I do not know Shakespeare, having seen only a performance of *A Midsummer's Night Dream* in Dublin before now. I think my education is in great need of advancement."

She smiled. "I know Dublin very well, though they are too obsessed with

Goldsmith and Sheridan. I played Hamlet there several years ago to much approval I think." She also preferred to forget a time twenty years earlier when the Dublin crowd had pelted her with apples and potatoes for a miserly performance.

"So," she continued, and indicating that they both should sit, "what pressing need brings you here today."

As she had walked from her dressing room to her brother's office several thoughts had crossed her mind. The most obvious was that the young man wished to discourse further on poor Josiah's death, but she was well aware of the excuses men would make to connive an introduction to her. And had she not recalled the young Irishman's handsome deportment in the church, perhaps she would not have been so ready to grant his wish. Looking at him seated across from her, she was pleased her first impression had not let her down – it rarely did. The young man's engaging smile, however, had disappeared. He glanced to make sure the door to the room was firmly closed before he spoke.

"You mentioned yesterday ma'am several matters concerning the late Sir Josiah. I would wish to discuss them further, if you will permit."

The lady was curious. "I recall you mentioned representing the place in which poor Josiah died, Mr Doyle. I would be grateful if you could elaborate." Her voice was hoarse from its exertions on stage and she gave a ticklish cough as she finished speaking, excusing herself.

Slowly but briefly Doyle explained his relationship to the Mahomets and his medical studies in London. Sarah Siddons listened intently though that was no great effort given the man who was speaking. He really is quite a handsome fellow, she thought – tis a pity he is so much younger. Her amorous musings were broken by his last sentence.

"We now suspect that Sir Josiah died from the poisoning of his food by a servant at the coffee house."

"I'm sorry Mr Doyle, did you say poisoning?" she asked, startled.

"Yes ma'am. My cousins engaged a kitchen porter a few weeks ago who seems to have added a very toxic root to the curry Sir Josiah ate ... that is what we think."

"But there has been no public mention of this."

"No ma'am. The doctor who attended the corpse ... my pardon, Sir Josiah, did not consider such a possibility ... and nor should he, given the circumstances at the time of death. It was only later that the poison was discovered and the kitchen porter disappeared."

"Should you not report this to the authorities?"

Doyle winced visibly. He knew they probably should despite the Honourable Basil Cochrane's instruction. "We are not at all certain of the facts, ma'am, hence my attending here today. It is such a confused situation, and the livelihood of my cousin and her family is at stake. I would not wish to make these suspicions public without great certainty."

He smiled weakly but the imploring look in his eyes seemed to entrap the lady that little bit more.

"Yes, Mr Doyle, I can quite see. All we have is our reputation, as I know only too well. So ... how can I assist?"

"Yesterday at the funeral you commented on the character of Sir Josiah's sons ..."

"Did I?" she interrupted.

Doyle nodded. "I was hoping you might ... expand on those remarks."

Mrs Siddons' eyes narrowed slightly. "If I said anything indelicate it must have been the grief of the occasion."

Doyle leaned forward in his chair, drawing Mrs Siddons into his gaze.

"That is as may be ma'am, but we ... I ... think the suspected porter was acting on behalf of another. It would seem highly unlikely there was a close connection between a gentleman of Sir Josiah's standing and such a coarse fellow. And his use of the Queen of Poisons was, frankly, surprising for such a rough fellow."

Mrs Siddons broke eye contact and looked towards the window.

"Yes," she said after some consideration. "Such an association is highly unlikely, given Josiah's excessive consideration of his own social standing ... though not impossible," she quickly added. "But who then do you think was instructing this servant?"

"Those who benefit the most from his death? His sons perhaps?"

To Doyle she seemed to take such a suggestion in her stride.

Sarah Siddons turned her gaze back to the young man. "Not sons, Mr Doyle ... son. George inherits all; it goes with the title. William is left with nothing. The same goes for Lottie, though I fear for how she is ever to get a husband now. The Harding boys are far too protective of her, which is probably Josiah's fault.."

"And what of George Harding ma'am?"

Mrs Siddons sighed. "Ever since he was a youth he has been a bad lot," she continued, then stopped herself. "No, that is unfair, not wholly bad, just easily led. He has most recently fallen in with a very bad crowd, much to Josiah's anxiety. Yet George was devoted to his mother and was crushed by her death when she gave birth to Lottie. Josiah claimed George went sour when he went up to Oxford, though I suspect it happened beforehand, when George stood up to his father's bullying. Yes there, I've said it; Josiah bullied his boys. But while George broke free, William remained dominated, even frightened of his father .... Where was I? Oh yes. Though he did not have the means, George gambled wildly in the full knowledge that Josiah would not disown him and would stand his debts to keep the family from scandal. I advised Josiah to refuse his son's creditors, but he did not heed me, and now he is dead. George is always in need of money. Yet to suggest he would murder his own father takes a great leap of the imagination, even for me."

Doyle sighed. His own relationship with Squire John was so close that he could only shudder at the mere suggestion of patricide, but he was also wise enough to know that all families were not the same. His Uncle Patrick was a barrister in Dublin and engaged with the most perverse aspects of life. Uncle Paddy's late night discourses had opened his eyes to the true nature of man's fall from Grace. Moreover Doyle's own experiences since attending the Hunterian, especially under the expert guidance of Dr Bunton, had only added to this education. So the newly knighted Sir George Harding was a front-runner, to use a parlance the gambler himself would understand.

Mrs Siddons broke his thought. "This Queen of Poisons ..."

"*Aconitum napellus* ..."

"Yes – I think I prefer the romantic name. Is it a common poison?"

"Not common ma'am, but seemingly well-known. It also goes by the name of monkshood or wolfsbane. My tutor says it is cultivated in gardens, and has pretty blue or yellow flowers, depending on the species. But it is poisonous, especially the root and seeds. I believe even touching the flower stems can cause severe irritation of the skin. Well diluted it can be useful for treating colds, quinsy, croup and the like – even laryngitis – and is still believed used by physicians in America I am told. But it is not often prescribed here because it is so poisonous. I would not recommend it for your throat."

The lady smiled. "After your description of its effect on poor Josiah, it will not be to the fore on my list of infusions. No, it's just ... I suppose someone with an interest in apothecary would know of it?"

"Most likely, ma'am. Why?"

"George ..." she paused. "His one redeeming feature is his interest in natural things. He is a frequent visitor to the Apothecaries' Garden in Chelsea ... he used to accompany his mother before she died ... I think he continued to do so after her death to honour her memory. And Josiah encouraged him and bought a small library of books on the matter, though if I recall it is William and not George with a propensity for reading, so I doubt what good they did. No, I was just thinking ... I would not be at all surprised if George were very well acquainted with this Queen of Poisons."

THE Honourable Basil Cochrane's coach and four drew into the park as night settled on the heath land. He would not return to Portman Square until the early hours of the following morning but his need was pressing, and the gentleman on whom he was calling had granted an immediate audience. Cochrane's destination was White Lodge, a mansion originally built as a hunting lodge for George II nearly a hundred years ago. It was in the English Palladian style, with a staircase on the outside taking visitors up to the grand entrance on the first floor. It was now the residence of Lord Sidmouth, the Deputy Ranger of Richmond Park, who had been granted the house for life by the current king, George III. The Deputy Ranger had, in turn, "acquired" some land from the park surrounding the house, turning it into an enclosed garden and keeping the park's deer and other wildlife firmly on the outside. It was through an entrance into this enclosure that Cochrane's coach now swept.

Having been shown into the Deputy Ranger's presence, Cochrane slowly and carefully detailed the errand on which he had come – the unfortunate death of Sir Josiah Harding – following which both men sat in silence for some time while the Deputy Ranger considered the details.

"I am truly at a loss with what you relate, sir," he said at last.

"I apologise, my lord, if my reasoning sounds confused," replied Cochrane gravely, "but Harding was closer to me than I first stated. He is, or was, a Brother of my Lodge, the Ancients. I cannot allow his suspected poisoning to go unchallenged but do not know how to investigate further."

"But I am no longer in government, sir, and my influence is ... constrained. Surely your suspicions are better placed in the hands of the local magistrates and Runners?"

Cochrane shook his head. "You retain the ear of the Prince Regent, sir, and those close to him, including Perceval. And this could be a State matter. I have to advise that we, that is our Lodge, count the Duke of Kent as a Brother."

The Deputy Ranger sighed. "Spencer Perceval is weak, and unworthy of the duties of a Prime Minister. The government is bogged down in Irish rebellion, a poor economy and the problems of making paper money legal tender. As for the Duke of Kent, are you saying that the King's younger son is threatened? If so sir, how? I would think the king's sons are in far more danger from themselves and their illegitimate offspring than any mad killer. Or are you suggesting that this is the work of one of Napoleon's agents?"

An exhausted and exasperated Cochrane looked pleadingly at the Deputy Ranger, who stared hard at his visitor. Sighing again, Lord Sidmouth stood and walked over to the door of the library in which they sat. Opening it, he spoke quickly and quietly to the footman attending on the other side who immediately departed on an errand. Returning to his guest, the Deputy Ranger sat and offered a pinch of snuff, which Cochrane gratefully accepted.

"This is indeed a troublesome business," continued the host after four fitful sneezes, "and one which warrants further investigation. Here you are fortunate. I have engaged a young gentleman recently arrived from the Virginias. His family are ex-patriots, and while the so-called United States are happy to call anyone Americans, some who still live there have an allegiance to an older country. His father provided the Crown with invaluable service in the North American colonies after the war, sending private reports on reprobates such as Washington, Adams, Jefferson and their like. Now his son wishes to follow in his father's footsteps, and I have agreed to take him under my wing. Your problem will be good experience for him."

There was a knock on the library door and a round-faced young man appeared with a distinctive shock of red hair. He made a low bow to the Deputy Ranger and his guest.

"This, sir, is William Rufus," introduced Lord Sidmouth, and the young man was invited to sit with them. There followed a long conversation where the main facts were once again discussed and the Deputy Ranger and his protégé mooted how best Rufus would approach his task. It slowly dawned on Cochrane that the young man's name was an alias.

"It seems obvious to me that your first step must be to find the servant who poisoned the curry," instructed the Deputy Ranger. "Who put him up to it and why? You understand that you might have to be very persuasive to make him talk. And the Indian? What of him? Can he be trusted? It is highly unusual for a native to be set up in such a trade, is it not? Perhaps we should be just as persuasive with him?"

Cochrane looked startled. He fully understood what the Deputy Ranger had meant by "persuasion". "But my lord, I can vouch for Mahomet. He worked in my household for many years before establishing his coffee house. He is married to an honest Irish woman and has a strong family. I consider him to be above suspicion."

Lord Sidmouth looked at his guest. "Do you? Or are you not fearful your good opinion might be misplaced? Very well, let us consider the Indian to be one of us ... for the moment ...but you, Rufus, will still need to speak with him. I hope for his sake that he is prepared to co-operate."

Rufus nodded. "I will speak to him, my lord."

"Good," replied the Deputy Ranger, "then you are going to be busy, young man. Keep me informed and I will act as a conduit to Cochrane ... and his Brothers."

Chapter 7

A Frenchman in his own country will dress a fine dinner of twenty dishes, and all genteel and pretty, for the expense he will put an English lord to for dressing of one dish. But then there is the little pretty profit. I have heard of a cook that used six pounds of butter to fry twelve eggs; when every body knows (that understands cooking) that half a pound is full enough, or more than need be used: but then it would not be French. So much is the blind folly of this age, that they would rather be imposed on by a French booby, than give encouragement to a good English cook!

The Art of Cookery Made Plain and Easy

London in the early autumn of 1811.

SAKE Dean Mahomet set out for Dr Bunton's house in Soho, where he had arranged to meet with Doyle, just after seven o'clock. Passing to the east side of Portman Square, it took only a couple of minutes to reach Oxford Street where he was brought to an untimely halt. Passing west was a large contingent of foot soldiers, and lining either side of the street were well-wishers cheering them on. Mahomet was taken aback by the sight of their red tunics – this was the very last thing he thought to encounter – and stood and watched as they marched slowly by, not entirely in step with each other.

"They're off south," advised a man standing next to him, perhaps assuming Mahomet was a visitor to these shores and in need of further explanation. "Heading for the camps at Brighton and the Channel no doubt. With all this heat it's cooler to march at this time of the evening."

Mahomet did not respond but seemed engrossed by the sight of the men, his mind drifting back to a march thirty years previously, when he was part of a battalion rushing to the aid of General Warren Hastings at the city of Benares. He could still see clearly the storming of the fortress of Patita under the leadership of his late friend and patron Captain Baker, and their raising the Company flag on its walls. Yet it was the part he played in the subsequent punishment of the natives of Ghazipur and Juanpur which had awoken in him a hatred for the waste of war.

"Everything is quiet on the Continent, eerily so," the sage next to him was continuing, "but you can't trust the French corporal; he's up to something, mark my words."

The shadowy figure of Napoleon Bonaparte seemed to hang above the country like a funereal shroud. Since the Austrians and Russians had signed humiliating treaties with the French two years previously, Britain had stood alone against the Glorious Tyrant who now held all of Europe in his hands. Like most Britons, Mahomet read the daily dispatches from Europe in the newspapers with both dread and awe. The one glimmer of hope seemed to be Wellington's campaign in Spain, but even that had turned into a stalemate. The British Marshal Sir William Beresford had been engaged in the siege of a French-held fort just in May, but despite the positive dispatches Mahomet had read of a British success the papers later revealed that the French had retaken the Spanish town, with nearly 6,000 British, Portuguese and Spanish soldiers lost. Like his compatriots, Mahomet thanked God for the Royal Navy.

It took some time for the soldiers and their trailing van to pass by, so it was well after eight when Mahomet arrived at Dr Bunton's residence. There Mrs Mac, who was deeply curious of the first Indian she had met formally, showed him into the doctor's library. As a native Londoner she was used to the sight of blackamoors, Chinamen and even the occasional exotically Indian servant in the street, but was still particularly taken by Mahomet's eloquent speech and fine manner.

Doyle and Bunton were waiting for him and the young Irishman soon recounted his meeting with the great actress. He wished to keep privy, however, of another engagement he had made with Mrs Siddons.

"So George Harding has an interest in herb-lore and apothecary," Mahomet mused on hearing Doyle's news. "In which case we can only assume he knows of the powers of monkshood."

"And if he is such a gambler, Mr Mahomet," added Bunton eagerly, "there is every chance he could have come across the likes of your man Walker." He paused. "Where on earth have I heard that name before," he chided himself.

"If he is such a gambler, doctor," Mahomet corrected, "he will be wanting his inheritance. Mrs Siddons seems clear that George Harding is in constant need of money for his gambling. The only person in his way of feeding his obsession was his father."

Doyle sighed. "Patricide, Sake Mahomet?" he queried.

Mahomet nodded. "It depends on how strongly his desire to gamble controls his mind, do you not agree doctor?"

Bunton, who took a special interest in diseases of the mind, concurred. "Uncontrolled desires drive men in many ways, to good and bad, Decimus. Perhaps I should arrange a visit to the Bedlam so you can appreciate this. Not every case in that hospital is a circus act to amuse those willing to pay and watch. Mr Mahomet is right; if George Harding is so driven by the need to gamble, I think it hardly likely he would allow his father to stand in the way."

With these words ringing in their ears the three men, accompanied by a porter from the medical school, headed for the less salubrious inns of Soho in their hunt for Mahomet's missing kitchen porter. Brewer Street was at the top end of Great Windmill Street and less than five minutes walk from Bunton's house. Although it was a street of craftsmen such as joiners, carpenters and masons, it was named after two brew houses which used to occupy the street, with only Ayre's Brewery now surviving. Mahomet's maid Sarah had mentioned that Walker said the beer did not have to travel far, so the investigative party started at the Coach and Horses at number 45 Brewer Street, given its proximity to the brewery. It was a miserable little establishment, which did not meet with Mahomet's approval. The straw on the floor was dirty, the walls rank with grease of all kinds and the air full of a noxious miasma created only partly by the frequent use of clay pipes. Sadly Mahomet could see Walker being right at home in such a place.

Although he did not drink alcohol, both Doyle and Bunton implored him not to ask for a sherbet or infusion, but to instead pretend to sip on a

small tankard of Ayre's best ale they provided for him, which Mahomet did
without allowing the froth of the beer to touch his lips. He could not avoid
the smell invading his nostrils, however, and soon felt intoxicated despite
his best efforts. They sat in a dark corner of the inn, but soon decided the
only way they would find news of Walker was to ask the other revellers.
Bunton readily volunteered for the task and, while Mahomet and Doyle
watched, the good doctor wandered around the room in his most effusive
manner, accompanied by the school porter. Within a quarter of an hour,
however, he returned disheartened.

"Either the fellow goes by another name or he has never been in this
tavern," he advised. Even repeating the sketchy description of Walker, which
Mahomet had provided, to the landlord drew little response.

They decided to move on, first to the small inn attached to Ayre's brewery
itself and then to an inn on the ground floor of Hickford's Room, the
concert hall and assembly room where once the child prodigy Mozart had
performed and that had fallen on hard times. It was now being used for
entertainments such as fencing duels and occasional lectures, such as that
being advertised on its doors by a Mr Lowe who would be demonstrating
"Various Acroamatical Experiments and Operations in Rhabdomancy,
Rhabdology, Pallengenesia, Capnomancy and Aleuromancy."

The inn was called Nelson's Eye, and it was here that the scales fell from
Bunton's own eyes, for at a table to one side of the bar were the two men
from whom Bunton had bought the body of the young farmer so recently.

"Of course," he hissed to his two colleagues as they sat down, "that's where
I've heard it before ... Walker is the name of one of the men who supplies
our cadavers."

It took Mahomet some moments to understand Bunton's statement and
then a look of shock and horror appeared on his face.

"You mean the man in my kitchen dug up ..." He did not finish the
sentence.

"I do not know if it was him," Bunton said hurriedly, "but I am sure those
two men in the corner had a compatriot named Walker." He dropped his
voice even lower. "They mentioned the name when delivering a body the

same night Sir Josiah died. They usually came with another, but said they could do with out him – Walker. It was definitely Walker."

The investigating party looked surreptitiously at the two resurrectionists on the other side of the room, who were engrossed in conversation.

"We will have to go and speak to them, Decimus," Bunton continued, "but they are hard men. I will need you to stand behind," he added, nodding to the porter. Mahomet was asked to remain as discreet as possible while the others crossed the room slowly. As they approached, the taller of the two body snatchers looked up, the scar on his face glowing in the candle light. He soon recognised the doctor and nodded.

"Gentlemen, may we speak to you," asked Bunton.

Such a request from a gentleman of authority would usually have made the body snatchers jump up and run, but they were cornered by the three large men now surrounding them, so the man with the scar nodded and kicked out a stool from beneath the table. Bunton sat.

"Do not worry, gentlemen," he said in as reassuring manner as he could, "we wish you no harm, no harm at all. It is something from when we last met of which I would now speak."

Neither snatcher had experienced a customer approaching them about an old body before, and both quickly looked around to see who was listening. While one or two in the inn had followed Bunton and his party cross the room, they had now turned back to their own company, so only a small dark man in one corner was observing them.

The taller man grunted: "What is it you want?"

Bunton smiled. "Gentlemen, I will not occupy your time for long. At our last meeting you mentioned that one of your party went by the name of Walker. I am correct?"

The gravediggers looked at each other then the tall one nodded.

"We seek a man by this name," Bunton continued, "and there may be a chance that your friend and our ... quarry are one and the same. Just a chance, mind."

The smaller digger took a draft of his ale.

"He's no friend of ours!" he spat and the taller one snarled.

"Quite so," said Bunton undeterred, "but he was your acquaintance. Where can I find him, gentlemen?"

Both paused before the taller one said: "It'll cost yer."

Bunton sighed. Not again, he thought, but before he could begin to negotiate a rate Doyle said: "A guinea each for leading us to him. Payment on results." Bunton bit his lip, annoyed at this interruption to his negotiation. He knew Doyle was a young man of means, but a guinea – each! They all looked up at the young man.

"Very well," Bunton confirmed, "a guinea each to be led to the man."

"What's 'e done?" asked the small one.

Bunton shook his head. "You know better than most, gentlemen. No questions."

"We 'aven't seen 'im for days. It could take some time."

"Then you will have chance to earn your guinea," retorted Bunton. "As soon as you find him, contact me at the Hunterian. And I warn you, gentleman, we will only pay if we find him alive."

WILLIAM Harding was suffering the effects of a restless night. He had returned to the forlorn looking Harding mansion late the previous evening and could see the library windows ablaze with light. He had been glad to be away from the house, if only to avoid the constant stream of visitors attending his brother. During the day it was lawyers and agents of the canal company. In the evening George's less salubrious acquaintances filled the dining and drawing rooms with inappropriate revelry – the family card table had never been so well used, nor the pocket billiards board George had installed in their father's cherished library. William made for the servants entrance to the other side of the house that would take him directly to his rooms, but still the sounds of raucous laughter carried along passages and under doors. When he reached the small dressing room connected to the bedchamber, he summoned his manservant. It took time for the old retainer to appear – he had been busy in the library and looked quite distraught. William asked for a jug of hot water to wash his face, and then enquired after his brother.

"Sir George is .... entertaining," came the reply, as the old man grasped for the correct form of words. "The master's compatriots and ladies ..."

"Ladies!" exclaimed William and the retainer nodded sombrely.

"Tell me no more!" the younger brother instructed, shaking his head.

After the servant had departed, William walked over to the window, staring into the night. There was no moonlight, and darkness seem to envelop the house, apart from some shafts of light coming from the other wing where his brother was at sport. William was still angry at George for the threats to Lottie and himself. Everything William held dear was beginning to slip from him: he guessed that George had all but completed the sale of the estate to the canal company. When his father had died he had foolishly not anticipated George's actions. Retiring to bed and blowing out the candles, for the first time he began to reflect on the nature of his father's passing. What a great shame George had not joined him on the floor of the Indian's coffee house.

The following afternoon William was sitting with his sister Lottie in the parterre to the front of the house. William was oiling his cricket bat, called a Little Joey, prior to what would be the last match of the year before the autumnal weather took hold, while Lottie was attending distractedly to her needlework. She was greatly occupied by George's intention of sending her to their Warwickshire family – people she did not know and did not care for. How could he be so cruel!

William heard the front doors slam shut, and looking up recognised the gaunt-looking gentleman leaving. Thomas Lord, the cricket promoter, was a bluff Yorkshireman and, like the late Sir Josiah, was in his fifties. Unlike the deceased, however, Lord maintained himself well and, while he no longer bowled at the matches he presented on his cricketing ground, he often eschewed a horse or carriage in preference to his own two legs.

William stood and greeted the visitor. "Mr Lord, sir!"

"My most sincere condolences, young man," replied Lord. "Your brother has just advised me of the tragic news ... and the likely consequences."

"This is my sister Charlotte, Mr Lord. Lottie, this is Mr Lord, the cricketing champion. Consequences sir?"

Lottie stood and curtsied. "Mr Lord."

"Miss Charlotte, please accept my deepest condolences. This is such a difficult time for you ... for you both. Your father was so generous in his support, and now your brother, it seems, is determined to sell my ground."

This was news William had expected since his last conversation with George, but had not anticipated him acting so promptly.

"I advised your brother of my contract with your late father. An eighty eight year lease," Lord continued, then paused. "It is such a shame ... your father's death, of course ... but the ground has only just settled. It takes time to prepare a proficient square of turf, William."

The young man nodded. "I am so sorry. I will speak to my brother, Mr Lord."

Lord smiled, but then shook his head. "He seemed very determined, William. Why, we have hardly begun playing on the ground. It was only last month we entertained Mr Aislabie's eleven. And the Mary-le-Bone members are still wary ... apart from finding able bodied gentlemen who are not taken with securing this island from that mountebank Napoleon, they say the bounce is uneven and are sure the ground slopes slightly. Cricketers are never happy ... now there is every chance they will never play there."

"I can only apologise, Mr Lord," William Harding repeated, "surely if George understood the consequences of breaking such a long lease ..."

"He seemed fully versed but determined nevertheless. You must not take yourself to task, young man, as your brother obviously has some personal ... feeling."

Unbeknownst to William but not to the late Sir Josiah, George Harding had been escorted from Mr Lord's previous cricket ground two years ago on suspicion of bribing batsmen to give away their wickets, obviously for some wager. There had been quite a scandal at the time, only quenched by Sir Josiah's offer to provide Thomas Lord with suitable land. Now William misinterpreted Lord's mention of bad feeling as concerning his own efforts to ensure their father guaranteed his own cricketing career.

"I will need to speak to my attorney," Lord was continuing, "but your brother must understand that breaking such a contract will not come cheap.

Take care William, for I have met the likes of your brother only too often on the boundary of the field. They gamble with everything and value nothing."

With that Thomas Lord bowed and made his way along the formal driveway towards the estate gatehouse and the village of Paddington. William stared forlornly as his great idol slowly disappeared from sight taking, it seemed, William's budding cricketing glory with him.

"Good day Mr Lord," said William softly as the great man departed, "though I think there is very little good about it."

He turned to see Lottie's flushed cheeks.

"Oh William!" she exclaimed, "what is to become of us? George has ruined everything. We are completely lost!"

"Come now Lottie, don't take on so. Sit and continue your needlework."

"I can pay no attention to it. You won't let George sell the house, will you William? You won't let him bundle me off to Warwickshire. I do not know those people. I will be all alone. If only I had some friends. But you are my friend, aren't you William? Please say you will protect me? Like you did from papa."

"Now, sweet Lottie, come and sit with me and do not dwell on what is past. Papa can no longer hurt us. But George ... he is another matter. It is a shame I did not witness him choke on his curry along with papa."

"William!"

"Well ... you know it to be true. Don't say you haven't thought the same. George is the now source of all our troubles ... yours and mine. If George were dead then Mr Lord would have his ground and we would be safe and secure in our home. I would take great care of you, my sweet. But George is going to destroy everything we hold dear."

"Then we must stop him ... you must stop him William," she replied in a low, determined voice.

"But I don't know how, Lottie. If only ..."

"I too wish he were dead," continued Lottie, now whispering. "Is that so very terrible, William?"

"No Lottie, no it isn't terrible. George is set to ruin us. If an accident could befall him in the same way as papa ...?"

"Challenge him William, fight him in a duel!"

"Brothers can't fight duels, Lottie."

"Why not? You're bound to win. He is such a dreadful shot. Papa was always saying so."

William Harding paused. Yes, George was such a dreadful shot. Now, what if he were to be challenged ...?

IT had now been some time since the unfortunate demise of Sir Josiah Harding and a routine, of sorts, had once more returned to the Hindostanee Coffee House. The number of diners who frequented the place became fewer by the day, and the Honourable Basil Cochrane's good intentions to frequent the coffee house had yet to materialise. While Mahomet had been able to raise some funds to pay pressing bills from the sale of the few books he still possessed together with some silverware, this did not address the fact that the quarter's rent would fall due on Michaelmas at the end of the month. Having already missed the Midsummer payment in June, Mahomet knew the landlord would not grant any further deferment.

He had just accompanied the last two diners to the door of the coffee house and was in the process of turning in for the night, when the main door opened and in walked a ruddy faced young gentleman who exposed a shock of bright red hair as he took off his tall hat, reminding the Indian of some of his wife's cousins.

"Good evening master," began Mahomet, "I am afraid we were just beginning to close ... though I am sure I will be able to provide some wholesome fare if you would take a seat. Can I take your coat sir?"

Mahomet held out his hands but the man made no move to disrobe.

"Do I have the pleasure of addressing Mr Mahomet?" he asked in an accent the Indian could not place – part American he suspected – and Mahomet bowed in acknowledgement.

"Then perhaps we could sit here," the visitor indicated to a nearby table, "as your house is now empty. My name is Rufus, by the way, and we have a mutual acquaintance." He bowed before placing his hat on the table and sitting down, still in his black coachman's coat. Mahomet, surprised by this familiarity, reluctantly sat down opposite.

The young man spoke quickly and softly, mentioning their mutual acquaintance as being the Honourable Basil Cochrane. It soon became clear to a shocked Mahomet that the visitor was fully conversant with the real nature of death of Sir Josiah Harding and that he was under the instruction of their mutual friend to investigate the circumstances.

"But our friend said we should not discuss the matter further!"

"Nor should you openly," nodded Rufus, "but your suspicions were such that he thought it best to consult me."

"Are you a Runner or thief-taker?"

Rufus smiled. "If it eases your mind, Mr Mahomet, then you should consider me so. Now, could you please recall for me once more the tale of Harding's last supper."

Mahomet disliked the young man's irreverent manner and was minded to ask him to leave. Yet Rufus' knowledge of Sir Josiah's death was such that he could only have come from Cochrane, so slowly he began to recount the events as he remembered them, up to and including the search of the inns in Soho and the meeting with the resurrectionists, which quickly gained Mr Rufus' close attention. Mahomet did not mention Doyle's meetings with Mrs Siddons, however, as he was wary of bringing too many people to Rufus' notice. He had already made up his mind that the ruddy faced, red haired young man before him was untrustworthy.

"So this Dr Bunton recognised Walker as a body snatcher?'

Mahomet shook his head vigorously. "No sir, I did not say that. Dr Bunton has never seen our Walker, but this other Walker seems to have disappeared at the same time, so we are guessing them to be one and the same. We can only confirm this when the body-snatchers ... the gentlemen in question find their own Walker." This statement confused Mahomet even as he said it.

"And have they confirmed he is one and the same?"

Mahomet shook his head again. "No, there has been no word. I have been to the cattle market along Oxford Street twice more hoping to see our Walker but without success."

Rufus asked for a description of Walker and of the body snatchers, and while Mahomet could not recall much about the shorter of the two, he still had a clear memory of the tall man with the scar; no doubt he would be easy enough to find.

"I assure you Mr Mahomet that I, and our mutual friend Mr Cochrane, have only your interest at heart and everything you have told me tonight will be held in the strictest confidence. But you must now leave this matter with me. Do you understand me Mr Mahomet? Put aside your amateur investigations."

Unfortunately this assurance had quite the opposite effect on the coffee house owner, and when Rufus left shortly afterwards Mahomet quickly locked and barred the main door in case the young man were to return. Cleaning up the dining room before retiring, he thought over and again about the meeting with his strange young visitor. Why had the Honourable Basil Cochrane changed his mind and who exactly was Mr Rufus? More importantly, was he expected to pay for his services?! He decided to call on Cochrane and ask these questions directly the following morning. Yet as he finished clearing the dining room and extinguished the last candles, he could not but fret that there was far more to the death of Sir Josiah Harding than any of them had feared.

Chapter 8

London in the early autumn of 1811.

OF all the private clubs in London, Almack's on King Street, between St James's Street and St James's Square, stood apart for two reasons. Firstly it was possibly the most exclusive to get into, particularly if you were a man. And this was because of the second reason – for Almack's was run by women, or rather Lady Patronesses, of which there were six or seven at any one time. Nor were these women insignificant in Society but included a Viscountess, three Countesses, a Lady and an Honourable. So vouchers costing ten guineas each for the Season and allowing entry to the club's Wednesday night balls were among the most sought after in town.

Yet the Lady Patronesses were less exercised by class than by the déclassé when considering those to be allowed into the club. The great socialite Lady Caroline Lamb was barred after she made a spectacle of herself over Lord Byron, yet the penniless Irish poet Thomas Moore was welcomed with open arms. Indeed London's leading theatrical lights were actively courted, and so it was that on the last ball of the Season the great Sarah Siddons held court in one of the Almack's withdrawing rooms, attended by a young Irish beau of impeccable breeding and dress. After engaging with her courtiers for some time Mrs Siddons, dressed in a demure deep pink satin dress with puffed sleeves which met her long white satin gloves above the elbow, indicated to the beau her desire to sit away from the crowd. She was escorted to the far side of the room, albeit their progress was closely observed by many admirers.

The actress and her escort sat on two gilded chairs. Ambient noise from the gaming tables in the next room competed with the orchestra in the assembly room to the far side. She turned to her attendant.

"You dance extremely well Mr Doyle, for such a young man." She cooled her face with the small feather fan she held in her right hand.

Doyle smiled. He did not care to mention the daily dancing lessons he had attended since being invited by Mrs Siddons, but was grateful the ladies of the Almack were yet to embrace the new quadrille and waltz dances – for decorum's sake they limited themselves to reels and minuets. "My dancing is still a poor reflection of my partner's grace, I'm afraid ma'am. I admit to not having made a step before I arrived in London."

"Then you are quick on the uptake, sir, a quality I find most admirable in a man, if sadly rare." She leaned forward to make a confidence and Doyle did the same, their heads coming close. "Thank you for providing my escort, Mr Doyle," she whispered. "I think myself to be the most envied lady here this evening."

Doyle blushed and breathed in the intoxicating smell of the great actress' scent he had first encountered at the church in St Mary-le-Bone some weeks previously. The musk seemed to take possession of his mind before he became aware of their closeness, and he quickly looked around to see if they were being observed. They were. He reluctantly sat back in his chair and Mrs Siddons, on seeing his caution, laughed.

"Do not worry, Mr Doyle, we will not be disturbed, though perhaps we should not give others reasons to gossip. I am an actress, after all. Come, let us speak of common matters. How does your investigation progress into poor Josiah's death?"

Briefly Doyle spoke of the meeting with the resurrectionists in the Soho inn, which brought a smile to her lips.

"The irony," she remarked, "that poor Josiah's life – one notable by its dreary routine – should end in such mystery. Yet I fear you are on a fool's errand," she paused, "though there is one fool I would gladly see depart this world. Wasn't it the Queen of Poisons which did for Josiah? I wonder where I could acquire some?"

Her tone was sharp and confused the young man. "Ma'am?"

"Oh disregard me, Mr Doyle. My patience is being tested by an impertinent clown."

Doyle was still none the wiser and it showed on his face.

"Mr Grimaldi," Mrs Siddons said at last, "or rather that idiotic clown *Harlequin* he plays. He can do no wrong, it seems. All of London would rather they were entertained by such tomfoolery, as they say nowadays. His mimes are quite *à la mode*, and my brother swoons at the money they attract. People would rather attend to such idiocy than be inspired by the noble Bard."

It took some moments for Doyle to understand her words. When he did he spoke softly. "Not I, ma'am."

She looked at her handsome beau and her face softened.

"Let us speak no more of it, but rather about you. Your family perhaps? Decimus is a curious name. I assume you come from one of those large Irish families."

Doyle was caught unawares, as he was unused to speaking about himself. He shook his head. "I am an only child ma'am."

Mrs Siddons raised one of her finely plucked eyebrows. "Even more curious then. Why Decimus? Do your parents have a quirky humour?"

Doyle looked serious. "My mother is dead ma'am. I never knew her as she died in giving me life." He then went on to describe his mother's difficulties in giving birth and the dead siblings who came before him. He concluded his tale by explaining that his father named him in honour of these. Mrs Siddons held her hand to her cheek in distress, gently wiping away a tear with a finger of her gloved hand.

"You poor boy. How dreadfully sad. And your poor mother, to lose so many children. I feel for her deeply. You should know, my dear, that I too have suffered the loss of children – my dearest daughters Elizabeth Ann, Maria and Sally. And I know what it is to miscarry. Such intimate death is the inevitable burden of women I'm afraid. Still, I have cherished memories of all my children. But you, my dear boy, have never known a mother's love …" Her voice trailed off and she reached over to touch his arm, before letting her hand fall into his and squeezing it tightly.

"I think you have suffered from too little female company, My Doyle, but I intend to remedy that."

NOT far from the ladies of the Almack club another of London's evening diversions was drawing to a close – but this was an entirely male preserve.

At number 13 Bond Street, less than half a mile from tasteful minuets, the pugilistic feats of England's best boxers had just concluded. Boxing had only recently come back into fashion. In the 1750s the Duke of Cumberland had shut down the boxing amphitheatres when he suspected he had been the victim of a fixed match, having wagered £10,000 on the champion Jack Broughton only to see him lose with an eye injury. So boxing was suppressed for thirty years or more before being revived thanks largely to Gentleman Jackson, whose academy in Bond Street taught the arts of self-defence to gentlemen. Jackson had been champion boxer of England, and his very popular boxing academy now included on its lists the likes of Lord Byron. Jackson had also founded the Pugilistic Club with a number of aristocrats, including the Prince Regent and his brothers.

At the heart of the boxing academy was the prize ring in the boxing hall, a square of 24 feet surrounded by ropes. While the fights themselves were bare knuckled, on one wall hung a number of mufflers – padded gloves the boxers used in training to avoid injury. English bare knuckle fighting was governed by a set of seven rules created by the same Jack Broughton who incurred the wrath of the late Royal Duke, but it was still a hard and bloody sport.

In one corner of the hall stood a sorry figure, a young man inclining towards a paunch and therefore not an obvious pugilist, who was clutching a large glass of ruby red claret in one hand. The evening had not gone well. The two boxers on which he had waged a considerable amount were nursing their wounds – and their pride – in the dressing area. Indeed one lay flat on the ground and from a distance it was impossible to tell whether he were dead or alive. A small man dressed in black and clutching a large book glided across the parquet floor of the academy towards the sorrowful young man.

"Sir George," he hissed as he reached his prey and spoke softly in the young man's ear, "I require three hundred guineas before the close of tomorrow's business. I would be most obliged if you would accommodate this ... request."

Sir George Harding looked dolefully at the diminutive collector.

"My luck is out," he lamented. "Perhaps I should keep to the card tables."

The collector smiled, if that was the correct term for the grimace that appeared on his face. "Luck Sir George? Perhaps you are too quickly tempted by the greater odds, but I would consider you to be one of the luckiest men in London today. Was it not fortunate that your hale and hearty father ... God rest his soul," he added quickly, "passed away so suddenly leaving you his sole heir. Luck, Sir George, is in the eye of the beholder, and I see a very lucky man before me."

"It does not compensate for this loss, sir."

"Does it not, sir? Then let me add that we make our own luck in this life, and you play fortune's fool very well, if I may say so."

Sir George looked at the man quizzically. "What are you saying sir?"

The sickly smile remained. "No more than you can now pay your debts like an honourable man without deferring to others. No more than that, sir. Why, we know well enough what can happen to men who find it impossible to settle their debts of honour. They have to flee, to dank quarters on the Continent no doubt, and only then if they are able to avoid some troubling accident beforehand. But you, sir, are a man of great respectability thanks to fortune smiling so bounteously. If I may make so bold it was less than two months ago when I brought news of the canal company plans to your attention, and now look at you. God moves in mysterious ways, the hymn says, His wonders to perform. And sometimes God gets a helping hand." The smile as it was remained on the collector's face but now he also seemed to wink at Sir George, or was it a nervous twitch?

The baronet found it most perplexing. But before he could respond the collector whispered "three hundred guineas" once again in his ear and had moved off, gliding across the floor towards his next victim.

MAHOMET had dawdled in clearing the coffee house while he continued to think on the disturbing appearance of Mr Rufus in the dining room the previous evening. Now, as Decimus' mantel clock struck the midnight hour in the small sitting room, he finally made his way towards bed, candle in hand, having just completed his evening ablutions. Neither he nor Jane were desirous of the chamber-pot, and they both preferred either the soil closet over the channel to the communal cess pit in the back yard or, when the coffee house was closed, the flushing water closet next to the dining room. This was regularly topped up by young William Mahomet for the sole use of patrons and which also ran to the cess pit behind the house. It had been installed at considerable expense in those optimistic days prior to the opening. Now Mahomet rued the cost, wondering why he did not simply provide the basic facilities of buckets and water behind a screen which were so often found in other coffee houses.

He was surprised to find his wife still awake when he entered the bedroom, as she had retired much earlier in the evening. She was sitting up in bed, straining to read a book by the light of a single candle. One of their first economies had been no lamp oil in every part of the house except the dining room.

"You will strain your eyes, my pearl," he said softly, not chiding but with a note of concern.

"I could not sleep," Jane Mahomet replied, looking up from her book to her husband undressing to one side.

Mahomet did not ask what disturbed his wife's thoughts though he could make an educated guess. There remained a disturbed atmosphere between husband and wife after their recent disagreement.

"What is your book?" he asked.

"Papa sent it to me. Mr Scott's poem *The Lady of the Lake*. Papa didn't care for it, but thought I might. It is set in Scotland. Some men are fighting over a woman, as usual. It reads very Irish, I have to say. Is Scotland like Ireland, do you think?"

"I've heard they do compare, though the Scots I have met go on about their lakes and mountains. Yet I doubt those compare to the Himalaya." He reached over to his nightshirt and pulled it over his head.

"It was good of your father to think of you," he continued, "when did he write?"

"Oh, some days ago."

"You did not say?" he queried as he climbed into bed.

"No," Jane replied and then fell silent.

Mahomet turned onto his side in bed and could feel Jane continuing to read behind him. A great tiredness came over him and he began to drift off to sleep.

"Husband. Are you awake?"

"Not for long," was his reply.

"Can we speak ... please."

Mahomet sighed. It was unlike his wife to be so disturbed at night. Usually the work of the coffee house combined with the demands of the children meant she was ready for bed as dusk settled. He turned over to face her but did not lift his head from the pillow.

"For a few moments, my pearl, then we must sleep. What is it, the children?"

"The children?" She was surprised. "Why no ... it's ... as well as the book, papa sent us his very sincere wishes."

"That was nice. Perhaps one day we will journey to Cork once more."

Jane Mahomet looked down at him and smiled. His eyes were half closed. It was now or never she decided.

"As well as his best wishes papa also sent his support."

It took quite a few moments for her statement to sink through the oncoming sleep, but when it did his eyes quickly opened.

"What do you mean, his support?"

"I mean he would like to make a small investment in the coffee house." There. She had said it at last, five days after she had received the book and letter with the wonderful news.

"Investment?" Mahomet's mouth had become dry, and he croaked out the word.

"Yes my love, investment." She could barely look at him. "He thinks it time he demonstrated his support ... his love for us by offering some funds."

Mahomet looked up at his wife. She had not! She could not! She would not dare! He was now fully awake and leant up on one arm.

"And why would he make such an offer without any prompting? Why?"

His voice had become loud and she shushed him, pointing to the wall.

"Well?" he demanded.

She sighed. "Yes, my love, I did mention our difficulties to him, but he made the offer of three hundred pounds without my asking, I promise you. Three hundred pounds, husband," she emphasised.

"But you mentioned our position, after I strictly forbade you from so doing."

"You did not forbid me husband. You said that you would not write to him. Can a daughter not confide in her father?"

"Not if it is against the absolute wishes of her husband. You have gone too far, Jane, and disgraced me in the eyes of your family. How dare you!"

He raised the arm on which he was not leaning as he felt a sharp pain move along it. Jane Mahomet flinched, the book falling to the floor and the stubby candle flickering wildly with her movement. Mahomet was horrified. Did she think I was going to hit her, he wondered aghast? In the gloom of the bedroom they stared at each other for some moments.

"I am too tired to discuss this," he said finally, and before she could reply he turned around in bed.

Jane looked at the back of her husband and started to speak. She was interrupted by his call of "Now now wife!" She paused and sighed. There was no reasoning with him. She would leave it until the morning, but they would accept her father's money. She blew out the candle and placed the pewter holder on the bedside table. Making herself comfortable in bed, she turned away from her husband and began to weep very quietly into her pillow.

WILLIAM Harding once more lovingly rubbed linseed oil into the face of his Little Joey, carefully caressing the blade of the cricket bat which had brought him so much success throughout the summer with the oily linen cloth. He was to play what probably would be the last game of the season and wanted to make sure everything was fully prepared. Other gentlemen relied on servants to attend to their equipment, but for William the anticipation of the game was as important as the match itself.

He was sitting on a bench in the small formal garden of the Harding estate, and from this vantage point could observe the comings and goings of the main entrance to the house. It also gave him space in which to consider the task he had set upon himself: how to remove his brother before he caused irreparable damage to both the family standing and his and Lottie's future prospects.

He also preferred the word "remove" as "fratricide" was harsh, if correct. Lottie had planted the idea in his mind and he was now unable to think of little else. He accepted that he would have to assume the role of Cain, but still hoped to create circumstances in which he would not have to do the deed himself. Yet how could he get another person to kill his brother? He could pay someone, but that would leave him open to later threats and blackmail when he assumed the baronetcy. Moreover, whom would he ask? He was sure there were many in London who would do the deed for a reasonable price and knew of one man in particular who would have been only too happy to jump out on George during one of his nocturnal visits to the brothels in Soho or the like. But his brother had to die honourably, like his father, so that no further comment would be passed on their family.

He was distracted by a noise and looked up to see a horse and cab approach along the drive. Who was this? Probably one of George's recent business associates. He watched the cab to the entrance of the house where a small man dressed entirely in black stepped down and spoke to the cabby. William recognised him immediately: a book maker, he identified with disgust, come to advise his brother on how best to dispose of his inheritance. He stared as the man walked to the door and, some moments later, entered the house.

The Harding mansion had become a den of iniquity, where gamblers and whores vied with bankers and lawyers for his brother's attention – when they could find him at home! George had now taken up semi-permanent residence at Watier's, the dining and gaming club off Piccadilly, and William could only imagine with horror what his brother had already lost playing at Macau, Whist and Loo. It was a shame their father had indulged George's gambling when he was alive: he should have disinherited him!

These thoughts kept churning around in William Harding's head as he prepared his cricket bat. Had George been unable to settle his gaming debts he would have been hounded out of Society, perhaps fled England or, even better, been challenged to a duel. William suddenly stopped applying the oil. Lottie was right. George was a dreadful shot and could never hope to win a duel and might be fatally injured in the process. In fact, William could be on hand as seconder to make sure George did not survive. And he would be blameless, perhaps even pitied for having to witness such a tragic scene, faithfully attending to his brother in his dying moments like Hardy on board the *Victory*.

What an outlandish thought! Yet how could William bring this about? George was one of nature's cowards, though like many such men was pompous and with an inflated opinion of himself, especially since taking on the title. George also knew any number of discreditable people, and William thought it highly likely that among them was a good shot who would willingly challenge his brother for a suitable wager. Of course to the challenger it would be proposed as a bit of fun, a way of taking George down a peg or two and make a pretty penny along the way. So long as the duellist was led to believe he would only need to frighten his opponent, William could attend to the rest. George would never survive the contest.

William returned to his loving care of the Little Joey, his brow furrowed with deep thought.

Chapter 9

London, Early September 1811.

SAKE Dean Mahomet sat in the formal gardens to the centre of Portman Square staring into space and oblivious to the bustle of traffic and business happening around him. He was suffering from a lack of sleep following Jane's revelation and had since risen early to avoid being alone with his wife for too long. Not that Jane seemed anxious to continue the conversation, but rather paid excessive attention to their children. This morning Mahomet had slipped from the house at the first opportunity to present himself at the Portman Square mansion of the Honourable Basil Cochrane. He was frustrated, however, when he learnt that his former patron was not there and would not return for some weeks, having journeyed to Scotland to stay at his ancestral home with his brother the Earl of Dundonald. Mahomet had questioned the housekeeper on whether her master had entertained a young gentleman with bright red hair in the past couple of weeks, but she could not confirm or deny this and Cochrane had taken his personal servant, Manjai, with him to Scotland.

He sat in the square deciding what to do next. He had no desire to return ito the coffee house. Although his anger had abated he still felt injured and betrayed by his wife's action. He could not understand why she would so openly defy him. Jane was a strong-willed woman, an aspect of her character that had kept his love so strong, but she had never acted so contrary. He needed more time to calm his mind and consider what to do for the best, but even now he knew he would have to accept the money as his debts were simply too pressing. But it came at a bitter price and how he would be able to look his father-in-law squarely in the eye again he did not know.

He stood and decided to call on Doyle at Dr Bunton's house in Soho. It had been over a week since they last met to discuss the Harding matter and he wished to tell him about the visit of Mr Rufus. He had mentioned both Doyle and Bunton to the thief-taker and now feared they might get an unwelcome visitor so wished to warn them – Jane's revelation had distracted him from matters in hand. He also wanted to know if there was any further news of Walker. It was an overcast, chilly morning and the warmth of the August heat wave was long forgotten. He pulled up the collar of his coat and set out for Soho, taking a route via the elegant Hanover Square and calling in at St George's for a few moments contemplation. As with many converts, Mahomet embraced his new religion with zeal back in Dublin when he had secured Jane's hand in marriage. He never questioned his choice – Mahommedans and Christians worshipped the same God, after all – but he retained many aspects of his first religious teachings, including abstinence from alcohol. Yet he was also deeply affected by Christ's self-sacrifice, and experienced great comfort in communing with such a Man, especially in the confines of an inspirational building such as the one in which he now sat.

It had just gone midday when he presented himself to Dr Bunton's housekeeper, who showed him into the doctor's library. From Mrs Mac he learnt that his wife's cousin had left for a short walk after a light breakfast but was expected back at any moment. The doctor was at the Hunterian and would not return until dinner that evening. Mahomet made himself comfortable and began perusing Dr Bunton's bookshelves, which seemed to be an eclectic mix of scientific and medical tomes combined with popular literature, including several volumes of poems but, thankfully, nothing by Walter Scott. He did not wish any further reminder of his wife's father, and was just about to try some Southey when the door opened and Doyle entered.

After they had settled down with a pot of green tea provided by Mrs Mac, Mahomet spoke of the visit by Mr Rufus.

"How strange, Sake Mahomet," said a surprised Doyle, trying to make sense of the news. "What can it mean?"

The Indian shrugged his shoulders and then nodded his head. "It can only mean ill. Why would Cochrane instruct such a man? Rufus said it was to protect my interests, but I strongly doubt this, otherwise Cochrane would have consulted me beforehand. No, Sir Josiah Harding's death has meant something to him that I do not understand and he has not been privy to reveal. Has Dr Bunton heard back from the ... gentlemen we met with the other day?"

Doyle shook his head. "Though he mentioned yesterday that perhaps we should venture again to their drinking room and seek them out."

Mahomet shuddered. The fact he had allowed a body snatcher into his house who had then murdered a patron struck to his very soul.

"Perhaps we should investigate the son George," Doyle continued, "after all Mrs Siddons did say he had an interest in apothecary."

"Yes," Mahomet agreed, "if we cannot find Walker at least we should establish where he could have obtained the monkshood. I recall you saying that George Harding frequented the Apothecaries' Garden in Chelsea. That would be a good start. Even if they do not grow it there they may know where in London it is cultivated or supplied. I assume there is a curator of sorts at this garden. So, Decimus, are you available?"

"When?"

"Now?"

Doyle raised an eyebrow. "Are you not required at the coffee house?"

Mahomet looked to Bunton's bookcases to avoid the stare of the young man. "I have a few hours before we open, and I do not think my presence will be missed until then."

Doyle did not know what to say. It was obvious something was amiss at the coffee house but it was presumptuous for him to question such a senior member of the family. Still, Sake Mahomet looked uncomfortable.

"My cousin Jane is well, I hope?"

"As well as can be expected," came the short reply.

Doyle paused in thought. Perhaps if he mentioned his own situation with Mrs Siddons then Sake Mahomet would be more confiding.

"I attended a ball very recently," he said.

"Really?" replied Mahomet, his thoughts still focused on his wife.

Doyle nodded. "I was invited by Mrs Siddons."

This gained Mahomet's attention. "You accompanied her?"

Again Doyle nodded. "It was quite the perfect evening."

For the first time Mahomet observed that the young man opposite was in a state of great happiness.

"Are you becoming ... acquainted with this lady?"

"I sincerely hope so, Sake Mahomet."

The Indian did not know what to say. This was one of the most unexpected things he thought he would ever hear, but then neither had he foreseen Jane's actions or the visit of Mr Rufus. Given Decimus was an ocean away from paternal advice, Mahomet immediately took upon himself Squire Doyle's responsibilities.

"I have heard say that this lady is of considerable years, Decimus," he said as gently as he could.

Doyle nodded blithely so Mahomet continued.

"Is it not correct that if your mother had lived she would have been of a similar age?"

Doyle smiled. "Yes, that is possibly correct. If Bunton is right with his gossip, there are a good thirty years between us. Yet if you saw her, Sake Mahomet, you would not raise such matters."

"Ah!" is all Mahomet could say.

"And she is not my mother," the young man continued, keen to state his case. "She is a gracious lady with a fine reputation and one of the leading ladies of the nation. And she is most handsome, both in body and mind."

The boy is earnest, thought Mahomet. He would have to step carefully.

"I do not know," the older man cautioned, "but I would think to carry on an acquaintance with such a person of profile and patronage would be difficult, Decimus, and fraught with problems. I would counsel great caution. And still you must not forget the age difference."

Doyle looked up sharply. "Like the age difference between yourself and cousin Jane, Sake Mahomet? Surely you, more than anyone, would understand the nature of love. You did elope, after all, and married without any of the family being present."

Mahomet realised he was not going to prevail. "They do say marry in haste and repent at leisure, Decimus ... not that I mean Jane, of course. Though at times our ages do produce some ... differences of opinion."

"But you remain a perfect match, Sake Mahomet, and an excellent example of how age does not matter."

Mahomet sighed. There was to be no reasoning with the boy so it would be best to leave it. No doubt his infatuation would go away as quickly as it came. In the meantime there was a question of journeying to Chelsea.

"If we set out for Chelsea now, Decimus, we should be there within an hour or so."

"Walk, Sake Mahomet? I would not hear of it. We will take a cab."

Love, it seemed, was in a generous mood.

FIRST recorded as a prison in 1329 when Agnes de Westhale surrendered herself to the local marshal for trespass on Richard de Chaucer, a relative of the great writer, the Marshalsea on the Southwark bank of the Thames was known to its inmates as "the Castle". It had a turreted entrance and for those who could afford it – ironic seeing it was a debtor's prison – life could be comfortable with chambers on the Master's Side. For those committed to the Common Side, however, prospects were not so bright but rather dark, dank and cramped, and when the smells of fresh bread from nearby Borough High Street filtered into the confines, a riot occurred more often than not.

Around the Marshalsea were set up lodging houses, of various levels of ill repute, where visitors attending on debtors inside the prison could stay. These lodgings vied with Southwark's more famous coaching inns, and in a very small room in one of the more meanly situated houses now paced a man who acted as if he were inside the Marshalsea itself, rather than a lean-too thrown up next to it. He had been placed in the room following the completion of the task he had been set. It was thought wise that he disappear for some time and he had been paid handsomely for his services. In truth he had rarely earned easier money, and it was now burning a hole in his pocket. This was more money than he had ever possessed at any one time and, once his master agreed he could depart this refuge, he planned to take himself away from London and the life he had led. He even dreamed of setting himself up in the trade his father had taught him. A butcher, perhaps, in a small town where no one knew of him or his past. For now, he had to rely on the occasional venture to taste the ales and steak pies of nearby coaching inns, but in the main had kept to his room for fear his new master might come calling and find him out.

Apart from money, the other thing he had plenty of was time. Time, that was, to think about recent events. He could not believe how easy it had been. When he turned up at their kitchen door with that letter as instructed they had taken him on without question. The mistress was a tart one to whom the little Indian should have taken a firm hand, but no doubt he was grateful for what he had. Where else in London was a native running a business and married to a white woman, even if she were Irish?

No, they were a queer pair and no doubt about it, but he had been able to quickly worm his way in and take charge. The original plan had been to bring the poison into the coffee house already made and add it when the opportunity arose. Yet it soon became apparent he could make it in the kitchen under the guise of preparing the horseradish, so had only to wait for the fat man to come in and dine.

With only the mistress to fool, and she so preoccupied with the kitchen and the children, it was a simple task. The challenge was to make sure it went into the fat man's food. After observing how he had been served on several occasions, he judged the best time to do it. The little Indian was always pushing his wife to serve up, so by delaying the "horseradish" he could add the poison into the food without anyone being the wiser.

It had also taken effect more quickly than even his master had guessed. The fat man was dead in a matter of minutes, barely giving him time to clear up. Still it had gone without a hitch, apart from that stupid shrewish housemaid accusing him of stealing. He left the root behind to avoid her squawking to the Indian. Surely they would realise it was not horseradish and throw it away? He hoped it had not gone badly for the Indian and his Irish wife. No one suspected that the fat man had been poisoned so how could it possibly affect them? He was glad in a way, as they had both shown some kindness to him.

He looked through the small, grimy window of his room onto the courtyard below and people busy about their work. He had to get out for some fresh air, he decided. Staying in this room was driving him mad. He ventured down the rickety stairs of the boarding house and out into the street, heading for the tavern at The George. Now he could afford the very best ale and steak pies he was not going to stint himself. In the public bar of the coaching house he found himself a dark corner and settled down with his mug of ale.

"So Walker, 'ow do you fare?" came the voice of a man who sidled up to him.

"You!" came the shocked reply. He could clearly make out the scared face in the darkened room.

"That 'aint no way to greet an' old pal."

"And that's news to me. Where's me money from the last job?" Walker had regained his composure.

"Oh, I've got a nice surprise for you."

"Well, where is it? 'and it over."

"Five guineas," Scarface continued. "But I aint got it 'ere. It's dangerous to walk around 'ere wiv money in yer pocket. You never knows what villains yer might meet. It's safe at me lodgings, just by the river."

"I didn't know you lived south of the bridge?"

"There's lots you don't knows about me Walker," Scarface smirked. "Like the fact your landlady told me you were 'eld out 'ere. She's 'olding your things. Don't be too long away, or she might sell 'em."

"And I told 'er not to say anything! Anyway, she can 'ave 'em now. I'm sittin' pretty."

"You wont want your money then."

"Five guineas! Of course I wants it," Walker replied, closing a hand over his purse which was safety sewn into his coat. The day was getting better and better.

"Come on. Drink up and we'll go an' get it, before I change me mind."

THE journey to Chelsea had been most pleasant, and a welcome distraction for Mahomet from the problems that awaited him back at the coffee house, even if he had been accompanied for most of the way by Doyle's incessant humming of a tune he had remembered from the recent ball. The cold grey morning had broken into a much fairer afternoon, and after the cab had passed through Sloane Square and struck the King's Road, Mahomet instructed the cabbie to divert to the Royal Hospital so Doyle could view the fine prospect of the military buildings. Here they had stepped down from the hackney and walked the length of the park, making pleasantries with some of the pensioners taking the air in their fine red tunics. They then instructed the cabbie to follow them as they walked the final quarter mile along Paradise Row to the Apothecaries', or Physick, garden.

As this was an impromptu visit they did not know what to expect, so Mahomet was relieved to find the garden open to visitors. A brief enquiry of the curator established that he was currently at the Apothecaries Hall in the city, but for a small consideration they were soon able to commission the services of one of the senior gardeners to show them around. It seems the garden was a major supplier of drugs and herbal remedies. Covering more than four acres, it was enclosed by a high brick wall and ran down to the river. This, explained their guide, gave for a more temperate climate that allowed exotic plants, such as a very large fruiting olive, to survive the harsh London winters. The garden was in fact divided into several smaller gardens, such as the pond rock garden that had been constructed using stones from, of all places, the Tower of London. And to the centre was a most glorious orangery. After walking around and paying close attention for more than an hour, Mahomet ventured to discuss the purpose of their visit.

"My colleague Mr Doyle is currently studying at the Hunterian and is especially interested in the effects of certain poisons, am I not correct Mr Doyle?"

"Most definitely," continued Doyle, continuing the deceit. "I assume you grow some poisons here?"

"Why yes sir," the gardener replied at his most helpful. "We have cultivated a specific area of the garden for such plants."

Doyle nodded. "Very good. I was curious about one plant in particular, the effects of which we have been studying. *Acontium napellus*. You may know it as monkshood or wolfsbane."

The gardener paused, slightly surprised. "I certainly know it, sir, though we do not currently grow it. I did not think it was now in common use, given its more contrary properties."

"You mean as a poison?"

"Rather because it is such an effective killer. We also found handling it rather tiresome … it can cause a very nasty skin rash … but really it is because it is no longer used that we stopped."

"How long ago?"

"Some years sir, though I do believe it is still grown in a garden in Hampstead. I am sorry we cannot help you, but the apothecary at the Hunterian should be able to purchase the root without difficulty, I think. If not, seek me out and I will acquire it for you."

So, thought Mahomet, it is readily available in London to those who know. He decided to mention the second reason for their visit.

"That is most kind, as has been the time you have given today. We had been advised that the gardeners here would be most helpful by a gentleman I spoke to recently … Sir George Harding … perhaps you know him."

The gardener smiled. "Georgie! Of course I know him, we all do, though we have not seen him here for some time. I am sorry for the familiarity, but to old hands like myself he will always be Georgie the curious little boy. He used to attend regularly with his mother, Lady Harding, until she sadly passed away. But he kept up his interest in plants afterwards. That is until he went up to Oxford. I heard about his late father's death. So sad."

"I did not know Lady Harding had an interest in plants," Mahomet responded, keen to encourage the gardener to continue.

"Not in plants, sir, but more in what they could do for her. She suffered terribly, though from what doctors could not say. She tried any number of concoctions but without any great relief. It is not always possible to help, don't you agree sir?" he asked pointedly of Doyle, looking for medical confirmation.

"Sadly that can be the case," agreed Doyle. "Still, she encouraged her son."

The gardener smiled. "I have never known a boy to have such an affinity with herb-lore. It is a pity he did not continued with it. The science of plants is an honourable study for a gentleman."

Mahomet nodded. "Yes, but he does seem to be easily distracted, if the rumours are to be believed."

The gardener looked sharply at Mahomet, annoyed at this remark. "I have heard the gossip about George Harding and, if true, I cannot rightly condone his behaviour. It is said he is in with a wild lot. But I remember the little boy with the questioning mind who would spend hours helping to plant out and could identify most species using the Latin names. Why, I now recall that as a boy he helped me plant out your own *Acontium napellus* with the care of a midwife. Perhaps had he been encouraged more in such studies he would not now be furrowing a wayward track. You have to nurture a seed, sir, to ensure it grows well."

BY the late 1700s shipping traffic in the Pool of London, which is that portion of the Thames between the cathedral of St Pauls and the Tower, was so great the West India Dock was constructed further downstream. The success of this off-river dock led to the construction of others – the London, East India and Surrey – but the Pool remained the commercial heart of the city. Around it were hundreds of tall warehouses to which thousands of Thames Lightermen transferred precious cargo between the ships and the shore. A curious scene was now taking place on an upper floor of one recently emptied warehouse. A man had been secured to a chair with twisted rope. To one side of him stood a tall thin man with a scared face while before him was a shorter, stockier gentleman with bright red hair. This man held in his hands a pilliwink, or thumbscrew, the crushing bars of which were studded with sharp metal points. The man in the chair was weeping with pain.

"Please sir ... I beg you ... leave me alone!" he cried.

"You beg me?" repeated the surprised torturer. "But you did not grant Sir Josiah Harding such courtesy, did you Walker?"

"Isn't that enuf ... sir?" said the scarfaced man from one side.

"Enough? Enough! This is government business, sir. Stop your ears if the noise offends you, or stand outside. No doubt one of my men will be only too happy to keep you amused."

The scarfaced man stepped back a pace. "But 'e's not speakin' sir, 'e's just yellin'!"

"Oh, he'll speak, won't you Walker? But first he needs to know pain. Hold his hand out again!"

Scarface did not move.

"Do not vex me sir, or I will summon my men. You have been paid very well for leading me to this reprobate so hold your tongue and do as you are told. I am surprised a man who handles the dead so readily could be so squeamish. You would have happily delivered him to the doctor in Soho for a guinea had I not intervened, so count your blessings that I ran you to ground when I did. Now, hold out his hand! He has still got plenty of fingers to work on, haven't you Walker. And I will ask one more time, what did the man who instructed you look like and where did you meet him? A name will stop the pain ..."

LATER the same day a message came to Dr Simon Bunton: one of his regular suppliers had a specimen available, and the doctor promptly agreed to take delivery. It had been some weeks since the Hunterian had been able to hold a practical anatomical lecture, so such a delivery was long overdue. He did not want students to start complaining, especially as Bart's had conducted two such lectures in the past week. What he really required was a change of judges at the Old Bailey, ones who would get the gallows at Newgate working again and increase the flow of legal bodies. Perhaps he should write to the Lord Chancellor suggesting this. Then again perhaps not, as he did not want any difficult questions on where their current supply was coming from.

He had assumed the specimen to be coming from a favoured supplier, so when the porters opened the doors to the rear of the school and in walked a tall man with a scared face, followed by a shorter colleague pushing a cart, he was taken by surprise.

"Why gentlemen!" he exclaimed, "this is a turn up. I thought you two had disappeared like your friend."

The tall one snarled. "Do you want this or not?"

Bunton held up his hand. "No offence, gentlemen, I am sure. Let us to this business then we can discuss the matter on which I sought your help some *weeks* ago." His emphasis on "weeks" brought about another snarl.

In the cart was a body of a man in his late thirties. With a cursory examination Bunton soon realised that there was so much damage to the head the man was hardly recognisable. He did not like it.

"How did this one die, gentlemen?" he asked sharply. There was no response.

Bunton looked for signs of burial but could find no soiling beyond a general grubbiness. For the entire world it looked like the man had been subjected to a violent death.

"I do not like all these marks, gentlemen, nor the general condition of the body."

"What wiv' it?" snarled the scarred man. "Wonce you get through wiv 'im e'll be even less a beauty. Do you want 'im or not?"

This sounded like an ultimatum, and Bunton was desperate for a body so had little room for negotiation.

"How much?"

"To you thirty."

Bunton weighed up the cost of the corpse against the likelihood of how they had acquired it. "I assume you mean guineas and I'll give you five for it and no more, so either take the money or the body. Which is it?"

The tall man looked over to Bunton and smiled, making the doctor's skin itch just slightly.

"We'll take it."

Bunton indicated to the porters to take the body away and quickly counted out the money, which he handed over.

"And our other matter gentlemen, what of him. Have you found Walker?"

Now the tall man smiled and tipped his hat to the doctor.

"Oh, we've found 'im all right."

"Then why did you not say?" Bunton challenged. "There is no money until we speak to him. Quickly now, tell me where he is."

The smaller resurrectionist chuckled as his colleague smirked. "But doctor, you already know were 'e is. You've just put 'im away."

Chapter 10

Richmond Park, Early September 1811.

THE Deputy Ranger started at the sudden movement of the deer, and looked around for the reason they had bolted. Such disturbances annoyed him – he was a man who expected order to apply as equally to nature as to society. From across the park he could see the figure of a man coming towards him. He paused his morning walk to await the approaching visitor, taking in the view towards Richmond Hill in the distance. It was a fine autumn morning, and the wide-open spaces gave him a greater perspective on life than the cloistered, stuffy rooms of Westminster Palace.

As the man approached his shock of red hair was as introductory as any calling card. What a curious young man, the Deputy Ranger thought. And why did he call himself after a medieval king? Aliases were common enough among agents of the Crown, but William Rufus? If the Deputy Ranger recalled his history correctly – and as a former Speaker of the Commons and Prime Minister he had made a special study of kingship – William II, or Rufus, was hated by his people. What did the *Anglo-Saxon Chronicles* say? "He was odious to God". Quite. His death was the most popular thing known about the king, shot by one of his own arrows while hunting. A typical piece of English understatement! His nobles had left him where he fell, and his body was carried to Winchester in the back of a charcoal cart. The Deputy Ranger shuddered at the thought, as he was one of those men excessively concerned with how history would judge him. Still, it was said Rufus had a ruddy complexion, so perhaps the choice of name by the young man approaching was not entirely inappropriate.

As the agent drew close he stooped and bowed low, which the Deputy Ranger acknowledged with a cursory nod.

"My lord," he declared.

"You have sought me out during my morning constitutional, sir, so what you are about to impart must be of very great worth." This sounded more of a warning than a greeting.

"It concerns the matter you presented to me recently with regard to the passing of a gentlemen member of a certain society."

The Deputy Ranger murmured to himself and look about; even the deer had moved out of hearing distance and the two men were quite alone.

"Well sir, and what have you found?"

""Many things, my lord."

The Deputy Ranger nodded. "Good, then join me in my walk and let me hear more."

William Rufus fell in beside his master and they continued on the pathway through knee-high bracken. The path was carefully maintained by gardeners at the Deputy Ranger's White Lodge residence to create a pastoral ramble for his lordship.

"I spoke to Cochrane's Indian at his coffee house. He, together with some other fellows, had attempted to track down the errant servant whom he suspected administered the poison to Sir Josiah Harding. His quest had led him to a couple of resurrectionists who supply the London medical schools with their cadavers. Seemingly the poisoner had a darker side to him and was an associate of these men."

"Had? You speak in the past tense young man."

Rufus nodded. "I will come to that, my lord. But thankfully I chanced on our poisoner before he shuffled off his mortal coil."

The Deputy Ranger stopped walking and turned to Rufus. "I find the lightness of your speech disconcerting, sir. Now tell me, was it as we thought? Was he working for another party and, if so, who?"

Rufus smiled at his master, only increasing the sense of irritation in the older man.

"I tracked him down to a lodging house in Southwark, my lord, and with a couple of men was able to persuade him to join me for a discussion in an old warehouse ..."

The Deputy Ranger raised his hand. "I do not wish to know the details of your ... discussion ... sir, simply the conclusions."

Rufus nodded. "My apologies, my lord. Yes, it was as we suspected. He was working for another party, and was not personally acquainted with the victim. After some … hard discussion, he confessed as much. A gentleman he knew from acting as a bodyguard approached him and, knowing of his night business supplying the medical schools, offered a handsome purse to carry out a special task. This gentleman arranged for his placement at the Indian's coffee house and taught him how to administer the poison. It was to look as natural a death as possible. Our body snatcher took to his new job expeditiously, it seems, and was rewarded handsomely. He was quite crestfallen that I had caught up with him."

"And did he know the gentleman who commissioned him?"

Rufus shook his head. "I'm afraid I did not get a name, my lord."

"What!"

"If I can explain my lord," begged Rufus. "He broke from me as I tried to … force his hand … and jumped from the warehouse. He did not realise or forgot we were on the third floor of the building. Death was immediate."

"Damnable man! And he gave no indication as to who instructed him?"

"Little except that the man is knowledgeable of the poison used."

"That would seem obvious!"

"Yes my lord," Rufus continued, "… yet I have also discovered that Harding's eldest son, George, is quite taken with herb-lore and gardening. I have spoken to one of the family servants, who say he often visits the Apothecaries' Garden in Chelsea. Moreover George has now inherited the title and estates. The family owns a large house north of Westminster and abutting Mary-le-Bone Park. It seems Harding senior recently refused an approach by directors of a company to sell the estate for an extension to the Grand Union canal. The late Sir Josiah was adamant in his opposition."

The Deputy Ranger's eyes lit up. "Mary-le-Bone Park, eh? You will not know but it is owned by the Crown and the leases on the small holdings which have farmed there for nigh on a hundred and fifty years have just lapsed. The Regent is most decided on building a great construction and processional way, running from the park through London to his palace at Carlton House on the Mall, to rival Bonaparte's designs for Paris. The King would be horrified if he could only understand what his son is up to. The plan is to build most well appointed properties around the park to provide an income, though I suspect that as with Carlton House itself, the Privy Purse will end up paying for it. I have not seen the plans but I believe the Prince's architect Mr Nash needs the new canal for the transport of materials. And Sir Josiah Harding was objecting to the Prince's grand design, was he? So what better than to replace him."

Rufus considered his master's revelation. "So you think, my lord, that Sir Josiah was removed to progress this project?"

"Oh, no doubt Parliament will approve the purchase of the Harding land in due course, but time is not on the Prince's side. What if the King recovers? ... he has in the past. The Regency Act would be revoked and our builder Prince frustrated. And before you ask, I do not consider the Prince capable of such a deceit, but he surrounds himself with the most dubious of characters only too keen to please him."

Rufus warmed to the Deputy Ranger's train of thought. "Like those who frequent gaming clubs and boxing matches?"

"Exactly. This, I think, is where your investigation should now turn. Look to the clubs. Find out where the elder son keeps company and what they say about him. That is where the answer to Harding's death lies."

"And should I speak to Cochrane, my lord?"

The Deputy Ranger shook his head. "He has headed north, according to a letter he sent me, to visit his Scottish clan and will not return for some weeks. By which time I expect you will have the answer. And before you go, what did happen to the poisoner's body?"

Now the young redheaded man smiled broadly. "There is the great irony, my lord. His resurrectionist friends knew exactly how to dispose of him."

THE fact Walker had turned up as a specimen at the Hunterian was a shock not only to Dr Simon Bunton. When Doyle rushed to the Hindostanee Coffee House the following day to advise Mahomet, both men sat in stunned silence. It was only after he was certain Mahomet had fully absorbed the news did Doyle venture to speak.

"What now, Sake Mahomet?"

The Indian looked at his young relative and shook his head slowly. "I do not rightly know, Decimus. You say Dr Bunton is convinced Walker had been killed?"

Doyle was cautious. "The resurrectionists claimed Walker was found at the foot of an old warehouse along the Thames, having fallen from a great height. But when Bunton examined his wounds – and some could be attributed to the fall – there were many which suggested they had been caused by a physical assault beforehand. Some of the flesh wounds had evidence of a metal weapon – a knife or such like – being used and the fingers of his left hand had been broken. If he was not dead before his body fell to the ground then Bunton thinks he was as good as. He said it looked as if he had been tortured."

"Dr Bunton is an expert on human biology so we must be grateful for his opinion," Mahomet sighed. "Did the resurrectionists kill him, do you think?"

Doyle shrugged. "I do not know. It is possible, but surely they would not place themselves open to a charge of murder by delivering the body to the Hunterian? Of course they knew we were searching for Walker, but did not know the reason why. Unless they fell out between themselves ..."

Doyle's voice trailed off as he became lost in speculation. Mahomet, however, was now considering another option. "Apart from ourselves, Decimus, who knew about Walker? Only Dr Bunton, Jane, Cochrane and the fellow Rufus."

Doyle drew in his breath. "Do you think Rufus found him?"

Mahomet stared at the young man. "Rufus has been charged by Cochrane with investigating Harding's death. I told him about Walker, the resurrectionists and where we last saw them. If Walker's body shows signs of physical abuse, could he not have been tortured by Rufus before being thrown from the building?"

"Sake Mahomet," Doyle whispered, "what have we got ourselves in to?"

The older man shook his head. "I do not know Decimus, but perhaps the delivery of Walker's body was a warning for us not to continue. Perhaps he was killed for what he did to Harding, and his death was meant to draw a line under the matter."

They both considered this for several moments. "Do you believe that, Sake Mahomet?"

Mahomet took out a handkerchief from his waistcoat pocket and wiped his brow. They were ensconced in the small sitting room with the door firmly closed and it had suddenly become very stuffy.

"That the appearance of his body was meant to conclude our investigation yes, but I do not think it is the end of the matter," Mahomet replied finally. "If anything, it is just another twist. Walker killed a valued patron of this coffee house at the behest of another, or so we assume. Although he initially dissuaded us, Cochrane has subsequently instructed a thief-taker, or whoever Rufus is, to investigate Harding's death, and within a matter of days Walker is found dead. In the meantime Cochrane has unexpectedly gone off to Scotland. It smells, Decimus, as rank as week old curried meat."

Doyle listened to the ticking of the mantel clock he had bought the Mahomets when he first arrived in London.

"Are we sure, Sake Mahomet," he said at last, "that Walker was acting under instruction. Could he not have held a grudge against Harding?"

"Enough to seek out employment here and then kill the man with a rare poison? I think not Decimus. Remember, you never met Walker ... but if I am any judge, he was simply incapable of devising such a plot. No, he was acting on behalf of another."

"Then perhaps Walker's master killed him to cover his tracks?"

"Yes, perhaps he was panicked by the appearance of ourselves or Rufus asking questions and decided to remove Walker. But that is simply another piece of speculation on our part. I think we need to keep with what we know rather than what we don't."

Doyle sat back in his chair, exhausted. "And what do we know Sake Mahomet? Very little, it seems."

Mahomet disagreed. "We know quite a lot Decimus. We know Sir Josiah was poisoned by Walker. We know Walker is now dead and had probably been beaten, perhaps tortured, before he died. We know that the only beneficiary of Sir Josiah's death is his eldest son George. And from our visit to Chelsea we learnt that George knows all about monkshood and its value as a poison. We also know that George Harding has serious debts of honour. So even though he did not actually administer the poison, he knew how to get hold of it and he has a strong reason for inheriting at this time. No Decimus, we know quite a lot and Walker's death, while unfortunate, does not detract from there being an unsolved mischief and by one who thought it game to use my coffee house for his purposes. I would disabuse him of his conceit, if I could."

"George Harding knew that his father frequented your coffee house and was partial to cousin Jane's curries, which would mask the bitter taste of the poison."

"Yes Decimus, you are right. And by employing Walker to commit the act but being present at the death as an innocent bystander he also had a perfect alibi. Matters are certainly leading us towards the son."

The two men looked at each other as the murderer revealed himself to them.

"But my question still stands, Sake Mahomet. What now?"

The Indian shook his head. "I am not sure. Our reasoning, as it stands, lacks substance. We have no actual evidence proving George Harding's guilt. We know it was Walker who killed Sir Josiah and now Walker is dead. We need to associate George Harding to Walker and place that evidence before a magistrate."

The two men sat in silence for some minutes more while they considered their quandary. Finally Mahomet spoke.

"I will have to call on George Harding."

Doyle responded quickly. "I do not think that a good idea Sake Mahomet. If we are correct then Harding is a killer, at least by proxy. It would be most unwise."

"We have no evidence, Decimus, and to make allegations against Harding to an officer of the law now would leave us ... me ... open to a case of slander. I would be ruined. No, the only thing is to put it to him directly."

"And what do you say, Sake Mahomet? Have you killed your father?" Doyle said incredulously.

Mahomet shook his head. "We need not be so direct. We could try and smoke him out. Say it has been brought to our attention that his father may have been poisoned, and that we have a good knowledge of the poison used and are going to the authorities with our suspicions. There would be no need to accuse him directly. Then wait and see how he reacts. I believe guilt shows in a man's face."

Doyle was far from convinced. "I am most unhappy, Sake Mahomet. You intend to tell a suspected killer that we know the details of his crime without actually accusing him. If he did kill Walker then he is unlikely to stay his hand with you. My Uncle Paddy says that once a man is decided on a journey of crime it is difficult for him to stop. He often finds the crime compels him forwards. Situations created by the first act lead him to commit more desperate measures. Or perhaps the man is emboldened by the fact he has not been caught, or that the fear of exposure drives him to excess. Should I not write to Uncle Paddy and seek his advice before we do anything more?"

Mahomet smiled for the first time. "Your Uncle Patrick is a generous and learned man; a well-respected man of the law. But I think I know what he would advise – let well alone. Yet I cannot do that, Decimus. I cannot stand by and watch a man profit from murder, especially when the one murdered was his own father and in my coffee house."

An image briefly crossed Mahomet's mind – that of a mother with two young sons being told their father had been killed. The Raja had assured her that her husband's killers, those evil brothers, would be brought to justice. Then less than one year later she saw them sitting at the Raja's side during the festival of Bakrid. This celebrates the day Hazrat Ibrahim was instructed by Allah to sacrifice his son, only to find a ram in his son's place. Mahomet's mother clearly saw the Raja pass meat to the brothers, signifying they were close family, and she knew then that there would be no justice for her sons' father.

He was shaken from these thoughts by Doyle's voice.

"I will still write to Uncle Paddy in Dublin," the young man was saying, "with your agreement. He may be able to help."

Mahomet nodded his assent, though doubted it would do much good. Yet the image of the murderous brothers and Doyle's mention of his father's learned brother Patrick had brought another thought to his mind.

"Wait! There is the second son, is there not? The younger one who accompanied Sir Josiah so often and was present when he died."

Doyle nodded. "William. Mrs Siddons did not speak kindly of him and says he is a malcontent – pernicious even."

Mahomet looked up. "Really? Why Decimus?"

Doyle blushed. "It seems he did not agree with her friendship of his father."

"Ah!" Mahomet considered speaking to Doyle again about his association with Mrs Siddons but then put it to one side.

"They were close then, Sir Josiah and the younger son?"

Doyle shrugged. "That is doubtful. If I recall correctly then Sarah said Sir Josiah bullied his sons. While George escaped to Oxford William was left at home and under the domination of his father. I think the father's treatment of his younger son was one of the reasons Sarah saw less of Sir Josiah."

He felt a strong desire to protect Mrs Siddons' reputation, but Mahomet had already moved on to a new line of thinking.

"It might be well to speak with William Harding first."

"Again, Sake Mahomet, to say what?" asked Doyle incredulously. "I think your brother killed your father?"

"No Decimus, no. But I have been amiss in not offering my deep regrets at the death of Sir Josiah. Such condolences are long overdue. I held back only out of respect for the family ... well that and the fact I feel guilty Sir Josiah was poisoned here. By speaking to William I might find something more about his elder brother."

"You must not mention the poisoning, Sake Mahomet. Just imagine what problems that could cause! I think I should come with you."

Mahomet had no intention of speaking the word "poison" out loud, but considered a meeting with William Harding to be the best way forward and appreciated his young cousin's offer of further support.

WILLIAM Harding had been waiting for the right moment before approaching his brother. Disposition was important, and it was at breakfast when he at last found George in good humour. It was rare for them both to be at the table together, yet William knew he had to get close to his brother if he was to seek out weaknesses he might be able to exploit. He also wished to meet with George's set in the hope of identifying a likely duellist.

"You seem in fine form this morning brother," complimented William as he finished his muffin. The Hardings kept breakfast better than most, and while the younger brother eschewed the ham and eggs usually found in the serving platter, both the late Sir Josiah and the new Sir George considered it important to have a solid foundation to the day.

"The tables were good to me last night, sir. I think my luck changes for the better."

I do hope not, thought William as he smiled and nodded, sipping on his tea.

"That is good brother. You deserve a change of fortune ... we both do. I would welcome some of that luck."

"How so?"

"I will shortly play in the last match of the season. Why not come along with your friends. You may find it diverting, and there will be an opportunity to place a wager or two. I believe there could be several hundred spectating, and you know what that means."

Indeed George Harding did. Several gaming books were likely to be open, with betting on everything from the final outcome of the match to individual scores and wickets. Why, he had once bet on the colour of scarf one of the batsmen would be wearing as he came to the wicket! Yes, cricket was good sport, and it had been a long time since George had attended, thanks to his father and Mr Lord. But now he was the landowner, and Thomas Lord could not deny him entry. It was also appropriate that he attend what was likely to be the last cricket match on Harding land.

"What you say is tempting, brother. I could arrange for a small party; friends from Watier's and Gentleman Jacksons. We can gather here."

"The more the merrier George," said William excitedly, hardly believing his brother had taken the bait so readily.

"I will make sure your party has entry to the players' tent," he continued, "though I would ask that, if you see him, you please allow Mr Lord every courtesy."

"But of course," spluttered George, his mouth full with a spoon of egg. "I have nothing but the highest esteem for the gentleman, even though he is taking a king's ransom for the broken lease. Papa was a fool to grant it on such terms, but I am a man who will pay what is due."

From across the table William smiled and nodded at his brother. Yes, he agreed to himself, we will all receive what we are due.

IT had taken nearly a week of strained silences and furtive glances, but in the end Sake Dean and Jane Mahomet finally discussed her father's offer. Jane was anxious that Mahomet reply soon while Mahomet had been visited by a number of creditors, including a very angry market gardener. In the end he bowed to the inevitable.

"We cannot continue in this vein," he said as they settled into bed, but keeping their backs to each other.

"It is not I being churlish, Mr Mahomet," came the reply from the other side.

Mahomet sighed. "Have you written to your father yet?"

"It is not my place to do so, it seems."

"Then I think I should write thanking him for his generous offer and say I will keep it under advisement. But I do not promise to accept it."

At last, cried Jane to herself, he is beginning to see sense. "If you think this appropriate husband," she said aloud.

He placed his head on the pillow before continuing.

"He is a kind man, and should not have been placed in such a position. But ..." he continued as he heard his wife gather breath, " ... what is done is done. Does he wish an interest in the business, do you think?"

"No husband, it is simply a loan, but I will show you the letter."

She went to rise from the bed but he turned over and stopped her with his hand gently on her arm. "Not now wife, it can wait until the morning."

For the first time in days Jane Mahomet looked into her husband's face. "I am sorry, husband, I truly am, if I have caused you distress. I acted only in the very best ..."

"I know, Jane, I know," he said softly. "None of this is easy, and the misfortune of the recent death has not helped matters. Perhaps I too was hasty. It is a most generous offer and your family has always been so kind to us ... to me. Yesterday I recalled my mother for the first time in years. I can still picture her face. She must be long gone I think or else reached at least eighty years. I visited Patna once just before I departed for Ireland and saw her in the market. She looked but did not recognise me – I was just another soldier to her, I suppose. I did not make myself known."

Jane Mahomet thought she had heard all her husband's Indian stories but this was new to her.

"Why did you not go and speak to her?"

Mahomet smiled at his wife. "I do not know. I wanted to but something held me back. I think I feared a repeat of the scene when I left home as a boy. I did not wish to cause her any more distress. My elder brother, I knew, had returned home with a wife and family so she was not alone. I should not have gone back ... it served no purpose as I was so determined to leave India with Mr Baker. Yet I still regret not saying goodbye once more. We should not deny our family, Jane, and I will not estrange you from yours. Next year we will travel to Cork so your father can see his grandchildren and beautiful daughter. This I promise."

Jane Mahomet, now in tears, turned fully in the bed and settled in facing her husband, gently stroking his brown cheek and kissing him softly on the lips.

The next morning Mahomet rose at first light to write to his father-in-law acknowledging the offer of three hundred pounds, and stating that while it was not required at the moment he would answer more fully in due course. Then he waited for Doyle to arrive at ten o'clock when they would venture the brief distance north to the Harding mansion. Doyle, as was his wont, arrived early by hackney just as the mantel clock struck quarter to the hour and together they made the final leg of the journey. They did not know whether William Harding would be in residence or prepared to receive them, but hoped they could surprise him, catch him unawares and encourage him to speak freely.

It was a clear morning when the cab passed the deserted gatehouse to the estate. As it reached the end of the short drive Doyle noticed a young man walking in formal gardens to one side of the main house. "If I am not mistaken, Sake Mahomet, that is William Harding yonder. I recognise him from the funeral. The other brother is much fatter." Rather than presenting their cards at the house and waiting for a formal introduction, Mahomet instructed the cab to hold on the forecourt of the main house and the two men crossed quickly to where the younger Harding had been observed.

"Mr Harding, sir," called Mahomet as they approached from behind.

William Harding turned sharply. "Who ...?"

"Mr Harding, sir, our sincere apologies for this intrusion." Both Mahomet and Doyle bowed low.

William looked at them bemused and slightly coy, having been caught in the process of plotting his brother's demise while walking.

"I am Sake Dean Mahomet sir and this is my colleague Mr Doyle."

Doyle cast a furtive glance at William Harding, who was now recovering from his surprise and recognised Mahomet.

"You own that coffee house?" he queried and Mahomet bowed again.

Harding was now fully composed. "Well sir, what of this intrusion?"

"My most humble apologises sir," Mahomet repeated and bowed for the third time. "We did not mean to impose but saw you walking alone from the carriageway. Please may we beg a few moments of your time?"

The Indian was so subservient and pleading that William Harding simply nodded.

Mahomet smiled. "You are most gracious, sir. I have come to offer my deepest sympathy and condolences at the passing of your late father. It was such a shock to all of us."

Harding breathed deeply as he was reminded of the dreadful evening so few weeks ago.

"I should have come before now, but delayed until the pain of your loss eased slightly. My colleague here, Mr Doyle, attended the funeral on my behalf."

Harding looked to the handsome yet sombre young man standing next to the small Indian but failed to recognise him as the gentleman with Mrs Siddons in the church.

"Is seems so long ago now," Harding remarked, and indeed to him it was, given all his brother had done since the funeral to dispose of the family estate. He looked to the small dark man again. "I thank you for your sympathies sir, though I feel you have been greatly exercised by submitting them yourself. A letter would have sufficed."

Mahomet quickly shook his head. "On the contrary Mr Harding, it is the least I can do given your father's ... illness ... took place on my premises. It was quite distressing to both myself and my wife. Sir Josiah must have been unwell for some time to have been taken so quickly."

So, thought William Harding, he wishes to make sure nothing can be directed towards his establishment, and he felt his cheeks flushing.

"My father was perfectly well sir. Indeed my sister considered it must have been something he ate which killed him that evening. It is fortunate for you that my brother dismissed this out of hand, despite her earnest pleading."

Mahomet stared at the man – this was the last thing he expected to hear and was taken aback, partly because it was so close to the truth. "I am deeply sorry if my presence offends sir. It is the last thing I would wish. The doctor attending made a close examination of the kitchen and found nothing amiss. He clearly stated that your father died from a failing of his own constitution, but I fully understand your anger. It was indeed a most grievous occurrence."

William Harding's feigned anger dissipated as quickly as it came. He was too occupied with other matters to argue with the coffee house owner. From the house a willowy young woman appeared dressed demurely in black, against which her bright blonde hair stood out.

"So you say," William Harding sighed, "it was a very great shock. Ah, here is my sister. Now, if you have finished your business, thank you for calling."

With this he bowed to both men, but before he could began to walk away Charlotte Harding was among them. "William, who are these gentlemen? Please introduce me."

"Lottie no ... oh well," William Harding sighed. "This gentleman is Mr Mahomet, the owner of the coffee house in which papa died, and the other is ...?"

"Decimus Doyle, Miss Harding, at your service.," said the dashing young beau who immediately caught the young lady's attention.

"Mr Mahomet ... Mr Doyle.." replied Charlotte, curtsying.

"Mahomet had come to pay his respects ... and his condolences.," explained her brother.

"That is so kind of you sir. So few people call on this house, except my elder brother's ... friends. Did you know papa well?"

"He dined regularly at my coffee house, Miss Harding, along with your brother here. And how is your elder brother? I think I should present my condolences to him as well."

"George is quite well and suffers his pain lightly," remarked William churlishly. "Come, if you must speak with him I will take you to the house."

"I do not wish to see George, William!" Charlotte Harding exclaimed, to the surprise of the others. "Please do not ask me to go!"

"Do not distress yourself Lottie. Stay here if you will. Mr Doyle, if you will be so kind as to keep my sister company while I attend on your friend?"

"Of course sir," said a surprised Doyle. "But may I have a word with Sake Mahomet before you leave."

Pulling the older man to one side Doyle whispered: "Be careful what you say Sake Mahomet. Did you not just hear Harding say his brother objected to suspicions about their father's death?"

"Do not concern yourself, Decimus," Mahomet replied in the same whisper, but smiling. "Now please attend to the pretty young lady yonder."

"I am ready Mr Harding," he called and the two men made their way towards the Jacobean mansion, leaving Doyle to stand uncomfortably with

Charlotte Harding in the parterre. "They won't find him," said Charlotte Harding to herself. "He often stays at his club. Will you accompany me around the garden, Mr Doyle?"

Doyle looked at the young lady but, noticing her staring at him, glanced down to the gravel path. "Of course, Miss Harding."

She smiled and, unexpectedly and most indelicately, took Doyle's arm and began to lead him through the garden. "Lottie, please Mr Doyle. It is the only name I know."

After some moments she paused and said: "Were you not at papa's funeral, Mr Doyle? With that lady?"

Doyle was taken aback that she had noticed him given the gravity of the occasion. "Why yes Miss Harding. But I did not escort Mrs Siddons. She simply sat next to me."

Charlotte Harding smiled and started to walk again. "Good ... I mean, it was good of you to attend, Mr Doyle. Papa had few friends and he did not consider it proper for me to entertain at home. He even dismissed my governess some time ago, though I did not feel her absence greatly. I see so few people, and now my brother is planning to remove me to the country." At this point Charlotte Harding halted again and Doyle could feel her begin to tremble next to him. "I am orphaned, Mr Doyle," she said in a shrill voice. "I have never known a mother and now I must do without a father. I am lost! Utterly lost!"

Doyle was taken aback by Charlotte Harding's uninhibited appeal to a stranger but then recalled Mrs Siddons remarks on the young woman's lack of guidance and want of a female companion. He gently eased her arm from under his and stood back slightly, looking at Miss Harding clearly for the first time. She was pale, even wan, but Doyle suspected it was not from the recent loss of her father.

"Please Miss Harding," he said gently, "I know it has been be most difficult for you."

"But you cannot imagine my loneliness, Mr Doyle. And now I am to be cast adrift by George. What is to become of me!"

Doyle searched his mind for consoling words.

"Please Miss Harding, do not take on so. There is always hope for the future. Why, I believe we already have something in common."

This statement caught Charlotte Harding's breath. "Really? Us? I mean you and I?"

"My mother died as I was born, Miss Harding. I understand the pain and guilt that this can bring."

Charlotte Harding gasped. "Really Mr Doyle, did she? Your mother? Of course it happens a lot, I know, but I've never met anyone else ... " She began to sob again. "Do families always become so unhappy when the mama dies?"

Decimus Doyle, unused to having to deal with a tearful young lady, did his best to create a bond of trust between them.

"No miss, I assure you that does not have to be. My father and I are very close. Please Miss Harding. I am sorry. I did not mean to upset you ... Here, take my handkerchief."

Reaching for the proffered comfort, Charlotte Harding slowly dabbed her eyes. "You are close to your father? Then I am glad for you. Oh Mr Doyle, I do not mean to be so weak. Papa was very forceful in his wishes, if you understand me. He would tell me to bear my duties as a daughter without complaint, and be strong with my emotions. But poor William. He was so badly affected. Papa would often berate him and I could hear ... angry noises ... too terrible, and poor William's cries ... I do wish mama had lived."

Doyle feared another round of tears. "Come now, Miss Harding, cry if it makes you feel better. I consider it a sign of strength, not weakness. Not to be able to shed a tear is the real weakness. Except, of course, when they dampen a pretty face. Perhaps you should dry your cheeks before your brother returns?"

At last a smile appeared on her face and she looked at the handkerchief, gently stroking the embroidered initials. "You are so kind Mr Doyle. DD. Are these your initials? What does the other D stand for?"

"Decimus, Miss Harding."

"Lottie."

Doyle smiled. "Miss Lottie."

"Decimus? What a magical name. Will you be my friend, Decimus?"

Again, the carefree nature of Charlotte Harding took him unawares. "Why of course, Miss Harding."

"Lottie!" she chided. "If we are to be friends then we must be on good terms."

"As you say … Miss Lottie. Now, I think we must return and wait for your brother and Sake Mahomet. And please keep the handkerchief … as a token of our friendship."

"Thank you Decimus," she said, taking a tight grip of her newly found keepsake. "You are so, so kind. And your friend is called Sake? What does that mean? Is it a title?"

"It is Oriental for prince, I believe."

"And is he a prince?"

Doyle laughed. "I would say so, yes. In many ways he can be considered a prince among men."

Chapter 11

Directions concerning the Sauce for Steaks.
IF you love pickles or horseradish with steaks, never garnish your
dish, because both the garnishing will be dry, and the steaks will be
cold, but lay those things on little plates, and carry to table. The great
nicety is to have them hot and full of gravy.

The Art of Cookery Made Plain and Easy

London, Autumn 1811.

THE gaunt-looking man stepped down from *The Flying Machine* and
stretched his arms. He had been travelling atop the coach for over three
days since leaving Liverpool, and even though he had tied himself securely
to the roof he could only catnap – especially after they had passed through
a downpour beyond Oxford. Being damp, miserable and hungry, he
decided on finding first a coffee house and then some lodgings. So when the
coach halted at the turnpike gate that marked the end of the Oxford road
and the beginning of Oxford Street, he headed east, and veered north.

He had no knowledge of this part of London, and was surprised by the
quality of row upon row of terraced residences. Yet even these houses did
not prepare him for the grandeur of the fine mansions in Portman Square
and, tired and hungry as he was, he stood for some minutes taking in his
surroundings. It reminded him of the Imperial residences in St Petersburgh,
and brought back painful memories of his time in Russia. He watched as a
large coach and four drew up outside a mansion close to where he was
standing, and two liveried footmen jumped down. From the coach a very
well dressed and superior looking lady appeared and swept up the steps of
the house and inside.

He snorted and turned on his heels, as if repelled by the square and its
elegance. Walking away, he came across a street parallel to the square but
further north that was occupied by a number of shops, and it was here he

came upon a quite unusual coffee house. He took in the name for some moments before entering. It was early evening, and the shadows of the day gave the dining room a mystical feel. On two walls were large painted murals depicting Eastern landscapes, and the wicker furnishings presented him with an Occidental scene he had not experienced since he was a young midshipman aboard the cutter *Hartwell*, plying its trade between London and China – and that had been twenty five years ago.

The dining room was empty of patrons except for two gentlemen deep in conversation in one corner. From behind a screen appeared a small Indian of mature years who bowed deeply and welcomed him to the coffee house. Handing over his coat and bag and being shown to a table, he requested a mug of ale and enquired about food.

"We keep a most choice table, sir, and can offer pies and stews made of the finest beef-steak, or you can have a steak broiled and with the most delicate of sauces. Or we have a cold kitchiri, which is a mix of rice, lentils, dried haddock and curry powder and is a delicacy of the house."

He decided on a warming pie to accompany his beer and sat back in the tall wicker chair, his eyes closing as the exertion of his travel caught up with him. Within minutes the Indian had reappeared with his order, which he fell upon driven by a ravenous hunger. Several minutes later and now replete, he again settled back into the wicker chair and took in his surroundings. His Indian host re-appeared.

"Thank you sir," said the man as the Indian cleared away the dish and spoon and topped up his beer from a large mug, "that was most welcome. This is a most unusual place, is it not?"

The Indian bowed. "I hope it meets with your approval master."

The man smiled, taken by the courtesy. "It does indeed. Who owns such a place?"

"It is my own, sir. Sake Dean Mahomet at your service."

The man looked surprised, not knowing whether to believe him. "Then my congratulations sir. In my time I have travelled widely and have seen many things. Yet this is one of the more amenable, as is this whole area of London, me thinks."

Mahomet bowed again and continued the pleasantries. Given the weather-beaten condition of the man's coat, he assumed him to be a traveller.

"You are a visitor to London?" he asked.

The man nodded. "Some parts of London I know well – as a boy I was apprenticed to a jeweller in the city before I went to sea. But this borough is new to me. I have just arrived on the Liverpool mail coach, and disembarked at the tollgate close by. I have an appointment in Westminster tomorrow and need to find a lodging house."

Mahomet smiled. "There are any number of inexpensive and clean lodging houses south of Oxford Street, and I can recommend a couple should you wish. Your business in Westminster is legal? To do with the government perhaps?"

This polite enquiry brought a bitter response from his guest. "You see before you a very wronged man, sir. Our government conspired to keep me locked up in a Russian gaol for six years. In the end I had to appeal to the Tsar himself to let me go, which he did when he learnt of my suffering. I am now petitioning these rogues and vagabonds in Parliament to compensate me for my very great loss. Yet no one will listen to my story."

He had become quite agitated and Mahomet looked across the dining room to his other two guests, but they were still in conversation. Deep down he knew he would come to regret what he would say next.

"If you have time, sir, then I will listen."

The man smiled at this kindness and gestured for Mahomet to sit at the table, which he did at an angle to keep an eye on his other guests. The man before him then told his tale which, to Mahomet, sounded quite confusing. He had been maliciously imprisoned in Russia for a debt he did not owe and the British ambassador ignored his appeals.

"I was held in Archangel, to the very north of that wintry waste they call Russia, while my young wife, with a child at her breast, remained in St Petersburgh. Neither the British consul nor ambassador saw fit to help. Not one claimant appeared to demand any debt against me yet still I was held, being moved from prison to prison. I obtained a legal decision from a

Russian court that I had been unjustly treated but still the Russian governor of Archangel demanded two thousand roubles for my release, which I resisted on account of the gross injustice."

"Is two thousand roubles a considerable sum?"

The man nodded. "But one I held. However, by paying it I would have admitted my legal case against the governor was false and would have been sent to one of their prison camps in Siberia! Only the British authorities could have interceded on my behalf but they were not desirous to so do."

"And your young wife and child? Were they alone in St Petersburgh?"

Again he nodded. "After nine months my wife managed to get passage back to England and her family in Liverpool – unescorted. Again, the British authorities were not prepared to assist."

Mahomet tutted. It seemed the man did indeed have a grievance. "And how did matters resolve themselves, sir?" he asked, now engrossed.

"By chance. The captain of a Hull ship arrived in Archangel and fell into dispute about a sum owed for pilotage. This matter was represented to the Emperor four times within a month by the British ambassador, something he failed to do once for me in six years! At length the Russian senate, tired out by these inequities, discharged both the Hull captain and myself and I was ordered to quit the Russian dominions. That was two years ago."

Mahomet shook his head in sympathy.

"When I returned to Liverpool I petitioned the local Member General Gascoyne to have my claims laid before Parliament. Yet he said they were precluded from interfering by the a suspension of diplomatic ties with St Petersburgh, caused by the Tsar's recent truce with the French. So I have in my possession a personal petition to the King's Prime Minister, Mr Perceval, which I will deliver to his offices tomorrow. It was the inaction of the King's ambassador in Russia, sir, which led to my continued incarceration, and justice demands I be recompensed. My affairs have been ruined through the fault of this man, my property all dispersed, my family driven to tribulation and want and a great suffering imposed on myself. I will make them pay!"

The man's voice had been rising steadily and as he finished with a flourish

Mahomet noticed his other two guests looking across the dining room. He quickly tried to calm him.

"I am sure, sir, that the just nature of your cause cannot long be ignored. Your tale is quite an extraordinary one. While I cannot provide counsel, at least let me offer you another jug of ale. I would be interested to hear how your meeting fares tomorrow."

The man smiled but shook his head. "No sir, I will settle my account with you and then find the lodgings you recommend. I start out for Liverpool again tomorrow evening but, as I will board the coach from the turnpike, will call in after presenting my papers to Perceval to say how it went."

"Then please leave a message with my wife," advised Mahomet. "For tomorrow I attend a cricket match."

THE once-rural game of cricket had in recent years become "exceedingly fashionable, being much countenanced by the nobility and gentlemen of fortune", according to Joseph Strutt's *The sports and pastimes of the People of England*, published in 1802. Three years later Lord Byron arranged a match between the boys of Harrow School and those from Eton College. Although Harrow was beaten, his account of the day recalled that "we dined together and were extremely friendly, not a single discordant word was uttered by either party. To be sure, we were most of us rather drunk and went to the Haymarket theatre, where we kicked up a row, as you may suppose, when so many Harrovians and Etonians were in one place ..."

The ground on which the boys played belonged to Mr Thomas Lord. In 1787 Lord, a Yorkshire labourer and bowler at the White Conduit Club, was approached by some cricketing nobles to set up his own ground, with a guarantee against any losses he might incur. He acquired seven acres just north of Mary-le-Bone village and the Mary-le-Bone Cricket Club was formed. When the lease expired and the landlord wanted the land for more profitable building development, Lord obtained an 88-year lease from Sir Josiah Harding, partly on the understanding that young William's name would be uppermost in the minds of those selecting teams to play.

However, when he moved his ground the aristocrats of the Mary-le-Bone club failed to follow, and Lord fell back to allowing sides such as the St John's Wood Club to take the field. Still, times were good for Mr Lord. He had introduced a six-penny entrance fee to exclude the more unruly – and generally poorer – elements in the crowd, yet his games still attracted four or five thousand spectators. And players were also benefiting, with the best commanding fees of six guineas to win and four if they lost. Moreover, around the playing field gambling and drinking were to the fore. So had George Harding not desired to sell the land to the canal company, he would have been well suited in following his father as a patron of Mr Lord's noble game.

It was to this ground that Sake Dean Mahomet and Decimus Doyle now made their way. Their journey to the Harding mansion had been unsuccessful, albeit Doyle had discovered a new "friend" in Charlotte Harding. Sir George was not at home, though William advised his brother was to attend the last cricket match of the season and, probably, the last match on Harding soil. Now both men were silent as they walked up Baker Street towards their destination. Doyle was very concerned about the course the day would take and what could be accomplished. He doubted George Harding would appreciate the suggestion his father had died through poison, whether or not he was a party to it. And he was anxious how Sake Mahomet would broach the subject. For his part, Mahomet had a restless night recalling the strange man who called at the coffee house and his story of Russian intrigue. For some unknown reason he was fearful for the man. It was very brave of him to challenge the conceits of government, but if they had already conspired to keep him locked up in Russia for years, they were perfectly capable of packing him off to the penal colony of New South Wales or the like.

It was with these thoughts still occupying their minds that they reached the entrance gate to Mr Lord's cricket ground and paid their sixpence each to the surly attendant. Inside a good crowd had gathered, perhaps two thousand or more spread around the boundary to the playing field.

"We must make for the tent yonder," Mahomet said, pointing to the only structure of any substance – a large white canvas tent he recalled from his days in India. It would have been at home in any British army camp. Around it had been staked a large wooden limed fence. There was one obvious opening to the front that led onto the field and was patrolled by two men in red coats, thus adding to the military feel, so Mahomet assumed there would be a similar opening to the rear. As they walked around the boundary there were clusters of men gathered around makeshift stalls selling beer and an assortment of pies – Mahomet hoped they were filled with recognisable meat. One stall was selling tea, but at six pence a cup there was a distinct lack of interest. There were also other clusters of men. In the centre of these were two or three, negotiating deals and taking money while writing transactions into a large ledgers.

Doyle had been to a number of cricket matches in Dublin, and had even played, albeit unsuccessfully, for a Trinity College team, but this was Mahomet's first time, and the crowd and noise reminded him of bazaars in the cities of the Bengal Presidency such as Calcutta and Lucknow. The atmosphere and noise was infectious, and heightened an anticipation of the play to come.

"It seems a great deal of money will exchange hands today," he called to Doyle, and nodded towards a group of well-dressed gentlemen in close discussion with a man holding a gaming ledger.

"A fool and his money are soon parted," replied Doyle dismissively.

Mahomet looked at his wife's cousin. He may be enraptured with Mrs Siddons, he thought, but at least he does not have Sir George's vice.

As they neared the tent they saw William Harding in discussion with two other players – or so Mahomet assumed them to be as they were without coats and cravats and wore white shirts and pantaloons. All three had red coloured scarves tied around their waist. They made their way towards him but the cricketing Harding, seeing their approach, made his excuses to the men he was with and turned, venturing into the tent. He had no wish to speak with Mahomet and Doyle, who looked at each other.

"We are obviously not welcome Decimus, but it is not William with whom we must speak. Come, let us go inside and find the elder brother, if we can."

As promised by the Harding servant the day before, their names had been entered on the admission list and they soon found themselves inside the large canvas structure. It was crowded and smelly, with scores of men grouped together in animated discussion. Being small, Mahomet had to rely on Doyle to guide him around.

"I cannot see Sir George," reported the young Irishman, his neck straining to see above the crowd. "But I can see William, speaking to a distinguished gentleman. They are standing near the opening onto the field and seem to be discussing the weather, if I am any judge. Perhaps we should make our way towards him and ask if his brother is hereabouts."

Mahomet nodded his consent and slowly they made their way through the throng. A shout went up "play to commence" and a number of players, distinguished by their white clothing, also headed in their direction towards the field of play.

"Careful," cried Mahomet, pulling at Doyle's sleeve, "or we might find ourselves in the game!"

They stood back as the crowd followed the players outside and slowly the tent cleared sufficiently for Mahomet to see about him. He now had a clear sight of William Harding, who had not joined the other players for the start of play.

"Is he not playing?" Mahomet asked, pointing.

Doyle smiled. "His team must be batting first, so he will be waiting his turn in the order. Now the crowd has cleared, it might be a good chance to ask him about his brother."

Steadily they made their way towards William Harding who, watching the commencement of play, did not seem them approach.

"Mr Harding, sir," said Mahomet quietly as they stood behind him. "You are a welcome sight in this crowd."

Harding turned and, realising who it was, thought quite the opposite to be true. "You came then, gentlemen?" he remarked dismissively.

Mahomet nodded. "We *do* wish to speak with your brother," he stressed.

"His party has not yet arrived. I am afraid you will have to wait."

"Then we will watch and enjoy the game ..."

Mahomet cut short his speech as he was tapped on the shoulder. Turning around, he was confronted by a shock of red hair.

"I thought it was you Mahomet. I did not know you enjoyed this pastime – India is too hot a place for cricket, surely?"

Mahomet tried to control shock showing in his voice or on his face. "*Mr Rufus*, sir!" he said exclaimed pointedly, hoping Doyle would understand who it was.

The agent bowed to all three men. "May I ask for an introduction sir?"

Mahomet quickly introduced both Doyle and Harding, the latter being partly distracted by the game taking place on the field behind him.

"My deepest sympathises on the loss of your father," said Rufus to William Harding. "He died, did he not, at Mr Mahomet's coffee house?"

These last words gained the cricketer's attention.

"Thank you sir," he replied. "You knew my father?"

Rufus smiled and shook his head. "I fear not, though I am aware of the circumstances of his death. Such a strange death, was it not, his falling from his chair and shaking so violently that he expired, just after eating one of Mr Mahomet's curries. I am surprised you did not think it most unusual."

Both Mahomet and Doyle were horrified by Rufus' words, but were unable to speak before William Harding responded. "What do you know about this, sir?!"

"I do not think ..." began Doyle before Rufus interjected.

"I know sir that such symptoms are displayed as a result of common poisons. Surely your brother, who is such an expect in these matters, would have realised this at the time?"

"My brother? But he dismissed such concerns out of hand!"

"He is versed in herb-lore, is he not? Perhaps the inheritance he was to receive dulled his senses. Or maybe he put his knowledge to good use at the time, and helped speed your father to a higher calling."

Doyle and Mahomet looked at Rufus shocked, and all four men faced each other completely still, as if frozen in time.

"You mean you think my brother poisoned my father?" whispered William Harding at last, hardly able to speak. But before another word was uttered a shout went up from the field and a cry went out within the tent: "Harding, you're in!"

THE King's Prime Minister lived in Downing Street in a house attached to the government's Treasury building off Whitehall, and so it was to this address that the man from the Liverpool coach made his way at the same time as Mahomet and Doyle entered the cricket ground. He intended, if he could, to gain a personal meeting with Mr Perceval, but if not then he was confident he could forcefully present his case to whomsoever would listen. As he strode through Charing Cross and into Whitehall he nerved himself for the task ahead. He had been wronged by the King's ministers and would demand justice.

Turning from Whitehall into Downing Street he found it to be a cul-de-sac and it took only a minute before he was at the door on which a brass plate proudly stated "First Lord of the Treasury" below a large white number ten. This was it, he decided, and rapped the lion's-head knocker. Some moments later the large black door opened and an imperious looking footman stood before him.

"Yes sir," he intoned.

"I am here to see Mr Perceval."

"You have an appointment sir?"

"Yes," the man lied.

The footman looked at him harshly. He had been told of no such visitor, and the man's weather-beaten attire did not imply social standing. "I see. Then you will know that Mr Perceval does not entertain business at his home. You should present yourself at the Treasury building."

Behind the footman two small children, possibly five years old, ran across the black and white chequered floor of the lobby laughing as they played a game of chase. Their presence unnerved the caller. "The Treasury building?" he asked distractedly, looking to see if the children were still there.

"Yes sir, behind this house. Walk back to the end of the street and turn left. The entrance will present itself."

He stood on the step of the house for some moments, taken by the presence of young children within the house. "Those children," he queried at last, "whose are they?"

The footman, although affronted by such an impertinent question, replied, "But Mr Perceval's, of course, whose else would they be? Now sir, please head to the end of street and turn left. You cannot miss the entrance to the Treasury building."

As he walked back along Downing Street his mind was still occupied by the children. He had never considered the Prime Minister to be a family man, and he did not know why the thought disturbed him. Had he only known, the Downing Street house was awash with children. Jane Perceval had conceived twelve in nearly as many years, now squashed into the London residence the King provided for his first minister of the British Dominions.

At the Treasury building, which overlooked the parade ground for the King's Horse Guards, the man quickly found the office of Mr Perceval's secretary and, after waiting for more than an hour, was allowed to submit his petition, together with a letter from the Foreign Secretary, Richard Wellesley, elder brother of the general fighting so gallantly on the Iberian Peninsula.

"I wrote to the Marquess Wellesley a year ago," he informed the secretary, a young man lately arrived from Oxford University, while waving the papers in his hand, "but he refuses to consider it due to the break in relations with the Russian Emperor. But, sir, this has nothing to do with it. My grievance lay with the King's government, and his ambassador to St Petersburgh. It was this man who allowed me to suffer so in an Archangel gaol. His Majesty's government seems determined to close the door of justice to me, declining even to permit my grievances to be brought before Parliament for redress. This is the birth-right of every individual and Mr Perceval must bend his will to my favour."

The young clerk had taken a step back from the man as his anger had built during the course of his speech, and now reached forward tentatively and took the papers from him. "I will make sure the minister is made aware of your papers sir," is all he could say.

The aggrieved man snorted. "Make sure you do, sir. I advise Mr Perceval to attend to my matter or I shall feel forced into executing justice myself!"

MAHOMET and Doyle hardly noticed William Harding depart for the cricket field, so aghast were they at William Rufus' remarks. The redheaded man himself stood by watching Harding walk to the wicket as if he had just wished him *bon chance*. It was Mahomet who finally spoke.

"Why did you say such a thing, sir?" he hissed, and Rufus turned towards him, quite clearly smirking.

"Oh, I think it is time we progress this matter, do you not, gentlemen? What other reason finds you here today?"

Mahomet looked around but they were set apart from the crowd, who were keenly watching the events on the field of play.

"But to make such a statement about Sir George, Mr Rufus?"

The redheaded man continued to smile blithely. "Come now, sir, you think very much the same, if I am not mistaken. Why else would you journey to Chelsea – to find some rare root for your curries? I have been a pace behind you, gentlemen, but a gardener at the Chelsea garden spoke in curious terms about a small Indian and a tall Irish beau who were so interested in Sir George Harding. As you know sir, I have been instructed in this matter and now it seems I have caught up with you. And here's the rub. You suspect Sir George of putting your servant up to the deadly deed, do you not?"

Mahomet gasped while Doyle, who had been paying keen attention, spoke angrily. "But why say this to the man's brother, pray? What mischief have you created? And what trouble have you caused my cousins by this?"

The thin smile finally disappeared from Rufus' face, his eyes narrowing as they looked at Doyle. "I suggest you let me to my business, sir, and you keep to your doctoring. As I perceive matters, the younger Harding is very unhappy with his brother's actions since their father's death. At this moment he is no doubt thinking that at last he has an ally. Let him think that. I need to establish who constructed events such that George Harding has been able to inherit a considerable estate, and William Harding might be able to help me in this task. I also advise most earnestly that you both leave this matter alone. Your presence can only confuse matters."

Another shout went up from the field and, across the tent, the next batsman readied himself to enter the field of battle. The reaction among the crowd was such that conversation was not possible for the moment between the men. Mahomet indicated that they should occupy a quiet corner of the tent where they would not be disturbed by the game, and both Doyle and Rufus nodded. In doing this they did not notice William Harding return after being defeated by the flight of a cricket ball – though in this he could hardly be blamed, his mind being on other matters. Nor did they see Sir George Harding and his party appear inside the tent, though William did and headed straight for his brother.

At first William had been shocked and worried to hear the allegation of poisoning, but soon decided this was the opportunity for which he had been waiting. His brother was being blamed for poisoning their father! It really could not have worked out better. If he told George then he would be duty bound to challenge him, especially if others in George's party were witness. His brother was late, but while taking guard at the wicket he saw him walking around the boundary towards the tent with several others in tow. So, following a wild and unaccustomed swing of his Little Joey that resulted in a simple catch, William made his way back to the tent determined to force George's hand.

Dismissing the few commiserations offered to him as he entered the tent, he made directly for his brother's party. Looking around, he saw the redheaded man with the Indian in a far corner. Everything seemed set so long as he acted quickly. He nearly ran towards his brother, who looked surprised at his approach.

"I am afraid I could not bring you luck, brother," replied George.

Yet William was dismissive. "Never mind that brother, I need to speak with you most urgently." George Harding sighed: what now, he thought.

"Brother," William continued, in a voice loud enough so that others of George's party could hear, "I have just spoken to a man who suggests that you are responsible for our father's death. That you poisoned papa!"

While George Harding thought he had not properly heard his brother, others in his party gasped at William's statement. "Pardon brother? I did not hear you correctly."

"There is a man here, in this tent, who makes a claim that you poisoned our father, George. He said it to me just before I went to the wicket. What are you going to do?"

George Harding looked at his brother and then at others in his party. What an outlandish statement! How could anyone say such a thing? He was now hearing words such as "outrageous" and "disgraceful" being uttered by members of his party, and he did not rightly know whether these referred to the claim or to him. Yet the speaking of the allegation openly confirmed in the mind of some the suspicion which had been circulating in the clubs to which Sir George Harding belonged. Many had noted how fortunate George had been to witness the passing of a wealthy parent so propitiously. Now matters had come to a head.

"What man and where?" is all George could say.

"He is standing in the corner, over there," continued William excitedly and pointing towards William Rufus standing with Mahomet and Doyle. "What are you going to do, brother," William repeated, anxious to force George's hand. "Surely he must be challenged?"

George Harding's head spun. He had already consumed a considerable amount of wine that day, one that up to this moment had been most amenable. Now he had his brother standing before him making the most ridiculous claims. He looked towards where William was pointing and recognised the small Indian who was the proprietor of the coffee house in which his father had died, talking to two others.

"You must be mistaken brother," said George, now angry with the messenger, but William Harding shook his head. "No sir, he said it before the others standing with him. He said that with your knowledge of herb lore you must have helped our father to meet his maker."

There were more gasps from the Harding party. "You must confront the blaggard, George," said one. "A duel" hissed another, and on hearing this William Harding could hardly believe his luck. Yet confrontation was not a word Sir George Harding commonly used, and all eyes were now on him. "This cannot go unchallenged George," said his brother yet again, "for your honour and that of the family."

"Yes honour," agreed Harding's party albeit they were not common with the word, while another said, "You cannot let this pass, George. Be a man."

Sir George was still confused. How had this come to pass, and if he left the tent now would it all simply disappear?

"Time is pressing, George," continued William. "What if he repeats his claims to others? There are gentlemen present of great quality. You will be forever shamed in their eyes if you let this pass – does our family name mean nothing to you?"

George Harding directed a sharp glace at his brother, but the claque was rising around him. "You have to challenge the man, George!" "Be a man, George!" "To not challenge this would be to admit its truth!"

"Now George," continued William, "you must go and challenge him."

George Harding felt a hand on his back pushing him forward and before he realised he found himself walking across the tent in the company of others. William stood back, satisfied that his work was done. If his brother were to issue a challenge to the redheaded man in the tent, it would not be seemly for him to be present. It might affect his standing with his fellow cricketers. By keeping back he would be perceived as an innocent party.

Yet as Sir George Harding approached the cause of his injury, goaded by others in his party, there was a flaw in William's scheming. He had not clearly indicated who made the statement, and there were only two men in the place indicated. Of these, George Harding was focused on the coffee house proprietor. To the injured party this was some comfort, as the other was considerably younger and more athletic.

Mahomet and Doyle had been trying to reason with William Rufus. They suggested he approach William Harding at the earliest opportunity to excuse his speech and say that it was mere supposition and should not be repeated. Rufus, however, was having none of it, and was sure the younger Harding would seek his help in handling his brother. A dismissive Rufus had taken his leave, leaving Mahomet and Doyle alone to rue their luck.

So it was with great surprise that when looking over Doyle's shoulder into the body of the tent Mahomet could see Sir George Harding approach accompanied by a bevy of beaus and bucks. He did not look happy.

"Gentlemen!" Harding announced, and made a great theatrical bow. Doyle turned to face the posse then stepped slightly to one side, giving them a clear view of Mahomet.

"Sir George ..." began Mahomet before being cut off by the aggrieved baronet.

"You courtesy is as unwelcome as it is false, sir," he snapped. "I have been made party to your recent statements. They will not do sir and I demand you take them back."

Mahomet glanced desperately around, trying to espy Rufus in the crowd. "But they were not ..."

"You will not but me, sir," interrupted Harding, "and I see you will not accommodate me!" he bellowed, attracting the attention of almost everyone inside the tent and some outside as well. Mahomet still struggled for words.

Someone had thrust into George Harding's left hand a pair of kid gloves. These he now raised and, to general astonishment, struck Mahomet firmly across the face. "I will have satisfaction!" Harding roared, driven on by the wine he had consumed earlier. "Now name your seconder!"

The blow had stunned Mahomet, though not because of the force. He looked to Doyle. "Decimus?!" he pleaded, seeking help in reasoning with the fury before him.

"Very well," boomed Sir George, "my man will contact yours before the week is out and make arrangements."

With that the bellicose baronet turned and walked away with his party in tow, every man gossiping about the good sport they had just witnessed. Behind them they left a shocked small Indian and a stunned tall Irishman. All eyes in the tent fell on Mahomet, who in turn looked at Doyle. "Oh Decimus," he whispered, "what has just happened? And whatever will I tell Jane!"

Chapter 12

London, Autumn 1811.

THE night's performance was by command of the Prince Regent himself, a man keen to show to his people an enlightened attitude towards the arts. And many in the audience thought the play to be entirely appropriate; had Macbeth not, after all, usurped the power of the lawful king? Obviously such inferences were kept well away from the Royal party, who were now settled in their box to the centre of the second tier. The Prince had especially come to see Mrs Siddons in her most famed role. They were of a similar age and he recalled their meetings at Windsor and Kew when she was teaching the younger princes and princesses in the finer points of the English language. While the Prince's grandfather and great-grandfather spoke little English, preferring their native German, his father had consciously "Anglicised" the House of Hanover – one of his few successes, according to the son who now ruled in his stead.

There was another royal command at the night's performance: one given to a young Irish student doctor by the leading lady. In select seats close to the stage in the first tier of the theatre sat Decimus Doyle and his tutor Simon Bunton. After he had received the summons to attend Doyle had agonised whether to ask Bunton to accompany him. After all, he knew what the probable outcome would be: salacious and unwelcome comments once the older man discovered the origin of the invite. But Bunton had been generous in his support to Mahomet regarding the death of Sir Josiah Harding and the unsuccessful pursuit of Walker, so he felt duty bound to extend the invite, especially given Bunton's admiration of the lady. So now they both sat enraptured as the glorious Mrs Siddons demonstrated her stagecraft – obviously for differing reasons.

There was a long interval after the second act for patrons to attend to their toilet and refreshments, though from the noises in the stalls it would seem this was unnecessary, as piss pots, bottles and mugs were passed around with abandon. Doyle and Bunton sat back in their box, which they were fortunate not to have to share – the lady took care of her own. The chandeliers were lit and a great noise ran through the house.

"This is capital!" exclaimed Bunton, looking around him at the theatre and towards the Royal box. "I have not seen him for some time, but I do declare he is even fatter than I remembered." They both knew to whom Bunton was referring. "I wish I had some glasses," he continued. "I am very curious to see his latest companion ... from this distance they look like a set of Toby jugs."

Doyle was grateful they were alone and he did not need to excuse Bunton's *lèsse majesté*. Reaching to pour another glass of claret from a small refreshment table the management had so kindly provided at the insistence of their leading lady, Bunton continued his discourse.

"This is indeed a most gracious treat, young man. I cannot thank you enough. It must have cost a King's ransom."

Doyle blushed, only too aware it had not cost him a penny. "Think no more of it. It is the least I could offer to show mine and Sake Mahomet's thanks."

Mention of his cousin's husband brought a tightening of the stomach. It had been over two weeks since the incident, if it could be so called, at the cricket match. Harding had taken Mahomet's plea to Doyle as him being named seconder, and since then had been expecting an approach by a gentleman acting for Sir George at any moment. But as the days passed and nothing more was heard, they both hoped it was simply bravado on Harding's part and the cold light of day had sobered his thoughts of a duel. Mahomet's report that Harding had departed to Brighton for his health only confirmed this in Doyle's mind, as he sought to re-assure his cousin's husband. Neither Bunton nor, more importantly, Jane Mahomet had been told what happened and they hoped to keep it that way. Yet Doyle still tensed when any stranger came near in case this was the messenger of doom. A loud rap on the door of the box made him jump from his thoughts, and he only relaxed when a young theatre footman entered.

"Mr Doyle sir?" the footman asked and the beau nodded.

"Mr Kemble requests your presence," and here he bowed to both men, "at a small reception following the performance. I will attend on you as your escort."

Doyle again nodded and the footman disappeared. Bunton looked in surprise at his colleague. "This is indeed a singular honour, Doyle. I wonder why we are invited?" Then he looked hard at his companion. "You have not become one of Mr Kemble's investors, I hope?"

Doyle smiled and shook his head. "I am as much at a loss as you sir."

Bunton snorted, not wholly believing the young man. "Well, I look forward to the second half with even greater anticipation, knowing that afterwards I might be received by fat George yonder ... or even better by Mrs Siddons."

Doyle was grateful when an attendant walked on stage ringing a hand bell to announce the re-commencement of the play. Yet sitting back in his chair as the chandeliers in the auditorium were dowsed, he was aware of the occasional curious glance from Bunton.

Whereas Doyle had previously watched Sarah Siddons rehearse scenes from the first half of the play, he was unprepared for what was to confront his senses in *Act V, scene i*. A doctor and woman entered and observed while Mrs Siddons, dressed simply in a white satin shift which demurely presented her buxom figure, wandered on stage as if sleepwalking. As she presented her nightmare scene, Doyle was taken at how little she compared with the lady with whom he had dined alone the previous week and had later taken to her bed. Was this marvellous, talented woman who how held all London in her sway really the same one with whom he had been so intimate? As she said the lines "all the perfumes of Arabia will not sweeten this little hand", he thought he could smell the musky scent she wore. And as she exited from the stage and the audience roared its approval, Doyle jumped from his seat applauding wildly, though his enthusiasm was less obvious given that Bunton had accompanied him with equal vigour.

As Macduff finally entered holding Macbeth's head and Malcolm was proclaimed King of Scotland, the young footman also appeared once more to the rear of the box to lead them to Mr Kemble's reception. They waited until the actors had taken their final bow, with Mrs Siddons being duly lionised by the Covent Garden audience – the same one that had been so hard on her during the Old Price Riots. Making their way through the myriad of corridors as the theatre crowd made its way onto Bow Street, Bunton was full of praise.

"She is like a new woman," he enthused. "I have never seen her more intense ... and with such passion! I do hope she is at the reception."

Doyle soon realised where they were headed; Mr Kemble's private office where he had his first audience with Mrs Siddons the previous month. Yet had Bunton anticipated a large public reception he was to be sorely disappointed. Only a few people were gathered, and there was no Prince and no Mrs Siddons. The theatre manager and impresario Kemble was welcoming the few guests there were.

"Mr Doyle, I presume," he called as Doyle and Bunton entered the room. Doyle bowed. "I am John Philip Kemble ... the brother," he said pointedly. Doyle introduced Bunton.

"I am glad you could come," Kemble continued, looking closely at Doyle. "Dr Bunton, sir, please partake of some wine and excuse me if I take a private word with your companion."

Bunton nodded and walked towards the refreshments, but glanced back more curious than ever. It seemed what he suspected was true: Doyle had put money into the theatre, no doubt encouraged by his recent meetings with Mrs Siddons. But Mr Kemble had other matters to raise with Decimus Doyle, and they did not involve money. He took the young man by the arm to a quiet corner of the room.

"It seems you have become familiar with my sister, sir," he said softly but bluntly.

Doyle did not respond.

"I assume by your silence I am correct."

The questioning annoyed Doyle. "With great respect sir, I think Mrs Siddons is capable of selecting those with whom she would associate."

Kemble looked hard at the young Irishman. A man in his late forties, the manager was in no mood to bandy words with young theatre bucks.

"My sister knows many gentlemen, sir," he continued, "but seems to be quite taken with you in particular. She is a passionate woman, but these passions can lead her in unexpected directions. I make it my particular duty in life to ensure she does not wander too far. And if I many say so, sir, it seems that this is now the case."

Doyle was taken aback by Kemble's tone. "I have only the very greatest respect for your sister, sir, and would not do anything contrary to her wishes."

"Then you will leave well alone?" demanded Kemble, but before Doyle could reply applause broke out in the room and the subject of their discussion appeared at the door with her maid. Looking around, she noticed her brother with the current object of her affections and quickly surmised the nature of the discussion in which they had been engaged. She had been delayed by a brief audience with the Prince, who was suitably gushing of her performance. Now, nodding to her captive audience in the office, she promptly headed towards her familial and fervent interests.

"John my love, and Decimus," she called as she approached, "and in such close confinement. I am so glad you have been introduced."

Kemble bowed. "Sarah, my love. Mr Doyle and I were having a moment of reflection. Now, if you please I have other guests to attend on ... and so have you, my dear, so please do not occupy Mr Doyle's time for too long."

With that Kemble withdrew leaving them alone but not unobserved by others in the room.

"So, my brother has been offering counsel?" she asked and Doyle blushed. "Yes, I see he has. Well let him think on this."

She turned to the room and clapped her hands. Across the way Doyle could see Bunton break off from an animated discussion with another guest and turn towards him.

"Ladies and gentlemen, thank you for attending," began Mrs Siddons, "and I hope you enjoyed the play." There was another brief applause. "I know you will understand how much it saps my strength so I am afraid I must make my excuses and retire. But please do not let my withdrawal prevent you continuing at your pleasure."

She turned to Doyle. "Come Decimus, please take me to my room," and with that placed her arm beneath his and marched him towards the door. From across the room the sound of a gentleman choking could be heard from a position approximate to where Dr Simon Bunton was standing.

TRADE might have been described as "quiet" at the Hindostanee Coffee House: in truth, and since the death of Sir Josiah Harding, it had been lamentably slow. For a London coffee house to be successful required two types of gentlemen: those keen to conduct business together with others and those gentlemen who who took in the daily gossip from newspapers, journals and polite conversation. The Hindostanee Coffee House lacked both, and Mahomet was torn as to whether he should accept his father-in-law's generous offer or not. While his head said yes, in his heart he was struggling to accept the inevitability in going cap-in-hand to his wife's family. So if Jane Mahomet expected a change in the mood of her husband, she was to be sorely disappointed.

Ironically there had been a few "sight-seers" in the days following Harding's challenge, but they had stayed only long enough to obtain a good view of Mahomet. One woman, indeed, had even traced a silhouette of him on paper, no doubt to be cut out later and placed on the wall for her own curiosity when guests called: "And this is the little Indian, my dear, who died in the duel not long ago". Thankfully, and Mahomet was indeed grateful for small mercies, his wife had not realised the nature of this grisly trade.

It had taken some time for Mahomet to appreciate fully that he had been the subject of a challenge. The dramatic events at the cricket match had been such a nightmare that he had to pinch himself to believe they actually happened. What had made that despicable man Rufus say such things to William Harding, and how had Sir George heard about them? Had Rufus been overheard? But if so, why did Sir George mistakenly believe that he, Mahomet, was the source of those allegations? Yet he did believe George Harding to be responsible for Sir Josiah's death, so had this been the reason why he had not immediately denied the challenge? Harding had been determined to bully him into a duel, and he had been struck across the face before he had the chance to refute anything!

The day following the cricket match he determined to seek out Sir George and explain the truth of what happened, but when he arrived at the Harding mansion had been informed that Sir George had gone to Brighton for his health that very morning! He did, however, see William Harding, but the younger brother was decidedly unhelpful. To Mahomet's pleas to explain to his brother the truth of what happened the previous day, William claimed he could not now recall who said what, so shocked was he at the allegation, but that the honour of the family had been impugned. Yet, he reasoned, was not Mahomet at the cricket match to speak to his brother on a private matter? About poison, perhaps? So far as William was concerned, Sir George's seconder would be sent to Mr Doyle at the Hunterian at the earliest opportunity to make arrangements for the duel. For Mahomet to refuse to fight would be tantamount to an admission of guilt and he, William, would ensure that no one partook of Mahomet's establishment ever again. Mahomet and his family would be hounded out of London and no doubt his brother would pursue an action for slander. Mahomet had left the Harding mansion more miserable than ever.

Doyle had agreed that they should not tell Jane until the approach from Harding's seconder had taken place, and to date there was no sign of him – Sir George was obviously too distracted in Brighton. Mahomet had considered following him to the coast, but on this William Harding had been as persuasive: to do so would only exacerbate his brother's mood, and there might be a fight there and then.

And what of William Rufus? Since the cricket match there had been no sign of him. No apology, nothing! Mahomet and Doyle had spoken at length about the man. As Rufus was acting under the instruction of the Honourable Basil Cochrane, so should not Mahomet appeal to his former patron for help? Yet it was something he could not commit to a letter, and Cochrane's family estates were some distance from Edinburgh. It would take more than three weeks for him to make such a journey and back, even if he was able to purchase a sea passage north on one of the coastal traders.

Apart from the fact he could not leave Jane alone for such a length of time to manage the coffee house, he did not like the thought of not being present should Harding's seconder appear for fear it would be construed as him running away.

The great injustice of his situation bore down on him, and he thought often of the customer who had been locked up in the Russian prison. That man, a Mr Bellingham by name, had left a note for Mahomet at the coffee house. He had been unable to see Mr Perceval but had given the papers to the Prime Minister's secretary at the Treasury building in Whitehall. Bellingham had returned to Liverpool, but mentioned in his note of his plan to return to London after Christmas and stay until his just claim was settled. He was very brave to challenge the government so, Mahomet thought – brave or foolhardy. Just like me, his thought continued, preparing to face a duel with Sir George Harding, a man whom I believe to be a killer!

It was while Mahomet was alone reflecting once more on the situation in which he found himself, and his head aching in sympathy, that he received an unexpected visitor – Dr Simon Bunton. Taking the good doctor to the privacy of the small sitting room on the first floor, it was not long before the physician addressed the purpose of his visit.

"It seems Mr. Mahomet, that our young Irishman has been swept away with a passion," he cautioned.

Mahomet coughed nervously. "Decimus is ..."

"The boy had been ensnared by a seductress of note, a veritable Aphrodite!" Bunton intoned.

"Ah ... you mean Mrs Siddons?"

Bunton was as dumbstruck as he had been days before when he witnessed Doyle depart with London's leading lady on his arm. "You know?"

Mahomet sighed, sitting back in his chair. "I suspected, doctor. He mentioned the lady to me some weeks ago ... he seemed quite taken with her."

"He is more than taken with her, Mahomet. He has not breakfasted at home for these past three days!"

This, Mahomet decided, was more knowledge than he wished to possess.

And Doyle's liaison seemed to agitate Dr Bunton more than Mahomet would have expected, given some of the tales Decimus had recounted about the man in the past.

"But what can I ... or you do doctor? Decimus is very much a grown man and reaches his twenty-fifth year in December. I do not think he would appreciate any interference from either of us."

Bunton was undeterred. "Yet he has fallen into the clutches of someone of dubious reputation Mahomet. Surely this must be of concern for his friends and family. Thankfully the lady is so old that I doubt there could be any issue ..."

Now it was Mahomet's turn to interrupt as he had decided the conversation had gone far enough.

"We really must not pursue these thoughts, doctor. I have a great trust in Decimus, which I am sure you have as well. He will come to see this ... dalliance as simply that, an event of whimsy to look back on in later years. If anything, doctor, I am grateful he has set his heart on an older woman – she has more to teach and less to lose. Let him have his will sir. As I say, any words of reproach from you or I would likely have the opposite effect to that we would wish to achieve."

Yet still Dr Bunton had concerns. "You do not know the woman, Mahomet. She is a powerful temptress of both guile and intrigue. And young Doyle has expectations. He is a wealthy young man who will inherit a very great fortune when his father dies, and he is a promising doctor, to boot, who could achieve a very high reputation ... if he does not throw it away now. How long, Mahomet, before mention of their liaison appears in the *The Times* or, God forbid, that tittle-tattle rag the *Morning Post*? You do not appreciate the power the lady has to command attention. Should not we write to his father at least, stating clearly the damage his son's association could cause?"

Mahomet was aghast. The thought of writing to Jane's uncle, so soon after their own contact with her father, was simply untenable.

"No doctor, no," he responded quickly, "that would not be a good idea. Jane and I strongly encouraged his father to support Decimus' move to

London. We would not cause such anxiety back in Ireland. No," he said firmly, then paused. "But if you think it will help," he conceded, "then I will speak to Decimus on the importance of keeping his liaison private, secret even."

Bunton snorted and quickly described the event he had witnessed at the reception. "It did not look like either party wished to keep their association within the confines of the bedroom," he concluded.

Mahomet shook his head slowly. "I promise I will speak to Decimus."

"When?" asked Bunton forcefully. "If the boy is not made to see sense soon he will end up with all the markings of a rake, flitting hither and thither. He is to attend a lecture at the Hunterian tomorrow. I will request he meets with me afterwards. If you are present at my house at, say, five in the afternoon then we can catch him before he wanders off again."

Mahomet did not think Bunton's words to be a suitable way of discussing his young relative, but he was still swayed by the force of his concerns so agreed to the request. As he showed the doctor to the door of the coffee house they were greeted by Jane who was returning from a walk with their younger children. She seemed curious, even anxious, at Dr Bunton's presence. And as he watched the doctor walk down George Street Mahomet realised he would have to keep the matter of young Doyle's love life, together with the expected duel, from his wife. He felt the ache in his head return with renewed vigour at the thought!

WATIER'S Club, on the corner of Bolton Street at 81 Piccadilly, had been established two years previously. While dining with members of both White's and Brook's, the Prince Regent asked what type of food they served at their respective clubs. He was less than impressed when told beef-steaks, boiled fowl and apple tarts, so summoned his chef Jean-Baptiste Watier and asked him to organise a dining club. This he did, and early members included Beau Brummell and the Prince's brother the Duke of York. Yet even though Watier's served the best dinners in London created by the finest Parisian chefs, it was the night-lay which attracted the members, and especially the card game Macau. And such were the large number of fashionable bucks who attended the gaming tables that Lord Byron called Watier's the "Dandy Club".

Macau was a variety of the French game *vingt et un*. At least two, and at the most ten, players were dealt five cards which ware played singly and in sequence around the table. Players, however, need not play a card but bluff and save it for higher points later. Cheating was encouraged, and when down to a single card the player had to shout Macau before playing it. If another player shouted Macau before him, then the player would draw another card rather than put down. The winner was the first player with no cards and it could become quite raucous. Stakes were high and became higher as the evening progressed, and Macau could clear out the deepest of pockets, including those of Mr Brummell and Sir George Harding.

Both gentlemen were absent in Brighton, however, on the evening a young redheaded man took to the Macau table. He had been allowed into the club after presenting a letter of introduction from the King's former Prime Minister and Deputy Ranger of Richmond Park, a close confidant of both the Prince Regent and the ailing King. While the redheaded young man – a visitor from the Virginias – had a pleasant enough manner, he dressed far too dowdy to be a full member of the Dandy Club. Still, he held a conversation well and played Macau with gusto, coming off the table after an hour with money to spare. He seemed interested in all aspects of the club, and fell into conversation with one of the older members who was sitting to one side with a bottle of claret watching the card tables.

"I was hoping to see a particular member here tonight," the young man began, "Sir George Harding. Do you know him sir?"

The older member snorted. "A bounder, sir, no doubt about it. Recently came into the handle when his father upped and died. Doubt there will be any more baronets, they way he carries on. George Porgie puddin' and pie, kissed the girls and made them cry. That's what they say of him here, if you listen close enough. Damn fortunate for him that his old man shuffled off when he did."

The young man smiled at the gossip next to him: he was in the right company, he decided.

"I really wanted to see the man who issued the challenge at Mr Lord's ground recently," he continued. "Quite a scene, I hear." Rufus had heard about the challenge while still at the cricket ground, and found it most diverting.

The older member turned to him. "I hear he challenged a foreigner – an Indian," he said, tutting and shaking his head. "The Indian owns a coffee house north of here, apparently. Trade! Not good form; one should only duel with fellows from one's own Society. Who challenges one's tailor? Now the man's off in Brighton with Brummell and that crowd, trying to avoid finishing the job! Typical of Georgie Porgie. When the boys come out to play, Georgie Porgie runs away. See what I mean? A bounder sir. Make sure you don't fall in with him. It'll do you no good, no good at all."

The two men were engrossed in their conversation, and the card play around them distracted others from coming over and joining in.

"Why did you say that it was fortunate his father died?" Rufus whispered.

His older companion tutted. "Debts, sir, and lots of them. It was becoming very uncomfortable for a while, especially after his father wrote to us and refused to honour them just before he died. I'm on the committee, you know. We had even been speaking of blackballing the bounder. Now, though … well, just let's say it was damn fortunate for him that his old man shuffled off when he did."

The redheaded man looked around the room before continuing. "You carry a very decided opinion of the fellow, sir," he said, in as dismissive a way a possible.

The older man growled. "He keeps close company with the worst kind. There was one particular book-keeper from Gentleman Jackson's boxing academy we had to throw out. Came looking for Georgie Porgie. No doubt the fool owed a bag full of money. You can't owe the wrong sort, can you sir? That's what clubs are for. The men who run the books at boxing establishments, cricket matches and the races, they'd sell their own grandmother for a profit and are not slow at calling in a debt. No, fall in with that lot and you deserve all you get. Be careful young man, and keep to your own … it's a good rule to follow. There are one or two other fellows here who sail close to the wind. You take that Mr Brummell, now! I know he is a friend of the Prince but ... tut tut."

"So ... Georgie Porgie ... associates with the wrong sort?"

"Absolutely" the older man exclaimed, now not caring who heard him. "I hear he's already sold the family land in London within days of burying the old man. And this was done after the father had set himself against a sale. What about honouring thy father? Bah! They had violent arguments I believe, according to Georgie Porgie's younger brother. Now there is a fine young man, and a masterful cricketer. Such an upstanding fellow. I often see him at the cricket and the like. Excellent shot."

"I do hear that George Harding has a scientific bent?"

"Flowers and herbs, you mean!" laughed Sir George Harding's fellow Dandy. "What use is that to a gentleman? He presented the club with a number of books on herb-lore and apothecary, as if any one here would be interested! Bah! Such books are only good for kindling in my opinion. Though there was one book on poisonous plants which might have been entertaining, had it not been partly in Latin and had so many pages missing at the beginning ... it didn't start until half way through the letter A!"

MATTERS had not gone according to plan for William Harding. Not only had his brother challenged the wrong man, but had then disappeared to Brighton the following day. This was typical of George, unable to face what he had set in motion, but William was determined not to let matters rest. The Indian had called to protest his innocence and, while William would have preferred George to face a more formidable opponent, at least the challenge stood and he would not allow either man to wriggle away. He had been hard on the Indian, threatening grave consequences against the man's family should he attempt to withdraw. But William knew that if he did not force George's hand then the challenge might peter out.

He waited a few days for his brother to return but, when there was no sign of him so doing, called for the coach and four and journeyed himself to the south coast. He ran his brother to ground at an assembly in Brighton's Old Ship Hotel and, after some prevarication, finally got him to agree to appointing William as his seconder. This was all the younger brother required. He returned to London shortly afterwards and began to lay his plans. To this end he obtained a copy of the *Code Duello*, a slim Irish volume that set out the government of duels by gentlemen. He called at the gunsmiths Wogdon & Barton and obtained a pair of duelling pistols, the barrel of one of which he had rifled to improve its accuracy: he was determined to weigh the odds in favour of the Indian. He also learnt that the Indian used to serve in the army of the East India Company, which meant he hopefully knew how to fire a gun – unlike George who constantly complained of headaches when taken on shooting trips by their father. Now all he had to do was to meet with the Indian's seconder to arrange the date and location and bring George back from Brighton to face his fate.

The Indian's seconder was sitting in the library of his tutor's house with Dr Bunton and his cousin's husband Sake Mahomet, and feeling like a naughty student about to be sent down. The summons had come in the form of a letter while he was attending a lecture on William Harvey's *De Motu Cordis*, the treatise on the motion of the heart and blood which had been published over one hundred and fifty years previously but still served its purpose. Decimus Doyle felt his own blood beginning to boil as two of the men he most respected after his father questioned him on a decidedly delicate subject.

"Dr Bunton is correct, Decimus," Mahomet was continuing, "when he says you really must take care. Mrs Siddons attracts a degree of comment which is most unwelcome for a gentleman making his way in the world." Doyle went to interrupt but Mahomet raised his voice. "And please do not mention my marriage to Jane. That was an entirely private affair among her family. Your association with Mrs Siddons is likely to be the subject of discussion at both assemblies and in salons – and sooner rather than later. Surely you understand this Decimus?"

Doyle sat back in his chair and put his head in his hands. He felt ashamed to be spoken to like this.

"Listen to your family Doyle," continued Bunton, "and, if you will not listen, then read this ... please."

Doyle looked up to the pamphlet the doctor held in his hand but did not take it; he already knew what it contained.

"I assume you refer to a copy of Mrs Galindo's public letter to Sarah. It is of no consequence."

Bunton disagreed. "Mrs Galindo writes that your lady infatuated her husband and indulged in a physical affair with him while in Dublin. Galindo abandoned his wife and their three children and followed Mrs Siddons here some six years ago. It seems the lady could not get a role for Galindo at Covent Garden, so lent him a thousand pounds to lease the Manchester theatre. When this failed and Galindo had been reconciled with his wife, your lady demanded back her money, threatening to ruin the Galindo family. There is also general talk of Mrs Siddons and the painter Lawrence and all this, bear in mind, while Mr Siddons lived. I warned you not to enter her lair with an open heart."

Doyle, now angered by Bunton's defamation of his beloved, stood and clenched his fists. "This is all in the past Bunton. She admitted her mistake with Galindo and did not pursue repayment to her great financial loss. And William Siddons died in Bath three years ago so Sarah is free to do as she wishes. I will not put her aside on account of gossip and rumour which has no basis in fact. I love her," he said pleadingly to Mahomet. "While I cannot expect you to understand this, I do expect you not to pass comment. And you Bunton, do you not still admire Sarah?"

Bunton coughed. "Sir, I worship the performance, not the performer!"

Mahomet looked to the young man with the pained expression. This really was an inappropriate meeting and he decided to conclude it before anything untoward was said which all parties would later regret.

"I think you ... we ... have made our thoughts known to Decimus quite forcefully, doctor," he implored. "It is for him to take his own counsel on affairs of the heart. We can say no more."

Bunton was about to continue disagreeing when there was a knock on the library door and Mrs Mac entered.

"Begging your pardon sirs, but there is a gentleman. There is no card."

Bunton snorted. "Very well," he sighed, "tell him I will be along presently."

Mrs Mac shook her head. "No, doctor, not you. He asks to speak to Mr Doyle urgently on a private matter."

All three looked at the housekeeper in surprise: had the rumour mill already started?!

Doyle nodded but Bunton, anticipating trouble, instructed his housekeeper to show the gentleman into the library. When she had gone to fetch him Bunton said out loud: "And so it begins. Do not say I didn't warn you."

They waited for the door to re-open and the visitor to be shown in. Yet all three gentlemen were surprised to see who it was.

The visitor bowed politely. "Gentleman," he began, "I did not anticipate finding you both together. I am here to discuss the arrangements for the duel."

Mahomet and Doyle swallowed hard at the sight of William Harding while Bunton, not understanding the words Harding had just spoken and thinking they concerned Doyle and Mrs Siddons, simply gasped.

Chapter 13

Rules to be observed in making Soups and Broths.
First take great care the pots or sauce-pans and covers be very clean
and free from all grease and sand, and that they be well-tinned, for
fear of giving broths and soups a brassy taste. If you have time to
stew as softly as you can, it will both have a finer flavour, and the
meat will be tenderer. You must observe in all broths and soups that
one thing does not taste more than another; but that the taste is
equal, and it has a fine agreeable relish, according to what you design
it for; and you must be sure, that all the greens and herbs you put in
be cleaned, washed, and picked.

The Art of Cookery Made Plain and Easy

London, Autumn 1811.

JANE Mahomet stood at the range in the kitchen of the Hindostanee
Coffee House stirring her latest creation: though for the life of her she did
not know why. They were serving fewer than a dozen customers each day,
and much of the food she now prepared she fed to the children the
following day to save on waste. Still, in the pot she was now attending was
her one saving grace – a variation on an Indian pepper broth first taught to
her by the cook of the Honourable Basil Cochrane. This man came from
the southern Indian city of Pondicherry in the Madras Presidency, and
called it pepper water or melligu thanir. It had a basis of dried peppers and
water to which were added carrots, onions and spices such as tumerick, as
well as rice to thicken. To her version Jane also added the remains of chicken
or other meats which were to hand, and it became an excellent, warming
dish for cold and wet days and far more wholesome than pottage. The
children loved it as did others, and she now took regular orders, supplying
earthenware tureens of the broth for sixpence a time to neighbours, and
which young William Mahomet delivered to their kitchen door.

She found ministering to the broth most efficacious, and she could stir away the troubles of the day. She had hoped the offer of her father's money would have calmed the stresses between herself and her beloved husband, yet Mahomet still seemed unduly distracted. Perhaps he could just not forgive her for writing to her father for help. Jane knew she needed no justification for her action if it kept her family from the debtors prison or the workhouse, but she longed for the affection, the closeness, which she and Mahomet once enjoyed. They had been through so much together and she had never once doubted him – until now. Perhaps in gaining her father's money she had lost something of far more value to her: a husband's love.

She looked around the kitchen: she was so proud of all that they – he – had achieved since they married. At first they had gone to work for Captain Baker in his house outside Cork and, following the captain's untimely death, Mahomet had secured a position with the Honourable Basil Cochrane in London. Jane recalled their leaving Ireland. Only William had been born, and they had taken the mail coach, along with her father and brother, to her Uncle John's estate at Mount Doyle near Dublin. After a few days of bittersweet parting, the family of three had boarded the mail boat for England. She remembered standing on deck and watching as Ireland disappeared over the horizon, clasping Mahomet tightly with one hand and William to her bosom with the other.

From the door that opened onto the stairway to the family rooms she could hear Sarah chastising the children. She smiled and turned to reach for a wooden salt cellar but jumped back in horror when she saw Mahomet standing behind her.

"Husband!" she cried, clasping her hands to her breast. "What! You surprised me!"

He looked horrified. "Jane, I am sorry. I did not think ..."

"How long have you been standing there?" she demanded, trying to re-compose herself.

He smiled, thankful at hearing the sharpness return to his wife's voice.

"Not long, my pearl. You looked so concentrated I did not wish to disturb you."

"You should not sneak around," she chided.

"I do not sneak, my pearl," he replied in a hurt tone.

She clicked her tongue. "No husband, you do not. I am sorry but you did frighten me so. I was distracted and did not hear you enter."

Mahomet tried to calm her with a smile. "A penny for your thoughts?"

"I was thinking of when we left Ireland," she said softly. "It was such a long time ago. Do you recall our journey, and our first arriving in London?'

"You were in awe, I think."

Her brow furrowed slightly. "As were you. Cochrane lives more in a palace than a house and you were to be in charge of it. I remember his Indian servants lining up to receive us. Whatever did they think when they saw me following you with William in my arms?'

Mahomet smile's now beamed. "That I was a very fortunate man," he said as he stepped forward and placed his arm around his wife's waist. He rubbed the small of her back with the palm of his hand. "I am so sorry I frightened you, my pearl. I would never wish you any harm. You know that."

She looked into his brown eyes as his face came close and he kissed her on the cheek.

"I know, husband," she whispered, before remembering the stove. "Oh, the broth!" she exclaimed and turned back to her stirring, her face hidden from her husband but displaying a large smile.

"Jane," said Mahomet, looking at the back of his wife again. "We must speak. I need to tell you something."

His words broke the spell of the last few moments and Jane Mahomet's smile slowly disappeared. She did not like the change in his voice.

"That sounds earnest, husband?"

"It is Jane. Come sit, I have something to say."

Removing the broth from the heat Jane turned to face her husband who was now seated at the kitchen table, and joined him reluctantly.

"Well husband," she said a lightly as she could, "I am all ears ..."

"Jane," Mahomet began, "I have something important to tell you and I do not want you taking on so, if only for the children."

She gasped. "Mr Mahomet, don't frighten me again. What is it?"

PARLIAMENT would not be sitting until the New Year, but the Deputy Ranger of Richmond Park preferred the House of Lords when it was all but empty. It had never been a kind place for him, and nor had the Commons – though not many others would agree with him. As the son of a physician and reverend's daughter, he had risen to the very top of the tree. Twenty years ago he had been nominated as Speaker of the House of Commons, and ten years ago, after the younger William Pitt fell out with the King, he had been invited to become Prime Minister. Yet war, famine, Irish rebellion and political in-fighting had made for an unhappy time. In some ways it was with relief when three years later he had been driven from office by an unholy alliance of Pitt and Charles James Fox, possibly the only time when these two foes saw eye to eye.

Still he was proud of his achievements during his Ministry. He had raised much money through Mr Pitt's new income tax, and had supervised the building of the Martello towers on the south coast to protect the country from Bonaparte. He had even raised enough money to be able to declare war on the French to defend the newly acquired island of Malta. But this was not enough. He never really liked cultivating friends beyond his own circle, and he had to admit he was dreadful at public speaking. Both Pitt and Fox could hold the Commons in their thrall, and this they did when they finally came to usurp him. Yet the King did not forget his faithful servant, and rewarded him with the title of Viscount Sidmouth.

Since 1807 he had been content to act as the Deputy to the Ranger himself, George III. It was with great sadness that Sidmouth had witnessed the Regency Act being passed the previous year and the Prince of Wales created Prince Regent in the King's place. For this he would never forgive his fellow Tory Spencer Perceval, and had refused a number of invitations to rejoin the Cabinet.

Today Sidmouth had commandeered the House of Lords, or rather a small antechamber to the Large White Chamber in which it sat, to attend to political business and catch up on gossip, but he also looked to more private business, including a meeting with William Rufus. He was becoming ever more pleased with the young man's skill at gathering information, though he was concerned at a slightly reckless, even aggressive, approach to his work that the young man displayed. Still, thought Sidmouth, this was no doubt due to his upbringing in the Americas and he would become more polished and refined with time. Moreover, Sidmouth had retained the services of the same private secretary for over twenty years – the Rev. Jonathan Williams was a man who did not suffer fools gladly – and his opinion was always sought on matters of character. Williams thought Rufus to be a most worthy prospect.

Sidmouth walked to the window while waiting for Rufus to appear. It was late afternoon, and he looked out over Old Palace Yard towards St Margaret's and the Abbey. With Parliament not sitting there were very few people around. A small group of soldiers were resting up against one wall of the church and their slovenliness annoyed the Deputy Ranger – where was their officer? Further on, two clerics were walking along the passageway between the church and the Abbey. It all looked so peaceful, but out there Lord Sidmouth knew were plotters and radicals peddling their seditious and troublesome thoughts. Perceval was a fool if he did not realise the danger the country was in, and yet the Prime Minister would not listen to voices such as his. There was a cough behind him and the Deputy Ranger turned to face a redheaded young man, who bowed low.

"My lord," said Rufus quietly, "your secretary said I could approach."

Sidmouth nodded, slightly disturbed that he had not heard the man's footsteps on the paved floor, and indicated they should sit on a velvet-covered banquette near the window.

"So young man, I have every expectation you have brought me comforting news regarding Cochrane's little business."

Rufus smiled. "My lord, I believe I can resolve the matter expeditiously."

He then described the events that had taken place, from the challenge at the cricket match to his attendance at Watier's Club and George Harding's debts.

"Of course, it is not conclusive," cautioned Sidmouth, "but news of these debts and his knowledge of the poison does seem suggestive. You will need a confession."

Rufus nodded then paused. "But if I cannot obtain one, my lord, even though I were convinced of his guilt?"

Sidmouth looked across the anti chamber towards the door to the Large White Chamber in which the House of Lords sat.

"Then he must be driven from Society, sir, as quickly and as painlessly as possible. I would not wish any scandal, particularly at the moment, but without a confession this is a case that could be difficult to prove in court now that the poisoner himself is dead. The country is uneasy, and even though we are not in government, it is our duty to hold the line where possible, for the poor King's sake. No, gentleman like Harding have no place here; he is an unwelcome distraction. We are at war with the French in Spain and in other dominions around the world, and while there is no armed action, we must also add the Tsar and his empire to the list of our enemies. Moreover, the Americans complain bitterly about orders given to the Royal Navy to stop and search their ships, and I am old enough to know what that could mean. Gentleman like Harding should be serving their King, not themselves."

Rufus smiled. "I understand, my lord."

"Good. And the Indian, sir, what of this challenge?"

Rufus shook his head. "I do not know. My guess is that it will not happen. George Harding – they call him Georgie Porgie at Watier's – is a born coward who would balk at fighting even a diminutive Indian of a certain age. Still, as I consider myself to be partly responsible, I have a mind to ensure the Indian's safety ..."

Sidmouth nodded. "Good. I would not want to disappoint Cochrane by reporting the loss of his man."

DECIMUS Doyle sat in the library of Dr Bunton's Soho house pouring over a slim volume that lay in his hands. "Rule 1," he read, "The first offense requires the first apology, though the retort may have been more offensive than the insult. Example: A tells B he is impertinent, etc. B retorts that he lies; yet A must make the first apology because he gave the first offense, and then (after one fire) B may explain away the retort by a subsequent apology."

Doyle groaned; how one earth was he to make sense of all this? He continued reading. "Rule 2. But if the parties would rather fight on, then after two shots each (but in no case before), B may explain first, and A apologise afterward."

An image came before him of Sake Mahomet lying in some muddy field, his cousin Jane pawing over her dead husband's body and blaming him for not stopping it. Nor had it helped when he spoke about it to Sarah. She seemed quite unconcerned, suggesting that George Harding could hardly hit a tree, never mind the diminutive Indian. "And make sure you stand well clear, my love," is all she would say in advice, though she did unhelpfully recall a number of duels supposedly fought over her during the years.

Doyle sighed and returned to the *Code Duello*. "Rule 4. When the lie direct is the first offense, the aggressor must either beg pardon in express terms; exchange two shots previous to apology; or three shots followed up by explanation; or fire on till a severe hit be received by one party or the other." He groaned again and, placing the book in his lap, put his head in his hands.

The arrival of William Harding the previous week had been a shock. It became even more confusing when Bunton had to be told it was nothing to do with Mrs Siddons but that Sake Mahomet had been challenged by Sir George Harding. "I do not know who is worse!" exclaimed the senior doctor after Harding had left. "How can you have been so foolish as to be challenged, Mahomet?"

"It was not by choice," was all Sake Mahomet could say.

Harding and Doyle had agreed they would rendezvous their men at the Lord Southampton inn on the Hampstead road north in the settlement of Camden Town at dawn on the designated day. William Harding had already spied out an appropriate field surrounded by trees to provide cover from prying eyes, and he had also purchased two duelling pistols. Doyle had questioned whether he should not supply a pistol for Mahomet, but Harding was adamant that those in his possession were newly purchased from London's most reputable gunsmith and could not be called into question. They had also gone through the procedure of the day and

William Harding had left with Doyle the book that he was now endeavouring to read.

"Rule 13. No dumb shooting or firing in the air is admissible in any case. The challenger ought not to have challenged without receiving offence; and the challenged ought, if he gave offence, to have made an apology before he came on the ground; therefore, children's play must be dishonourable on one side or the other, and is accordingly prohibited."

There seemed no way he could get Sake Mahomet from facing the duel and, for his part, the Indian had resigned himself to the fact. "I could not stand down and live with the dishonour," he told Doyle earnestly, "as I would be broken as a man. This may all seem ridiculous, but my only concern is how to tell Jane. I must do so in case I do not return."

Doyle looked down to the *Code* again. "Rule 19. Firing may be regulated – first by signal; secondly, by word of command; or thirdly, at pleasure – as may be agreeable to the parties. In the latter case, the parties may fire at their reasonable leisure, but re-presents and rests are strictly prohibited."

Doyle sighed. There were twenty-six rules just like this. He closed the book and threw it to the floor. He could not do it, he simply could not. He would go to Mahomet straight away and demand a withdrawal. If the family suffered financial loss because of it then he would help out himself, or write to his father. Yet even as he thought this he knew it was useless.

Doyle's thoughts were disturbed by a knock on the door and Mrs Mac entered. "Begging your pardon sir, but there is a lady …"

She did not complete the sentence as Jane Mahomet pushed past her and into the library in a great deal of distress.

"Oh Decimus, how could you?!" she cried, heading straight for her young cousin. "You should have stopped him! You must stop him!"

Doyle jumped up from his chair and rushed to comfort his cousin. Mrs Mac, who was quickly becoming as equally distressed, was sent to make tea, and he ushered the weeping Jane to a chair, forcing her to sit against her will.

"Calm yourself, cousin, please. Surely you did not come across the city in this state?"

"And why should I not?" she cried, sobbing once more. In truth she had been fully composed until entering the hallway of Dr Bunton's house.

Doyle knelt down before her and took her hands in his. His association with Mrs Siddons was paying a beneficial interest in his handling of the fairer, and older, sex.

"Come cousin, we can only speak of this if you are calm."

Jane Mahomet sniffed and then, reaching for a handkerchief in the sleeve of her dress, blew her nose quite hard. Doyle sighed and stood, trying a smile to lighten the mood.

"He has told you then?"

Jane Mahomet breathed in hard. "Of course he has told me. When is it to happen?"

"In two days."

"What!" she exclaimed, and Doyle feared for a return of the tears. Instead she drew in her breath.

"It is unthinkable," she announced. "I will not have my husband chancing with death in a duel. He can't even hold a sword!"

"Pistol," corrected Doyle, which elicited another cry of anguish.

"Oh Decimus, this is too much. How did you let this happen? You are the sensible one, the clever one. I rely on you to keep him out of trouble. He is not a young man anymore, though he would like to think so. The next thing he will be sailing back to India to fight in some Company war. You must make him see reason!"

Doyle shook his head. "I have tried, cousin Jane, believe me I have tried." He did not add that since their heated discussion over Mrs Siddons he had hardly spoken to Sake Mahomet except to confirm the details of the duel. In any case, he knew any remonstrance would be worthless.

"He is determined, cousin Jane, and I think you know this."

Jane Mahomet certainly did know this. After Mahomet had told her in the kitchen there followed a good two-hour conflagration in which, and in turn, she had heaped scorn, begged, threatened, implored, chided and even blasphemed. All to no avail.

"He is going to leave his children fatherless and me a widow. I will have to throw myself on the mercy of the family or the workhouse." She paused for a moment. "No, it will be the workhouse, as I could not witness the pain in my father's eyes seeing his daughter so distressed."

Doyle, who held a very high opinion of his Uncle John Daly, knew he would care for his daughter and grandchildren if presented with Mahomet's death. Sake Mahomet's death!

"They say cousin, that only one in ten duellists die ..." as he was speaking that his words he knew they were unlikely to ease the situation.

"Dead! One in ten dead! And we all know who the tenth man will be, don't we. That stupid, pig-headed ... loveable ..." and again Jane Mahomet broke down in tears and could not now be consoled. Doyle was grateful when Mrs Mac arrived with the tea and he asked her to stay to comfort his cousin. When, after some minutes, the room was calm again, he said: "I will do all I can for him, cousin, and Bunton has also agreed to attend. If he is injured he will have two doctors on hand."

"And his loving wife," she added.

"Pardon?"

"His wife, Decimus. If he is determined to go through with this then I intend to be there as well."

Doyle was flummoxed. "But cousin, you cannot. Ladies are most strictly forbidden. It is in the rules."

"What rules?" she barked.

From the floor he picked up the *Code Duello*. "These cousin. They govern the rules for duelling and make sure for a clean contest. They may be laws of chance and danger, but they also protect Sake Mahomet." He opened the book. "Yes here, Rule twenty seven," he lied. "Gentlemen only shall attend at a Challenge. Ladies are strictly precluded and on no account should attend." He slammed the book shut. "Sake Mahomet considers his honour at stake, cousin, that is why he accepts the challenge. Do not compromise him on this."

Jane Mahomet put down her teacup and grasped the hand of Mrs Mac sitting next to her on the sofa. "Oh Decimus, how can this be? How can he do this to me, to our children ... and to our unborn child?!"

DECIMUS Doyle continued to muse on the visit by his cousin. Jane was pregnant and he doubted Sake Dean Mahomet knew about it. How would this affect him? Would it lead Mahomet to seek some compromise with Harding and make him apologise for words he did not utter, bearing the humiliation this would cause. Or would the fact his wife was pregnant embolden him to see the duel concluded to protect his reputation for the sake of their unborn child. He was more confused than ever, and beginning to suffer from an aching head, when Bunton's housekeeper again entered the library.

"Yes Mrs Mac, what is it," he asked weakly.

"You are indeed popular today sir," she started. "You have another visitor." Another?"

Mrs Mac nodded. "A young lady accompanied by her maid is waiting in the hallway."

"A lady?" he queried, and hope rose that Mrs Siddons was calling unannounced, unable to be apart from him. Then he realised that Mrs Mac had said "young".

"A Miss Charlotte Harding, sir. She said to say that Lottie has come to see her friend." Mrs Mac's arched brows said more than any words.

Doyle was completely flustered. "Miss Harding? Here?"

Mrs Mac nodded once more.

"Oh dear. I suppose you must show her in, Mrs Mac." He paused. "Do you think you would act as her chaperone and stay here?"

Now the older woman smiled. "I am sure she will be safe, sir. And, after all, her maid will only be the other side of the door. No sir, I am sure she will be safe."

Doyle sighed. "Then show her in Mrs Mac and I am afraid you will need to raid Dr Bunton's tea caddy once more."

Smiling broadly, the housekeeper showed Charlotte Harding into the library then, with what Doyle thought was a slight wink to him, firmly closed the door. Doyle escorted his visitor to a chair then sat in a two-seat sofa opposite. He was surprised to see colour in Charlotte Harding's cheeks, and it did not take long to get to the gist of her visit.

"William has told me about the duel Decimus. It is horrible, simply too horrible!"

Doyle sighed. He was being asked to console another distressed lady. "Please do not vex yourself, Miss Harding … Lottie … these things happen but I am sure no harm will come to either party. It is all bluster and display, no more than that."

"But you cannot be a party to it Decimus. You simply cannot. I will not allow it. Oh I wish I did not mention it to William …"

"Mention what?" interrupted Doyle, curiously.

The question stopped Charlotte Harding in her tracks. "No matter, Decimus, it is not important. But you must not attend this duel."

"Must not? I am afraid I must, Miss Harding … Lottie," he caught himself as she looked at him plaintively.

"But you might be injured, even killed!"

"I think not."

"Oh, I know George is a dreadful shot but he could be lucky. What then? A stray shot is all it takes, so William told me."

Now Charlotte Harding stood, crossed the room and settled herself on the sofa next to him, reaching out for a hand and holding it tightly in hers. Doyle was embarrassed by the action but did not pull away for fear of causing too great a reaction in his young visitor.

"We have only just become friends, Decimus. You must not fight my brother."

Doyle smiled, some relief to an indelicate situation dawning on him.

"Do not concern yourself Lottie," he said gently. "Sadly, it is not I who will be fighting your brother, but my honoured friend and relative Sake Mahomet."

He now tried to pull his hand from hers but she held on tight, relief clearly showing on her face.

"The Indian!" she exclaimed, her relief now palpable and squeezing his hand once more. "Oh, William did not tell me that at all, just that he had called on you. Well then, that is splendid!"

Doyle was both shocked and irritated by Charlotte Harding's irrational behaviour. "I would not say it in such terms, Miss Harding, I really would not."

"Oh forgive me Decimus," she smiled as she continued to squeeze his hand, "I did not mean to dismiss your friend so lightly. But this is good news, it really is. And your friend can hardly be troubled by a challenge from George. He is quite without sense when it comes to guns. Your friend will surely prevail."

"Forgive me Miss Harding if I do not consider matters as clearly as you. Both your brother and Sake Mahomet will be standing in a field taking shots at each other. This can only end ill for either party. Surely you are concerned for your brother's wellbeing?"

"Ha!" she exclaimed, throwing back her head. "And why should that be. He is packing me off without the slightest care. He has never been a true brother to William or me. An elder brother would have protected us from papa, not abandoned us. No Decimus, I am sure your friend will prevail."

At that the library door opened and Mrs Mac re-appeared with a pot of Dr Bunton's finest green tea. Doyle, realising his compromising position, at last pulled his hand from Charlotte Harding's grasp, much to the housekeeper's amusement.

THE house on Liverpool's Rodney Street was similar to the one on which the man had called in London when submitting his papers to the Prime Minister Mr Perceval: a substantial and terraced brick house in the style popular throughout the last century. Perhaps politicians preferred such houses, he thought, as he ascended the steps and rapped loudly on the large black door. In any case it compared most favourably to the one-room of his in-laws' house in which he, his wife and child now resided near to the Salthouse dock. As he waited for a reply he spat on the step, partly to expel the taste of poverty into which he and his family had sunk and partly to mark his disgust at those who had put him there – like the man on whom he had come to call.

It was the residence of Issac Gascoyne, a Tory Member of Parliament for Liverpool who succeeded his brother Bamber to the position in 1796.

Gascoyne was an army man, and lieutenant-general of the 7th West India Regiment. With interests in the West Indies, he had been strongly opposed to the abolition of the slave trade, and consistently voted against it in the House of Commons when the Slave Trade Act was passed four years previously. In this he was encouraged by the Liverpool ship owners, whose profits from the so-called Triangular trade (textiles and rum from Liverpool to West Africa in exchange for African slaves to the West Indies and then back to Liverpool with the same ship full of sugar and cotton) had set the town up as one of the principal ports of the British Empire. Indeed, so important was it that the newly formed United States of America opened its first-ever consulate here twenty years ago, and the Liverpool Customs House was the single largest contributor to the British Treasury.

Liverpool had grown from a borough of 20,000 to a sprawl of over 80,000 souls in the last fifty years, though most of these people had no property and therefore no say in the election of General Gasgoyne, including the man now standing on his step. But at least Liverpudlians had a member to petition – two in fact, as they had done since the last time Parliament was reformed in 1295. Nearby Manchester, of similar size and prosperity, had no one. And both of these Lancastrian successes looked in despair at the bucolic borough of Newton-le-Willows that lay between them. With just over fifty electors (depending on the time of day, of course), the tenants of Newton happily returned their man to Parliament. As most of these electors were in the pay of the local landlord and directed to vote as he saw fit or lose their livelihood, then you could understand why the merchants of Manchester said that there was indeed something rotten with the British Parliament. Not that General Gascoyne subscribed to this view.

The man banged on the door again, not noticing the rather elegant bell pull to one side, and after another pause it slowly opened, revealing a young man with a pitted face, evidence of a skirmish with the pox.

"Yes?" he virtually spat at the visitor.

"I am here to see the general."

The young man, his eyes adjusting to the light, now recognised the caller.

"You again! Can't you give up? He wont help, you know."

"He's the Member of Parliament and I have a right to speak to him ... again. And I have an appointment. He agreed to see me after I returned from London, where I saw the King's Prime Minister."

The confidence and force of the man's speech swayed the pock-faced man into allowing him into the hallway. Instructing the visitor to sit in a nearby chair, the attendant disappeared up the main stairs of the house. The man looked around him: the hallway displayed many of Gascoyne's acquisitions after a long life in the service of the King. On the wall opposite was a flag, a regimental colour displaying honours won in Dominica, Martinique and Guadeloupe. Next to it was a large oil painting of a tropical island, full of vibrant green foliage and a vivid orange setting sun. It prompted him to recall with great bitterness his time in the Russian gaol, and the freezing cold which got into every sinew of the body and which had cost two toes to the frost.

From the top of the stairs he heard a great noise, as a deep baritone voice indicated a protest at being summoned to attend to a matter it really had no care for. The voice was followed by an immense body standing to the top of the stairs and which was lit from behind by a picture window, casting a long shadow down the stairs and into the hall.

"Well sir!" it boomed, "Have we not had sufficient of this nonsense?"

The man in the hallway stood and turned to the shadow.

"I said I would return following my meeting with Mr Perceval, sir, and here I am. I would ask you to receive me with civility."

There was a great "harrumph" from the top of the stair. "Would you now? Well, we'll see. Oh ... you had better come up. I'll not give you long, mind, and don't expect anything different from before. Show Mr Bellingham up, John, and be quick about it. I have far more important things to attend on than this nonsense."

With that the shadow, also known as General Gascoyne, turned and walked into his library on the first floor. The general's manservant began running down the stairs but was met by Bellingham already on his way up. "This way," the servant hissed, to which Bellingham replied, "I know the way only too well."

General Gascoyne's gait demonstrated that his battles were now fought in the mess hall rather than on the field of Mars. He had positioned his ample bulk in a large and commodious wingback chair as Bellingham and the servant entered, and instructed his visitor to sit in a much less substantial version some feet away. He also indicated to his servant to remain. The last time he had granted an audience to Mr Bellingham the air had become thick with gestures and bile.

"So," the general intoned, "what did Perceval have to say?"

"The matter is not what he said or did not say, sir, it is whether you are now prepared to lay my petition before Parliament."

Gascoyne groaned inwardly. "Did you speak with the Prime Minister?" he asked incredulously.

Bellingham nodded.

"And what did he say?"

"That you must present my petition to Parliament," Bellingham replied, and the general immediately doubted the veracity of this statement.

"Did he? If this is truly Mr Perceval's wish, then no doubt he will instruct us in due course. Did he say nothing of the fact we are at war with the Tsar?"

"As I have explained several times, sir, my petition has nothing to do with the Russians and everything to do with the King's ambassador in St Petersburgh. My claim is against the King's government here, not the Tsar or his viceroy in Archangel."

"But it was they who kept you locked up Bellingham, not us!" exclaimed Gascoyne, "and I fear I am repeating myself but you will not listen. We ... that is our Foreign Minister Lord Wellesley cannot present your case to the Russians while we are at war with them. See the sense of this man!"

But Bellingham was adamant. "It is you who do not listen sir, so I will state my case once again in the hope you can understand. After I was seized and thrown into prison by the military governor of Archangel, I applied to the British Consul in Archangel to ask Lord Gower, then at the Russian court, to press my case most urgently. Gower wrote to the military governor but was told I was detained in prison on a legal cause, and that I had conducted myself in a very indecorous manner!"

General Gascoyne was already beginning to commiserate with the said Russian governor.

"From that time Lord Gower and the British Consul positively declined any representation on my behalf, and I was held for two further years despite my efforts to induce Gower to address the Russian Emperor."

"But you were held on a legal cause, man, as you have just yourself said! What else could Gower have done? The Tsar was not likely to gainsay his man in Archangel. There is no point bandying words on this."

"Yet I, sir, was bandied from prison to prison, dungeon to dungeon, fed on black bread and water and treated with the utmost cruelty. I was marched through the streets with other criminals, even before the residence of the British ambassador. All he had to do was to look from his window to see the degrading severity in which a British subject who had committed no crime was being held, to the disgrace and insult of the British nation!"

General Gascoyne sighed and sat back in his chair. He was sure that the government would never consider Bellingham's detention to be a *casus belli* with the Russian Empire. Nor was the man's tale unusual in a Europe wrecked by war and the ambition of the French. Lord Gower was no doubt more concerned with keeping the Tsar from signing a truce with Bonaparte, which sadly had now come to pass. Yet this was not going to assuage the man before him.

"Perhaps in less grievous times your case would have attracted better attention, sir, but do remember this nation stands alone against the French tyrant. Men of commerce such as yourself have to take especial care when trading with the Continent, as I often advise others in this town."

His words had little effect on Bellingham, who hardly heard them. "I instructed a procurer in Archangel who investigated and obtained judgment against the military governor. But I was still sent into another prison and a demand made on me of two thousand roubles. I refused to pay a debt I did not owe and continued to be held in prison. Lord Gower refused to help and the British Consul told me to pay the money. He said they would even accept just twenty roubles."

Gasgoyne was exasperated. He had been through all this before. "Why on earth did you not pay, man? Could you not afford it?" he barked. "Surely anything is better than languishing in a Russian gaol?"

Bellingham shook his head wildly. "I had the money sir, but why should I pay a debt I did not owe? It would have justified the conduct of the military governor, against whom I had a legal decision. If I admitted the debt then I would have also admitted the falseness of my claim against him. Such an admission would have sent me to Siberia! No sir, Lord Gower should have continued to represent my case to the Tsar. It is his inaction that led to six years of suffering and it is against him, in his role as the King's ambassador, that I seek redress. Now, sir, will you lay my claim?"

Gascoyne looked sternly at the man before him. "I have already told you, sir, that I cannot. You seek financial redress and as your petition is of a pecuniary nature it can only be brought to Parliament by one of his Majesty's ministers. If, as you say, you have brought this matter before the Prime Minister then no doubt we will all be advised in good time what steps he intends to take."

To Bellingham the general's words were simply another example of the obfuscation he had come across since his return from Russia. "I warn you sir that this will not do. If my grievances continue to be ignored and redress refused me, I will be obliged to take steps against those responsible for resisting my applications. The King's ministers must listen, to avert such an abhorrent but inevitable alternative."

General Gascoyne now failed to hide the contempt he felt for the man. While he did not consider Bellingham to be a danger, those last words were chilling and intended to intimidate. "And I must advise you, sir, to leave the past where it lay. No good can come from all this if you approach it with such a mind. You have my advice: wait until you hear from Mr Perceval and in the meanwhile get about your normal business. Whether you take my advice or not, I will not entertain you again. Now good day sir."

He nodded to his servant who stepped forward to where Bellingham was sitting. Reluctantly the visitor stood and looked to speak again, but Gascoyne quickly raised the palm of his hand in a final gesture. After Bellingham and his servant had withdrawn, the general sat alone for some time. He had not liked what he had heard, especially at the end. While he was disinclined to help Bellingham – the man was a complete fool, after all – he was concerned that no one in the government was attending to his matter. After his opposition to the Slave Trade Act, Gascoyne had found himself out of favour with Mr Perceval's government. But there was one friend who, while not in government, kept a watching brief from his position in the House of Lords. He would write to him, explaining Bellingham's case as best he could and mentioning his own concerns. Gascoyne did not know whether Bellingham really wanted money or simply a recognition of the wrongs against him – probably both. Perhaps a fresh mind of great learning and guile could settle the issue and relieve him of Mr Bellingham. The general walked over to his desk and began to write.

Chapter 14

London, Autumn 1811.

SARAH Siddons lay back on the chaise lounge and gently stroked the dark wavy hair of the young man who was sitting on the floor with his back to her. It had been a difficult week for both of them. Two days ago she had informed her brother of her intention to step down from the stage at the end of the current season. He was less than pleased, and accused her current "dalliance", as he put it, as being the real reason for her decision. There had followed a great *contretemps* between the two, in which some harsh things were said. She disliked such upset, especially with a brother to whom she had been so close, but was consoled by the thought of another evening with Decimus.

She looked down at her handsome beau, his lithe legs stretching out on the carpet. Why was he here, and what did he see in her? Despite herself, she knew there was one truth in her brother's words: it would not last. How could she contain a young man's amorous wants when every day it became more taxing? Maintaining a performance both on and off stage was already exhausting her. Presently she would have to say no when he asked to call, if only to gain some rest. For the moment, though, she wallowed in the warmth of the unconditional love of a handsome young man who wanted neither money nor position in exchange.

For Decimus Doyle, stretched out in such abandon on Mrs Siddons boudoir carpet while she caressed his head, thoughts were focused far from the bosom of the aging beauty behind him. He and Dr Simon Bunton had arranged to call on Sake Mahomet at six the following morning, and together they would journey east to the rendezvous just north of Camden Town. As the fateful day drew close, the more anxious Doyle had become, and yesterday he had insisted on taking Mahomet to open land west of Hyde Park. Here he made his cousin's husband practice with a duelling pistol borrowed from Bunton. Doyle had been surprised by the accuracy of

Mahomet's shot, but the Indian had just shrugged and smiled, reminding the young man that for many years in the East India Company a rifle had been like his third arm.

"It will not help if you fret so much," Sarah whispered into the ear of her young lover.

Doyle turned his head slightly in response. "I do not expect you to understand, but I look upon Sake Mahomet like ... an elder uncle, I suppose."

"Is that not a curious description?"

Doyle paused, confused by the question. "Curious? ... Perhaps, but he is close kin, no matter where he was born. And cousin Jane is like my aunt, and their children my brothers and sisters. If anything goes untoward with Sake Mahomet, I do not know how I will account for it."

He sighed and dropped his head, so Sarah leaned forward and kissed him softly on the crown.

"My poor sweet, how sincerely you consider things. Oh!" she exclaimed, "how I wish we had met many years ago."

"But I would have been just a boy," Doyle replied, not realising the insult.

Sarah Siddons smiled. "As are all men, no matter their age. But in my own experience I would say that you are a rare creature, Decimus. There are not many men who place the interests of others before those of their own. Your innocence is quite intoxicating."

If she could have seen past the back of his head she would have noticed her beau's face flush slightly.

"Now come Decimus, we must dine ere it gets too late. I have a table laid with cold meats and warm broth next door."

They rose and, with delicacy, both adjusted and smoothed their dress before making their way through to the dining room. They sat opposite each other but she found it difficult to engage him in conversation, so soon reverted to the previous discussion.

"You say your Mahomet is a fine shot?"

"Yes, but what of that? I fear for the health of Sake Mahomet, but what if he kills George Harding? How will he live with himself?"

Sarah Siddons sighed. "If, as you say, he has served in India for many years, then he will not be a stranger to death. Your only task, Decimus, is to keep your man safe. Make sure George Harding, or that pestilent William, does not gain an advantage. Remember I know those boys, and I still contend they drove their father into an early grave even if there is a question about who fed him the poison. No, do not take anything they say as the word of the Gospel."

Sarah's words brought up a concern that had nagged at Doyle since the visit of William Harding.

"William is providing the pistols. He said he purchased them for the very occasion."

Sarah tutted. "By the pricking of my thumbs, something wicked this way comes. Then make sure you take the one not offered to you," she advised. "And take a spare, just in case."

GEORGE Harding looked at the grandfather clock in the main hall of the Harding mansion as it struck. Half past the hour of five, George groaned to himself. It was usual for him to be retiring at such a time after a most enjoyable evening at Watier's, not completing his lave and making his way to the breakfast table. He entered the dining room and headed for the sideboard where covers hid the early, and cold, breakfast cook had prepared for the brothers. Taking two slices of boiled ham and some cold scrambled egg, he made for the table but did not sit at the head. He was still hesitant at taking his father's place, fearful some ghostly admonition would descend from above – especially since the house had now been sold and would be demolished sometime next year.

His father's elderly retainer appeared carrying a cup of hot chocolate: yet another servant who, come the New Year, would be looking for a new master.

"Good morning, Sir George," said the old man sonorously. "Master William is attending to the horses and will be at the front of the house presently. He asks that you join him there."

George Harding snorted. William! Why did he ever agree to that idiot being his seconder, when he knew so many more able men at his club. His mind became fully occupied with the thought that within the hour he would be standing in a field north of London and expected to aim a pistol and fire on another man. Moreover, he would be expected to stand firm while that other man shot back! He looked at the plate of cold ham and eggs before him and pushed it to one side. He sipped slowly at the cup of chocolate and then closed his eyes, still in the hope that he could wish this day away. He heard someone enter the room and knew who it was before he opened his eyes.

"Come George, we cannot dally. The horses are ready," chided his brother.

He slowly opened his eyes to see his brother standing across the room, dressed for the journey and carrying his, George's, riding coat in his hand.

"I have loaded the pistols. It will take a good half hour to reach the rendezvous so please finish your breakfast."

Sir George Harding frowned: William was in an excitable mood, as if he were enjoying this.

"I will take as long as I wish, brother. Your haste does not become the occasion."

William Harding bowed low. "I beg your forgiveness, brother. I did not mean to press, but punctuality is important. The rules state ...."

"Do not quote from that God-forsaken tome any more William!"

George sat back in his chair and rubbed his temples to dispel the anxiety of the moment. How had it come to this? That infernal cricket match! And what of the Indian who so blithely made those gross allegations. George knew that he had been driven partly by guilt that day after so promptly disposing of his father's London estate. The old man was probably looking down on him now, in a mixed state of contempt and apoplexy. His brother broke his thoughts.

"George, it is nearing six. We have to be there by seven. At first light, remember!"

The elder Harding sighed: it was likely he would also shoot William before the morning was out. The man had been an irritation ever since he brought news of the slander at the dreaded match. He took another gulp of the chocolate, which was now only lukewarm, and stood.

"Very well William, I understand your purpose."

This statement surprised William Harding and had the dining room not been so dark George would have witnessed his brother's face turn a light shade of red. Instead the elder brother walked over and took his riding coat from his sibling's hands. As the brothers left the house and walked over to where a stable-lad was holding their horses near a stone step, George looked up into the darkness.

"When will it be light?" he asked.

"Another hour sir," replied the boy.

"And how will be the day?"

"Fair, I think sir. It was a red sky last night. It will be a good omen, sir."

"Will it?" Sir George Harding quipped. He had not noticed the weather the previous evening; he had far more pressing concerns. Then, as he mounted, his mind slipped to the small Indian he was about to meet. Did he see the sky, he wondered, and did he think it a good omen? They could not both be right.

From her bedroom Charlotte Harding could just make out her brothers ride off along the gravel drive. This was to be a momentous day, and she felt nervous but with a sense of expectation. When William had first told her of the duel, and led her to believe it was to be with Mr Doyle – Decimus – she was beside herself with fear and anxiety and had rushed to the student doctor's lodgings as soon as she had been left alone. The thrill of seeing him again, of being close to him, was beyond anything she had experienced in her young life. And when he advised that it was to be the old Indian duelling her brother, Charlotte Harding was beside herself with relief.

She continued to stare into the darkness, all shadow of her brothers now gone. She might never see George again and, while this was indeed sad, it was becoming more and more necessary and no less than he deserved. Charlotte was determined not to be packed off to Warwickshire, and with George out of the way and William as her new guardian, this would never come to pass. William had spoken to her just the previous night of his intention to make sure the duel would not go George's way. What did he say to her? Just as justice was served on papa so too will it be on George. Then William would stop the sale of the estate or purchase another property in London for them, and she would convince her brother to allow her to brought out into Society. In her mind she had already planned her first assembly on the arm of the dashing Mr Doyle, who would take her in his arms and lead her around the dance floor. And as she continued these thoughts and looked through the darkened window she gently caressed the gentleman's handkerchief she so carefully held in her hands.

LIKE Sir George Harding, Sake Dean Mahomet had not seen the red sky the previous evening, though he had watched through the night from the window of the small sitting room, reflecting on his life and his beloved family. There had been a decided change in his wife since he had returned from the shooting practice with Decimus. Instead of berating him at every opportunity, accusing him of abandoning his family for want of a silly feud, Jane had sat with him until the early hours, holding his hand as they both observed life rolling by on George Street. Not that there was much; in fact George Street was as quiet as a churchyard.

After sitting in silence for some time, husband and wife began to talk ... and talk and talk and talk. It was as if words dispelled their anxiety about that which was bound to follow. It was when Jane heard Decimus' mantel clock chime two that she tried to persuade Mahomet to take at least a couple of hours sleep.

"It is no good, my pearl," he replied softly. "I will not sleep tonight. I remember as a young man staying awake for hours prior to a battle, while many around me snored and slept. But I felt fresher than most, and afterwards would partake of the sleep of the blessed. So will it be today. I will face my fate with a clear mind, and will meditate for the remaining hours if you will allow."

So reluctantly she left her husband to his contemplation though she knew she would not sleep herself. Yet she did drift off, and woke with a start when she heard a coach draw up outside. Fearing Mahomet would leave without saying goodbye she jumped up and quickly dressed, rushing down the stairs though careful not to make a noise and wake the children.

In the dining room of the Hindostanee Coffee House she was greeted by her husband, her cousin and Dr Bunton.

"Jane," said Mahomet quietly, "Decimus and Dr Bunton have arrived, as you can see. We will depart shortly."

She gave an involuntary squeal of fear before rushing over to her husband and holding him in a tight embrace.

"Come now Jane, please do not make this any more difficult. I have two good fellows standing with me."

So the Mahomets' took their parting. Jane accompanied the men to the door and watched them climb into a coach and four Dr Bunton had acquired from the Hunterian's stables in Coventry Street. It was fortunate that neither of the Mahomets knew of the special adaption to the carriage, which now included a large box attached to the rear that could accommodate a body of ample size. Yet as she watched the coach turn the corner of George Street and head north along Baker Street, Jane Mahomet quickly looked the other way along the street and then disappeared back into the coffee house.

Inside the carriage, however, the disposition of the three men was decidedly calm given their destination, and it was only when the coach turned east onto Islington New Road did any man venture to speak.

"We are in good time, Sake Mahomet," Doyle advised. "Cousin Jane was calmer than I expected her to be, given her obvious distress when last I saw her."

Mahomet smiled at the young man. "She is resolved, as am I. It is strange, but at this moment I feel closer to my Mohammedan upbringing than I ever expected to be. You know I was brought up to say the Arabic *Insha'Allah*, which means if it be of God's will. We say this not in the expectation that we will succeed, simply that every act is a part of His divine plan. So no matter what happens today, it will be God who has determined what shall be and we must all place our trust in Him – *Insha'Alah*."

Doyle, who was sitting next to Mahomet with Bunton opposite, grasped the Indian's arm in comfort and re-assurance, and wondered if cousin Jane had told her husband of her pregnancy.

From across the carriage Dr Bunton, whose face was hidden in shadow, spoke up. "That is very well and good, but I think the Lord might also expect us to put our best foot forward, Mr Mahomet. Doyle here has told me you are a good shot ..."

"Excellent," interrupted Doyle.

"Yes excellent shot," repeated Bunton, "but he also says that the Hardings will be providing the pistols. I was not too pleased when I heard this. Both Doyle and I think you must be able to choose first, but I think you should wait until one is proffered to you and then select the other."

"You do not think ..?" began Mahomet, surprised.

"I think nothing, sir. However I do know that you think George Harding responsible for his father's death. I put nothing beyond him or his brother."

The three men fell back into silence until Mahomet turned to Doyle and asked: "Did you lodge the papers?"

Some days previously Mahomet had spent time putting his affairs in order and had drawn up a last will and testament. This, together with the coffee house accounts, he gave to Doyle to lodge with a solicitor. The younger man nodded.

The coach slowed as it turned again, this time north towards the Hampstead Road. There had been a handful of buildings beside the main road to Hampstead for years immemorial, but it was only twenty years previously that Camden Town, named after the first Earl Camden who owned the land, became a recognisable settlement, with a number of terraces being built. The Lord Southampton inn was named after another notable landowner and had become a regular starting point for those travelling north.

The coach stopped before the inn and a stable boy ran out to attend, only to be shooed away by the coachman. It was still dark, though the first flecks of light could be seen breaking in the eastern sky. Bunton drummed his fingers on the windowsill of the coach door, adding to the tension inside the carriage.

"Are they late?" he asked, but Doyle shrugged and the men again fell into their own thoughts.

They had been waiting nearly half an hour, and dawn was most definitely beginning to break, when the coachman knocked on the roof and they looked out to see two mounted horses nearby. Doyle quickly stepped down from the coach and crossed over the road to the brothers.

"Dr Doyle," said William Harding in a stage whisper, his breath creating a mist in the cold morning air. "Please follow for about a mile further north. There you will have to leave the coach and follow on foot into a field I have chosen for the duel."

Mahomet's seconder quickly glanced to Sir George Harding but could see little: Harding had drawn up his coat collar to hide his face. Doyle instructed the coachman to follow the horses and, as he got back into the coach, noticed a small pony and trap making its way up the road. The Hardings had left it late and before long they would be exposed to prying eyes. North of Camden Town the land opened into countryside, and they passed a sign pointing to a lane that said "Chalk Farm". Some ten minutes later the coach stopped again, the knock on the roof announcing they had arrived. They stepped down into the grey light of dawn. The sky was clear of cloud and the sun would rise in less than half an hour. They saw the Harding brothers take a bridle track off the main road and followed. Five minutes later they stood in a harvested but unploughed field, surrounded by thick woodland. To the west and just above the tree line stood Primrose and Bloody hills, a popular viewing point from which to survey the British capital and, it seemed, they could also watch a duel taking place to the east should anyone be there at this early hour. It was not the most secluded of places.

"This is very open," said Doyle as William Harding dismounted and started to untie the pistol case from the saddle.

"It will do," came the response, "we will be only a few minutes. There are few places of complete privacy in London. Now, shall we?"

The Harding brothers, Mahomet, Doyle and Bunton gathered together in the centre of the field. Sir George Harding was particularly aggrieved that his opponent had two seconders: surely a baronet should have a larger retinue than a coffee house proprietor? William Harding presented the pistol case to the men and, opening it, proffered the gun with the rifled barrel to Mahomet.

"He will have the other," interrupted Bunton, taking William Harding aback.

"But they are both the same sir," he countered angrily, "in every way."

"Then it will not matter if he has the other," supported Doyle. "Rule 16 clearly states that the challenged shall have the right to choose his own weapon. You decided on these pistols Harding without our agreement, so we will select which one to fire."

Mahomet, meanwhile, was looking blankly at the gun case.

"This is most irregular, sir," William was continuing, pushing his chosen pistol towards Mahomet's hand. "Surely it should be for the injured party to chose the weapons ..."

"Nonsense!" barked Bunton. "Our man will not have that one!"

Mahomet, now aware of the argument, was about to intervene when Sir George spoke on his behalf. "For Heaven's sake, William, it does not matter. They are both the same. Give them their choice!"

Reluctantly the younger brother handed over the pistol still in the case. As ever, events were not happening according to William Harding's plan, which was flimsy at best. He was hoping that a superior shot would kill, or at least maim, his brother. So long as he could take away an injured party, he was quite prepared to finish George off back at the house, and he knew exactly how this could be achieved and had made preparations. Yet he had been so concerned with delivering his brother to the duelling field that he had not considered what would happen if George emerged victorious. Now, even though he might not be the better shot, he did hold the better weapon.

While Bunton stood to the centre of the field, the Harding brothers took twenty paces west while Mahomet and Doyle took the same east. The four men then stood and faced each other and the doctor walked off to the side, making sure he was a good distance from the line of fire. William Harding and Doyle also retired, while Mahomet and George Harding cocked their guns but continued to hold them in an upright position.

From across the field William Harding shouted to Mahomet. "Do you sir, apologise and take back the words you spoke recently?"

Mahomet had now composed himself for the challenge. "I cannot take back words I have not spoken," he replied.

This confused George Harding but it was his brother who quickly spoke again. "As you deny the charge then my brother shall take first aim. George, in your good time discharge your weapon."

For Mahomet the next few seconds seemed like a lifetime. He watched as Harding pointed the pistol towards him. For the briefest of moments he thought Harding had changed his mind then he heard the discharge and instinctively closed his eyes. The next sound was Doyle's voice.

"Are you unharmed Sake Mahomet?" he cried.

Mahomet opened his eyes to see George Harding standing forty yards away with the pistol hanging limply at his side.

"Sake Mahomet, are you hit?" cried Doyle again and this time, choking back an overwhelming feeling of relief, the Indian replied, "No! No Decimus, I am not injured."

William Harding was the quickest to take up on these words. "My brother has fired, now it is your turn Mahomet. Doyle, instruct you man!"

Doyle paused, hardly able to utter the words. "Sake Mahomet, you know what you must do."

Mahomet turned to look at the young Irishman and smiled. He had no intention of shooting George Harding but knew he had to discharge the weapon in accordance with custom and do so in a way which did not imply a feint. He nodded to Doyle, turned back to the baronet who had so contemptuously struck him a few weeks ago, and called: "Do you withdraw your challenge, sir?"

George Harding had been struck dumb since firing the pistol, so shocked was he at his own action. William, sensing a change in mood on the field following his brother's miss, answered for him. "He does not and cannot sir! This is about family honour! Continue with the challenge!"

Mahomet sighed to himself: they were determined to play this out. He held the already cocked pistol towards George Harding but sufficiently to one side to clearly miss. Then, as he began to squeeze the trigger, a number of things happened. From the corner of his eye he could see a shape, which quickly transformed into Jane Mahomet, running from the cover of the trees towards him and shouting his name. This shocked him sufficiently to jolt his arm in discharging the weapon as he turned his head towards his wife. Almost immediately he heard what he thought was another shot, and a man's cry from across the field. And as he looked back towards his opponent he saw a body prostrate on the ground.

Chapter 15

Richmond Park, Late October 1811.

LORD Sidmouth leaned forward in his chair and re-read the report in *The Times*:

> BOW STREET:– At an examination into the recent death of SIR GEORGE HARDING BART., the magistrate directed that Sir George died from of a shooting accident, the result of an unfortunate series of events involving gentlemen at sport in fields close to the Hampstead Road.
>
> THE FACTS:– Sir George was a member of a small party, which included his brother (now Sir) William Harding, taking part in the shooting of small fowl and game. During the course of the morning Sir George appeared in the line of another gun about to discharge with the most unfortunate consequences. Albeit the party included a senior registrar of one of London's medical schools, little could be done and Sir George died from his wounds shortly afterwards. The registrar attested to the accidental nature of the incident. Sir George is to be interred at St Mary-le-Bone church to rest along side his beloved mother and recently deceased father, the late SIR JOSIAH HARDING BART.

The Deputy Ranger of Richmond Park sat back again considering the report. When he first read it he immediately summoned William Rufus to attend on him, and now the young man sat opposite.

"Well," sighed Sidmouth, "this seems to conclude the matter. And you are sure he was responsible for his father's death?"

"As much as I can be without a confession, my lord. Having so much gambling debt, to the extent that he was about to be black-balled from his club, he was tempted with the proposal from the canal company to buy the estate and moved against his father."

Rufus might have added that at their last meeting his lordship had all but given instruction for the removal of George Harding from society. This wish had been executed with the minimum of fuss thanks to the duel, yet he suspected his lordship might not have appreciated such a literal interpretation of his words. As it stood, Lord Sidmouth was still unsure and looked hard at his instrument of truth.

"So you say sir, so you say. And are you confident there was no other party involved? Perhaps gentlemen concerned with the Prince Regent's proposals for Mary-le-Bone park?"

"I am most decided, my lord, that Harding was alone in this, along with the servant at the coffee house. As I have just mentioned, he had a great number of debts. He was most contrary with money."

Sidmouth nodded. He quite understood the dissolute nature of the deceased man: there were far too many of them in London, and most were encouraged by the behaviour of the royal princes. But his lordship was still unhappy with the outcome. "This is all very arbitrary, I must say. You have witnessed the death of the poisoner and now we are made aware of the death of his master in this duel. The rule of law is most important and it would have been far better for these two men to have been served with justice, even if this were at the end of a rope outside Newgate."

"If you feel I should have intervened in the duel ..."

"No sir, no," interrupted Sidmouth, anxious not to dishearten his valued agent. "Please do not mind my thoughts. I am dissatisfied that our quarry escaped justice, that is all. You have acted in a most exemplary fashion, for which your honoured late father would be proud. No, both killers received justice, albeit summary. Yet death seems to have stalked this matter: first the father, then the servant, then the son. Three deaths is quite a count."

Rufus shook his head. "Harding's was most unfortunate, my lord, but hardly unexpected. The Indian, I believe, is a fine shot while George Harding was as useless with a gun as he was at the gaming table. It takes courage to both stand and shoot and then stand and be shot at. But if you issue a challenge then those are the consequences."

"Gentlemen duel too readily," said Sidmouth shaking his head, "and it does not help when politicians do not lead by example. You may have heard of the furore some time ago with your Vice-President, the man named Burr, who killed his former Secretary to the Treasury. Of course we can expect this from your fellow Americans, but gentlemen in this country should restrain themselves. When Castlereagh wounded Canning in the leg on Putney Heath two years ago ..." Sidmouth paused, as if the memory still overwhelmed him. "Two of the King's Cabinet fighting in such a way, I would never have imagined it! The Minister for War and the Foreign Secretary! I'm afraid it has opened the floodgates to such nonsense. Look at Harding. A shooting accident, bah! I hope the magistrate admonished the Indian but I see the matter has been taken no further. I believe the two seconders were doctors and stood for him at this informal inquest. Still, Cochrane will be satisfied when I advise him. Harding's death concludes the threat to his freemasons, and as for this Indian ... well, let us say he has been excessively fortunate."

"And the matter is concluded, my lord?"

Sidmouth paused in thought and then nodded. "Yes, for you this chapter is closed. But now I have two other matters. First, there are disturbing reports of workers in the county of Nottinghamshire damaging machines in their care – cotton and wool looms and the like. These are isolated incidents they say, but I am wary. I wish you to travel north and bring back your own report. I will provide letters of introduction to the Lord Lieutenant of the county and the like, and even speak to the troublesome workers if you think fit. Perceval does not understand that prompt force is the only answer to such sedition. He says the country suffers great hardship because the war with the French depresses trade and causes distress in the nation, but I suspect he would like to reach an agreement with Bonaparte if he were allowed. I sometimes question whether the Prime Minister is not a greater danger to the country than the French corporal. Perceval has asked me yet again to serve in government but I cannot ... and will not until he is gone from power."

The Deputy Ranger was distracted by the machinations of government and stopped speaking, though William Rufus had been hanging on his every word, especially those mentioning the removal of the Prime Minister.

"And the other matter my lord?"

"What? ... Oh yes. I have received a letter from the Member for Liverpool, General Gascoyne – a good man who shares my views on Perceval. A merchant, though not an elector mind, has approached him with a grievance against the government after being locked up in Russia for some years. He made supposed threats against the King's ministers, and Gascoyne seeks my help. Either let us obtain evidence that will place the man in court for seditious comment or see if he has a just cause. The matter is confusing, but as you are journeying north I think you should also visit Liverpool and speak to Gascoyne and this man. I will ask my secretary to furnish you with the letter but do not unduly exercise yourself: it is only a small matter but one I would honour if I could."

SAKE Dean Mahomet sat in the small living room above the Hindostanee Coffee House watching his youngest, three-year-old Horatio, play on the floor with a small rag doll their servant Sarah had made. The boy was named after the *Saviour of the Nation* and had been born on the anniversary of Nelson's death, so the Mahomets considered the name highly appropriate. Horatio's doll had black needlepoint eyes and mouth, a brown jacket and even black woollen hair, and he called it "papa". Mahomet failed to see the resemblance though Jane thought her little boy highly observant. The father smiled as he watched his child play. He spent too little time with any of the children – after all it was a man's role to provide for and not nursemaid them – but secretly he looked forward to those times when both Jane and Sarah were busy in the kitchen and he was able to volunteer to sit with the baby of the family. Not that Horatio would be the baby for much longer: Jane had told him of her pregnancy soon after they returned from the duelling field.

The duel! The thought of it still made his blood run cold. How had he found himself in such a position? He remembered turning to see Jane running across the field towards him shouting "Husband! No!", and the pistol going off in his hand. When he turned back he saw the body on the ground – the body of Sir George! William Harding was looking down at his brother's body some feet from him and both Bunton and Decimus were running over to the fallen man. How had he hit him? Even now he could not believe it. He had aimed away from Sir George so the shot should have passed safely by? Yet there was his body crumpled on the earth and, shortly afterwards, Decimus standing and walking slowly over shaking his head while Bunton covered the body with his coat.

It was only after the late Sir George Harding had been lifted over the saddle of his horse and led to the coach and four, where it was placed in the body box to the rear, that Mahomet recalled hearing what he thought had been a second shot. Yet neither Decimus nor Bunton could recall such a sound, suggesting Mahomet must have heard an echo, and William Harding was so pre-occupied he would not respond to even the simplest question. He followed the carriage on his horse while Mahomet, Doyle and Bunton sat inside with Jane.

Jane! There had been another mystery. How on earth had she turned up in the field? She was as unresponsive as William, and Mahomet was in turn angry and anguished. The coachman reported that soon after they stopped and the gentlemen headed towards the duelling field, the lady appeared in a pony and trap accompanied by a gentleman, and had followed the duelling party. After the coachman heard the shots, the gentleman re-appeared without the lady and in a hurry, departing in the trap and heading north towards Hampstead. The coachman did not think this strange: after all, it was better to depart a duelling field promptly. Yet he could not make out much about the man, except that he seemed young and was dressed in a large black coachman's coat. The collar of the coat was drawn up about his face and all that could be seen was a shock of red hair stickling out from beneath the hat. William Rufus!

After they returned the dead body to the Harding mansion, Bunton headed for Bow Street magistrates to inform the authorities of the incident while Doyle and the Mahomets returned to the coffee house. Here Mahomet quizzed his wife until she finally confessed. The day before, while Doyle and Mahomet were beyond Hyde Park practicing with the pistol, the redheaded man appeared at the coffee house saying he was from the Honourable Basil Cochrane. Jane knew him to be the William Rufus of whom her husband had spoken. He wanted details of the duel which Jane agreed to supply so long as he took her with him. It was agreed that he would wait along George Street until the duelling party had left the coffee house, and as the coach left Rufus arrived in a trap and together they made their way to the Lord Southampton. They saw the coach waiting for the Hardings so held back along the road. As the brothers passed they followed and arrived at the designated place only minutes later. The redheaded man told Jane to stay nearby. She did not see George Harding take aim but heard the shot, and as they approached through the trees saw Mahomet take aim himself. She could not bear it so broke away from her escort and ran into the field to stop him. She could not confirm if the man had been armed.

On this evidence Doyle decided Mahomet could have possibly heard a second shot, and both men became convinced William Rufus was involved somehow. But why would he have shot at George Harding? When Bunton returned from the Bow Street court some time later he was not happy to learn of their suspicions. He had persuaded the magistrate, a good drinking friend, that Harding's death had been a tragic accident. Duelling deaths were still considered killings of honour by many in the judiciary and very few, if any, were prosecuted. Yet Mahomet had to submit himself before a court of inquiry and offer due abeyance, which might include the payment of a nominal sum to the Harding family for their loss. To now say that Sir George Harding died at the hands of another would cause great controversy and might find Mahomet, Doyle, Bunton and even Jane in the dock! Dr Bunton was adamant: no mention would be made of the presence of William Rufus or Jane Mahomet, and both he and Doyle would stand for Mahomet in front of the magistrate in his chambers.

And so this is what happened. Mahomet was summoned and the magistrate greatly chastised him for his part in the duel. That he had not spoken the insult in the first instant, and suspected his shot had not killed Sir George, he did not say in his defence. Instead he stood with Doyle and Bunton on either side while the magistrate accused him of all manner of things, stupidity being the mildest. Yet while he bore these words with equanimity, he found it much harder to bear the consideration that he was instructed to pay Sir George Harding – five hundred pounds! Dr Bunton advised that not to agree to this sum meant the possibility of a charge of murder, so he signed the paper presented to him. The magistrate explained this promissory note would be passed on to the newly ennobled Sir William Harding who would decide what to do with it. Outside the court Bunton advised that while the sum was far greater than he imagined, the magistrate had taken into account the killing of a gentleman of much greater standing than Mahomet. In any case, it was to be "a gesture" only. William Harding would not seek enforcement – gentlemen never did and it was very bad form to try and do so. Mahomet, however, was not so sure that Harding would stay his hand and the gesture hung over him as surely as any noose.

Mahomet was overwhelmed by the injustice, and the story of the man who had been imprisoned in Russia often came to his mind. How similar their situations were. They had both been falsely accused and sentenced: Bellingham in a Russian gaol and Mahomet forced into the charade of the duel. They were both charged with paying an unwarranted fine, and they were both "inferiors" – the Englishman in Archangel and the Indian in London. Mahomet knew this had been the real reason for the magistrate levying such a penalty. Most times Mahomet could ignore petty prejudices brought on by the colour of his skin, but in a society overwhelmingly white he sometimes wondered if certain people saw him as carrying the mark of Cain. And not only did his family have an Indian half, but the other was Irish! He often thought this to be an even greater burden in England. Yet he had also been shown great kindness by Decimus, Dr Bunton, the Honourable Basil Cochrane and, in the early days, Godfrey Evan Baker. It was gentlemen such as these who had offered friendship – even kinship – that Mahomet found most comforting and helped him bear injustice.

And what of William Rufus? Like an unlooked for ghost he had again disappeared into the mists, where Mahomet hoped he stayed. However he was determined to take the matter up with the Honourable Basil Cochrane when he finally returned from Scotland. How could his patron commission such a man? Mahomet suspected Rufus had killed Walker, and given Jane's testimony was almost certain he shot at and killed Sir George Harding. While there might have been some purpose in the former there was no justification for the latter, despite all their speculation that George Harding may have been behind Sir Josiah's poisoning. Did Rufus know otherwise? Mahomet was unsure. What was not in doubt, however, was that beneath the boyish exterior William Rufus seemed to display all the attributes of a madman. The man had felt foul when he first turned up that night at the coffee house and this had proved to be the case. The thought his wife had been alone with Rufus for some time as they journeyed to Camden Town, and that he had engaged her in such danger, made Mahomet shudder.

Then, like a revelation, it came to him. In shooting Sir George Harding Rufus had performed a summary execution on a man against whom no case could be brought. Of course! Rufus must have some evidence of George Harding's involvement in the death of his father; had he not said as much at the cricket match? They had been right all along. So Rufus allowed Mahomet take the blame for the killing, knowing nothing would come of it because of the duel. His wife's young cousin, however, was far from convinced by Mahomet's reasoning. They had no proof that Rufus had taken a shot at Sir George Harding and Jane could not even say if the man was carrying a gun. So Mahomet persuaded Doyle to accompany him once more to the duelling place in the hope it might give up some secret.

When they returned to the field north of Camden Town the farmer had still not ploughed it over. Taking long sticks, they stuck them in the ground at an approximation of where they all stood that day. It was easy enough to establish where George Harding had fallen. The ground was badly scuffed from their attempts to help the man and bind him. He had been shot in the chest and, given there had been no rain since the fateful day, the ground was still stained with his blood. Once more taking his place, Mahomet raised his arm as if to shoot and became more confident then ever that his pistol had not caused the death. He walked towards the trees where Jane had appeared. She said she had broken away from Rufus, so he must have been standing nearby. From the trees he again looked towards the sticks. From where he estimated Jane and Rufus to have been hidden there was a clear sight of both Harding brothers and Mahomet. From this standing point there was no doubt William Rufus could have easily shot at, and killed, George Harding. Yet beyond this supposition their visit had been inconclusive.

Mahomet was left to ponder these matters as he sat smiling at little Horatio, playing on the floor with his rag doll that Jane said looked like her husband. The bond between a baby and a mother was always so tight, though it was sadly common for babies to die when young or, even worse, for mothers to die during accouchement, such as Decimus' mother Frances May. That had been nearly twenty-five years ago, and Mahomet could not now properly recall her. She had very dark brown wavy hair and a beautiful aquiline face, but this was not difficult to remember as Decimus had inherited both features. He remembered first meeting her in Cork when he and Jane had eloped to Dublin and returned as a married couple. He smiled at the memory. He had been so fearful, far more so than when he faced George Harding in that field. In Cork it had been a different kind of fear: that of losing their chance of happiness if Jane's father disowned them. At the duel he feared not for himself but for his family should he be injured or killed. But thankfully he had not been harmed. It was William Harding who had suffered the loss – that of his elder brother – to leave him as the sole remaining Harding heir to whom the title could pass.

THE new Sir William Harding was far less distraught than Mahomet might have imagined at the demise of his elder brother. Indeed, he had been more than grateful it was George lying on the ground and not him, and could not but inwardly rejoice in the grim satisfaction that his plan had worked so well. The luck which started with the redheaded man accusing his brother remained with him at the duel. Lottie had run from the house towards the carriage bringing home the body of their brother and William was at first disturbed when she displayed no sign of shock or grief. Indeed, she had embraced the young Doyle in quite an indelicate manner when he stepped down from the carriage, but the other gentlemen seemed too distracted with handling George's body to notice her actions. William had quickly pulled her to one side and told her to put on a suitable act of grieving when in public.

His time since then had been taken partly with the arrangements for his brother's interment at St. Mary-le-Bone church. It had been done quickly and with the minimum of fuss. William had expected some of George's supposed friends from his club to attend the funeral, but they had not appeared. Obviously that particular supply of money had dried up for them, so it was left to William and Charlotte, together with the family servants, to grieve their loss. Not that William had any pity for a man who had brought disgrace and shame on the family. His only sadness was that George's death came too late to delay the sale of the London estate. Still, at least the proceeds would not be frittered away at the gaming tables and he would purchase an appropriate gentleman's house for him and Lottie – in close proximity to Mr Lord's latest cricketing field, of course.

Charlotte Harding had indeed been greatly relieved when she saw Doyle appear from the carriage, and was irritated by her brother's chastisement. After all, who was he to tell her how to act when he had agitated for the duel in the first place! Still, she did understand the need for caution, and soon realised that she could play the grieving sister to her advantage. Shortly after George's funeral she wrote, on black-edged notepaper, to Decimus Doyle requesting he attend on her, as she needed to hear a first-hand account of her brother's last moments. Ever the gentleman, Doyle reluctantly agreed to this request and appeared at the Harding mansion the following day. Charlotte Harding was dressed in mourning, but unlike when they first met or when she had called on him unannounced, he immediately noticed that she had slightly rouged her cheeks and lips and had gathered her hair in a bob and with ringlets falling down the back of her neck. After some polite conversation he addressed the purpose for his call.

"I must caution, Miss Harding, that I am most hesitant at speaking on such a delicate matter as your brother's death."

Charlotte Harding smiled. "My brother has spoken of it in general terms and I do not now wish to dwell on the matter. Yet I was most relieved to see you unharmed Decimus."

Now it was Doyle's cheeks that showed signs of reddening.

"Your concern, while appreciated, was misplaced Miss Harding ..."

"Lottie, please," she interrupted.

"Ah ... yes ... Miss Lottie. As I previously said, it was Sake Mahomet who duelled your brother though on a most unfortunate pretence. I am only sorry neither Dr. Bunton nor I could help Sir George when he fell."

Charlotte Harding sighed. "Never matter, Decimus, you were not to blame. George brought this upon himself, with William's help. He was too like papa, I think. And like papa he has fallen in an accidental death."

"It has indeed been a most grievous time for you Miss Harding ... Lottie. You must feel very much alone."

Yet Charlotte Harding smiled. "Alone? Why do you say so Decimus? Why William is far more of a guardian to me than either papa or George. And now I have your friendship, do I not, which is something I value above everything in the world."

Doyle felt distinctly uncomfortable.

"William says we have to leave this house," she continued, oblivious to her visitor rubbing his palms, "but we will not move far and he had promised me I am not to go to Warwickshire. So you will be able to call regularly and accompany me to assemblies. We will have such a jolly time. George's death at the hand of your relative has tied us together in so many ways, Decimus."

Doyle was at a loss what to say to his new friend. "I am glad you consider your situation so well, Miss Harding ... Lottie, though I must advise that my studies keep me from much entertaining. I hope you will not be too disappointed if you find our ... friendship ... less than constant."

Charlotte Harding looked askance. "You will not abandon me Decimus, not now, after all that has happened!"

He was taken aback. "Of course I will not abandon you Miss Har ... Lottie. I value our friendship greatly. It is just ..." He did not get the chance to finish his sentence.

"Good, then that is settled," she interrupted. "Now, I will ask for some tea and afterwards we can seek out William and you can advise him on which assemblies we should attend."

Decimus Doyle silently groaned to himself and wondered in desperation how he was going to withdraw himself from Charlotte Harding's bond of friendship.

SARAH Siddons was also in a quandry, and considered the suite of jewels laid out before her on her dressing table. It was handsome, no doubt about it, and consisted of a necklace, bracelet, earrings and brooch, made of red gold and pearls except for the brooch where diamonds framed a small cameo of herself made, she assumed, from shell. The suite had been delivered that morning from the Prince Regent's own jewellers, Rundell and Bridge on Ludgate Hill, and while there was no message she was quite confident who commissioned them. They must have cost him a small fortune. During their time together the extravagance of his gifts had increased. First a recent print of Shakespeare sonnets taken from the original 1609 publication. He had starred sonnet 18, comparing her to a summer's day, and sonnets 127 to 152, written to the "dark lady". Sarah re-read them with some amusement, especially those verses which her tutor some forty years ago had considered unsuitable for a young lady. Then came a number of items of clothing; a pair of beautifully soft kid gloves; a less than impressive though no doubt expensive bonnet from her milliner; and finally, and beautifully crafted, a reticule bag and matching parasol. Oh yes, and a swans-down tippet. If he continued in this vein she would have a completely new wardrobe, none of which would have been selected by her. She wondered who was advising him, and had questioned her maid Melissa at length though she adamantly denied any collusion. It seems if she mentioned any wish or desire when they were together, it would magically appear over the following days. Oh Decimus, she cried to herself, and recited the words of her greatest character: "I fear thy nature; it is too full o' th' milk of human kindness to catch the nearest way."

The appearance of the jewels was far more serious, and Sarah now suspected they presaged a proposal of a particular kind. She had to avoid this at all cost! Matters had gone too far. At first she had been flattered by his attention: what woman of a certain age would not be by such a handsome and innocent young man? Perhaps she had been too permissive. Within a short time he was comfortable in her bed. She thought she could control his ardour, and flattered to deceive herself that they would both tire in time. Sadly she had, and all too quickly as her age revealed itself to her. In the first days he had taken her back thirty years, and she allowed herself a freedom she had not known since the early years of her marriage. But since then she had begun to feel increasingly uncomfortable when they were together, embarrassed by the natural blemishes on her skin which, for a woman in her fifties, still retained alabaster-like qualities – but only with copious amounts of lotions and powders concocted by her favoured apothecary. A young man expected so much of a woman, or rather did not take consideration of her limited energy and resource. And why should he when for him the susceptibilities of age were still so far away.

Yet she would fain put him to one side, if only that in so doing it would have proven her brother right. John had been constant in his opposition of their friendship, and not without cause. She had decided to cancel three performances of *Macbeth* because of tiredness, though not simply because of the attentions of her young lover. She was finding the role to be a greater strain than she expected, and more than ever looked forward to next June and her final curtain call. Her brother was still convinced she would change her mind about retiring, but it was something she now longed for. But would she retire into Decimus' arms?

She tried to picture herself arriving at the Mount Doyle estate beyond Dublin – he had described it so vividly! The servants would be wondering that if here were the mother-in-law then where was the daughter? The face of her new father-in-law would be so wracked with confusion and shock; it would be worth taking her friend Thomas Lawrence to paint it in oils. She smiled to herself. No, she would not place herself up for such display, though she knew women who would be quite prepared to do so for a young beau with considerable fortune. And he did indeed have wealth if he could commission such a suite of jewels.

The only thing she could do was to return them, and quickly before he appeared at her door. She would write him a letter, being as gentle and considerate as she could. She would say her affection to him is earnest, but her first and only love is the stage, and that following the death of her husband she vowed to take no other. She would mention to him that as a young woman she played Hamlet to great acclaim. In the play, Hamlet watches a performance in which is said: "The instances that second marriage move are base respects of thrift, but none of love." These lines have stayed with her throughout her life. In truth she had been married to the stage from the day she was born – her father had managed the Warwickshire Company of Comedians, after all – and no man could ever replace the theatre, as poor Mr Siddons was to learn. She would not impose such an injustice on Decimus. He must find a wife who is happy to play the part yet she, Sarah Siddons, would cherish forever the weeks they had together and they would always remain friends. She would finish with the words of Miranda in *The Tempes*t: "I would not wish any companion in the world but you."

And so the deed was done, and Mrs Siddons wrapped the letter and suite of jewels together and sent them, in the hands of her maid, to the Soho residence of Dr Simon Bunton. Yet as the maid departed a sudden anguish overcame Britain's greatest actress, and she stood to call back her servant before pausing with yet more Shakespeare coming to her mind: "Things without all remedy should be without regard: what's done, is done."

Chapter 16

To make a Boiled Plum Pudding.
TAKE a pound of suet cut in little pieces, not too fine, a pound of currants, and a pound of raisins stoned, eight eggs, half the whites, half a nutmeg grated, and a tea-spoonful of beaten ginger, a pound of flour, a pint of milk; beat the eggs first, then half the milk, beat them together, and by degrees stir in the flour, then the suet, spice, and fruit, and as much milk as will mix it well together very thick. Boil it five hours.

The Art of Cookery Made Plain and Easy

London, Christmas 1811.

THE children loved the plum pudding which, as in many gentlemen's houses across the Kingdom, had become an essential part of the Christmas Day dinner. Jane Mahomet had risen especially early to make preparations for the day, and to be ready before the family went to church. The Mahomets prayed at the Portman Chapel in Portman Square, established thirty years previously for the residents of west London's fashionable new developments, and it fell within the jurisdiction of the parish church of St Mary-le-Bone, where most of the Harding family now lay at rest. Sake Dean Mahomet made sure his family prayed together at the Chapel at least twice a week, and the older children also attended Sunday school nearby.

In fact Sundays were regimented. The family rose early and attended the Honourable Basil Cochrane's vapour baths for their weekly ablutions. Mahomet was decided that his family should be physically cleansed before attending the ten o'clock service at the Chapel. It had taken some time to convince their maid Sarah of the value of a weekly washing of the body, but she finally fell into the family routine and, secretly, enjoyed the tingling sensation of the water vapour on her skin as she sat inside the muslin tent which covered her modesty. This year Christmas Day was on a Wednesday, and Mahomet decided his family should bring forward their Sunday bath to ensure they were at their very best to celebrate the birth of Christ. This was less than convenient for Jane, but after the angst of the past few months she had made a personal vow to support her husband as much as possible. Hence her three o'clock start.

The main celebration of Christmas was Twelfth Night, for which Jane would be making light sugared cakes, and in one of which she would place a bean. The person who ate the cake with the bean would be king – or queen – of the Hindostanee Coffee House for the day, with the others attending on them. The children loved the game, which seemed a fitting celebration of the Arrival of the Magi. Of course there had already been some excitement. William had rushed into the kitchen the previous day saying a group of comedians were performing in Portman Square. Sarah had taken the children to see, and they all came back an hour later in a highly excited state.

"The men had funny, horrible masks mama, and paper hats with coloured ribbons around them," explained nine-year-old Amelia, her second eldest. "They did the most silly things mama, and hit each other. They were very naughty men, and even frightened Henry ..." At this the three young Mahomets – William, Amelia and Henry – set off in fits of laughter, soon accompanied by young Horatio from his chair in the corner of the kitchen. Calm was only restored when their father appeared to take the older children to gather greenery for the dining room and kitchen. It was unlucky to bring foliage into the house before Christmas Eve and, looking around the kitchen at the ivy and holly garlands the children – under Sarah's supervision – had painstaking made, Jane smiled.

The children had been rewarded when Mahomet presented them with their gifts before they retired on Christmas Eve, as was accepted tradition. For Henry there was a bag of clay "marbles" (he had been using his brother's cup and ball since William had become too grown up for it); a bone hair-comb for Amelia; and a jigsaw of Britain for William. His parents had an expectation he would be apprenticed in the Post Office at Paddington next spring and hoped the puzzle would help him with the geography of the country. Horatio was considered too young for a present, though not by cousin Decimus who, as usual, spoilt the children. For William he bought a simple but effective spyglass, for Amelia the most delicate shawl, for Henry a wooden sword and shield, and baby Horatio was given wooden blocks with the alphabet and numbers painted on. He had sent them round by messenger and would by joining the family for dinner later in the day. Last year he had stayed on Christmas Eve and joined them at the Portman Chapel, and Jane wondered if the events of the Autumn had placed some distance between them: she had seen him only once since then.

Sake Dean Mahomet, however, had a much clearer understanding of Decimus' absence, so when he arrived to much acclaim by the children later in the day, Mahomet asked if they could speak privately before the Christmas meal. Settled in the small sitting room with a glass of Portuguese wine for Doyle and a cup of perfumed Chinese tea for Mahomet, the older man smiled benignly.

"Jane was beginning to voice concern for you Decimus, though I knew you to be well."

Doyle smiled weakly. "I have not been in the best of humours, Sake Mahomet, though my symptoms are not physical."

Mahomet nodded. "I suspected as much. I met with Dr Bunton earlier in the month and he said you had ... *la maladie du couer*, I think he called it. You know he speaks in rhymes and riddles and I find him hard to understand. My French is poor, but I think he meant love-sickness ... well, this is how I interpreted it given the wink of his eye." Mahomet did not add that he had been quietly relieved by the news.

Doyle groaned. He could just picture the meeting and cursed himself for confiding in his tutor. But Mahomet smiled.

"Would you like to speak of it?"

After some moments Doyle looked up at his cousin's husband. "There is little to say, Sake Mahomet, and believe me when I say I wish there were more. I have been passed over, it seems, for another."

"Another?" asked a startled Mahomet.

"No, not another suitor ... her first love."

This was grave news and Mahomet quickly became indignant for his young friend. "But no, Decimus, this cannot be. Who is this man? Her first love? Surely not ... he must be at least sixty if he is a day ..." Mahomet suddenly realised the sensitivity of his speech and paused.

"I did not say it was a man, Sake Mahomet."

The Indian was now truly confused. "But ..?"

Doyle raised another weak smile. "The stage Sake Mahomet – the theatre. She believes she can never truly give herself to a man. That it would be unfair. She says she treated her first husband abominably and would not repeat that particular performance. When she is not playing Lady Macbeth she is playing Mrs Sarah Siddons. She could not play Mrs Decimus Doyle as well."

"You had proposed?" asked Mahomet, shocked at the suggestion, but Doyle shook his head.

"I was never given the opportunity, Sake Mahomet. She wrote ending our ... friendship before such a situation could arise. Though I have to say, it never truly crossed my mind. I always assumed marriage to be for other people. I am not excessively naive, cousin, and know the disappointment with which such news would have been received by my father. We all have expectations, I think."

Mahomet shook his head. "Mrs Siddons is a very particular woman, I think. A widow who can command men's hearts, though if Dr Bunton is to be believed her marital status did not stay her hand previously. I am truly sorry Decimus, that she has caused you such distress. You do not deserve it. But if, as you say, you are not naive enough to imagine marriage, how did the subject arise?"

Doyle now managed a sincere smile. "You may ask, Sake Mahomet. I received a letter from the lady enclosing a suite of jewellery that included a very fine diamond and gold necklace, and a brooch that had a small cameo of Sarah at its centre. The letter said she could not accept the gift, which she interpreted as an overture from myself prior to a proposal of marriage. She writes a fine letter, Sake Mahomet, albeit one laced with tragedy."

"We must always give and take with care. Mahommedans believe that if you dream of being given a gift then it is a sign of joy and happiness. Except of course, if it is Allah Himself giving the gift. Then it is a mark of sickness and hardship, though you will be rewarded at the end by earning Jannah, or Paradise."

"And what do they make of a gift you do not give?"

Mahomet was confused. "I do not understand Decimus."

"I did not give the jewels, Sake Mahomet. They did not come from me. I tried to return them, but she would not see me. When I called again the house was firmly shut up. So I called at the theatre in Covent Garden and was turned away. They said the lady had departed for the country and would not return before the New Year. I approached the theatre manager Mr Kemble, who is her brother, but he simply laughed when I explained the mistake, and suggested I hold the necklace as a keepsake of what was not to be. To say the truth Sake Mahomet, I nearly attacked him, so angry did he make me with his spiteful remarks. He made it obvious he would not intercede with his sister on my behalf."

"Then where did the jewellery come from?" asked Mahomet, now captured by this Christmas tale.

Doyle sighed. "I was confused and also angry that another was sending her such gifts, so I approached the jeweller and he was horrified. They had been commissioned by the Prince Regent himself, to be presented to Sarah after she had advised him that her final performance was to be next June. It is usual of the Prince to make such gestures, I was told. They should never have been sent out, but stored until Carlton House called for them. Old Mr Rundell, the senior jeweller, was beside himself, and thanked me greatly for returning them. He would contact the lady immediately, he said, and I have been hoping that his intercession would lead to a rapprochement between us. But I have heard nothing more, and the waiting has drained my spirit. I do not even have an address to which to write, and suspect the brother will put anything I send to the theatre to one side. This is Bunton's *maladie du couer*."

Mahomet sighed, his heart going out to the young man sitting opposite. He remembered the dreadful meeting in Bunton's library, which concluded with the arrival of William Harding, and Decimus' earnest plea for support. He had not shown it then, even though the young man had subsequently stood by his side at the duel, but he would do all he could now.

"If in the New Year you wish me to represent your interests, I will gladly request of Mrs Siddons an audience, if she will grant it."

Doyle looked up, both surprised and relieved. "Thank you Sake Mahomet, thank you. That is a most gracious Christmas gift, and one I will take under advisement. I need just an hour with her, to hear from her own lips the same words she wrote in the letter. If you can help me secure this ... though perhaps it would be better to call on your help with another lady."

"Another!" cried Mahomet.

Doyle nodded. "Charlotte Harding. She seems to have adopted me. I have been pressed down with daily missives from her describing the most intimate details of her life, how William Harding treats her and how deeply she holds my friendship, as she calls it."

"My, this is a turn of events," exclaimed Mahomet. "And are you good friends with the young lady Decimus?"

Doyle blushed. "At first I did not wish to upset her and had great sympathy with her plight. After all, Sake Mahomet, she had just lost her father and elder brother in most contrary circumstances.'

Now it was Mahomet's turn to wince. "Do not remind me Decimus!"

"I am sorry Sake Mahomet. She persuaded her brother to take her to an assembly and insisted I accompany them. It was her first, and I felt duty bound to do so, although I should never have agreed to it. She should have still been in mourning for her father and brother, and we most certainly should not have danced. Yet if I danced with her once that evening I must have danced with her ten times. I made a very grave mistake but she can be very persistent. Then there was a ball last week but I was able to make my excuses. But no matter how often I decline her requests to call the daily letters still come. Bunton's housekeeper finds it all most amusing."

"If I recall correctly then Miss Harding must be, what, sixteen or seventeen, and has lived a very sheltered life. You should not be surprised if you are the object of her affections."

"But I have not encouraged them Sake Mahomet!"

"That is beside the point Decimus. But you are right to be cautious, and I have to say that the closer you are to the Hardings, both brother and sister, then the less likely it might be that William Harding will try to collect on that promissory note. I am sorry if this is selfish, Decimus. If you must let the lady down, please do it gently."

Doyle smiled for the first time. "The irony of it, Sake Mahomet. The love of my life does not want me and I do not want to be the love of another's life!"

"Oh what a tangled web we weave when first we practice to deceive!"

"Pardon, Sake Mahomet?"

"Oh, do not mind me, Decimus. It is from a poem by Walter Scott. Jane's father sent her a book, *The Lady of the Lake*, by the Scotsman. She has now become a fervent fan and reads out passages of his work when we retire. We were both taken by that line from one of his poetic works. It sums up, I fear, what has happened to us over the past few months. But I am sure better times now lie ahead. And speaking of Jane, we had better return to the family or she will be sending William to look for us. Come Decimus," he said, reaching for the young man's arm and squeezing it gently, "and Merry Christmas."

London, New Year's Day 1812.

SPENCER Perceval considered himself to be a loving man. He doted on his children – Jane, Frances, Maria, Spencer, Frederick, Henry, Dudley, Isabella, John, Louisa, Frederica and Earnest – yes, he even got them in the right order, and nor did he forget Little Charles, who died a few weeks after being born. And he loved his wife Jane. He and his elder brother Charles had rented a house in Charlton while studying at Lincoln's Inn, and the brothers fell in love with the Wilson sisters Jane and Margaretta. Yet while the ladies' father, Sir Thomas, agreed to Charles marrying Margaretta – his brother had just succeeded to the tile of Lord Arden, after all – Spencer, an impecunious barrister, was told to wait until Jane came of age. Yet when she reached her majority Spencer's career was still not prospering, so the couple eloped to East Grinstead, before setting up home above a carpet shop in London's Bedford Row.

And twenty years later they were still living above the shop – at the home provided for him by his latest employer – the King, or rather the Prince Regent. Number 10 Downing Street was a ramshackle place, built by the miser George Downing in the 1680s. To maximize profit, the terraced houses were cheaply built, with their foundations on boggy ground, and the houses suffered continually from damp. Robert Walpole had moved in as the King's first minister eighty years ago, and since then most Prime Ministers had used the house, though recently not many had lived there, preferring their own London residences and using Number 10 as an office. Sadly for the Percevals they enjoyed no such luxury, so moved in *en masse*. Perceval preferred to keep his formal office in the Treasury building located behind the house and overlooking the parade ground of the King's Horse Guards. Yet he did use for business the main room on the ground floor which had been extended by William Pitt some fourteen years ago to provide for Cabinet and government meetings.

It was in here that the Prime Minister now sat with an unexpected guest. Perceval also considered himself to be a generous man, to his family and especially to his political colleagues. Indeed this generosity extended to his master the Prince Regent, whose bickering with and personal dislike of ministers meant keeping the government together was a constant feat. Now Perceval's generosity was extended to Lord Sidmouth, the man who had given him his first position in government ten years previously. Yet they had not always agreed, especially on foreign policy, and Perceval was relieved when his close and dear friend Mr Pitt had ousted Sidmouth from government. That was 1804, and within two years Pitt had died tragically young. Perceval had been an emblem bearer at Pitt's funeral, and subsequently stood down from government until asked to become Chancellor of the Exchequer. Now, as Prime Minister as well as Chancellor, he had more sympathy but less time for the gentleman sitting at the Cabinet table, whom he had invited to re-join the government without success.

"So, sir, this is an unexpected but not unwelcome call. I know you would not ask for my time without great cause."

The older man opposite nodded. He had set out from his home in Richmond Park early that morning after considering the latest report he had received from the north.

"I thought it wise to come and speak with you as soon as the matters at issue were brought to me."

The visitor looked down at some papers he held and Perceval groaned to himself. This looked like becoming a drawn out affair unless he could head the man off.

"If it is a report I should consider then perhaps it would be best if I take your papers and read through them at leisure," he offered.

The older man looked up. "Do not concern yourself sir, I will be brief. You will know, of course, of the troubles experienced by local magistrates and the militia in Nottinghamshire?"

Perceval nodded. "You have spoken on this before. They are but isolated incidents brought about by the price of grain and the general economic malaise."

"Quite," retorted the older politician, "but I still decided to dispatch my man ..."

"Which man?'

"No matter. He journeyed north to Nottingham and has now returned with his report. We know that in March letters were sent to owners of lace and hosiery factories in Nottingham in the name of a General Ned Ludd and his Army of Redressers, complaining of wage reductions and the use of non-apprenticed workmen. An estimated two hundred stocking frames were destroyed."

"As you say I know this my lord. We offered £50 to anyone giving information on any person wickedly breaking these frames."

"And were you successful?"

Perceval shook his head. "There were few suspects, and it was too difficult to prove. Yet the Nottingham magistrates enrolled four hundred special constables at great expense and now the incidents have all but ceased."

"Have they sir? It is my contention that far from quelling the disorder, the Nottingham magistrates have pushed their troubles elsewhere. There are seditious noises coming from mills in Derbyshire, the West Riding of Yorkshire and Lancashire."

Perceval sighed. It was going to be a long meeting. "Machine-breaking is not new sir, as you well know. This Ned Ludd, in whose name the March letters were sent, is known to be one Edward Ludlam, who broke two stocking frames in Leicester thirty years ago. Since then, whenever frames are damaged people say Ned Ludd did it. It is folklore and the like. You see sir, I am fully conversant with the problem, but it is not a major question of sedition. I hope you will concede to me on this matter. Remember, I was junior counsel for the Crown in the trial of Thomas Paine, and led in the case of John Binns. I will have no brook with seditious matter."

But the visitor was far from satisfied. "Yet you have presided, sir, over the most disadvantageous of governments. This all started with the Slave Trade Act, mark my words, and you were the instrument of the reformists in that aggrieved matter. Now every man jack of them sees how they can influence, even change, the policy of the nation by agitation and challenge."

"Let us not relive old battles Sidmouth, and your evaluation of our ills is out of step with the opposition. The Whigs would have it that the Orders of Council I introduced, restricting trade with the French and which our ships so expertly enforce, to be the reason for unrest and economic despair. They say the Orders will bring us into conflict with America. But it is neither the lack of trade in slaves nor the boarding of ships on the High Seas that is to blame for our current despair, but this continuing Continental war that drains us so. The country is depressed sir – economically, physically and emotionally – and yet it is our duty to see it through to better times."

Lord Sidmouth was not swayed by Perceval's oratory. "We would do our duty better if we looked to the law regarding these machine-breakers, sir. You cannot fight a war abroad if the enemy within defeats you first. They do not call themselves the Army of Redressers for nothing."

"Then what would you have us do? We have the Riot Act, and there are laws on the book which provide remedies for machine breaking ..."

"They are from the King's father and grandfather's time!" interrupted Lord Sidmouth, now agitated. "You know as well as I that it is difficult to lead juries to convict on such old law. The seditionists must see the government act decisively if they are to desist."

"So what would you suggest?"

"A law against frame-breaking punishable by death."

"And am I to instruct a new Judge Jeffries to ride through the land dispensing this justice?"

"Of course not. The courts are suitably disposed to administer such a law. But you must bring this before the Prince and Cabinet in a timely manner and then before Parliament. This is a cautionary measure. And with so many men under arms and resting idle in the southern ports, it would be wise to send a few detachments north. Our greatest danger does not come from across the Channel sir, but from the streets of our northern mill towns. Men need to know their station in life, and that disturbing the King's Peace will not be tolerated. And I am far from alone in recommending this."

Both men sat in silence for some time, and from beyond the Cabinet room door the high-pitched voices of the Perceval ladies could be heard in distant conversation. It was New Year, after all, and a certain frisson ran through the old house.

"Very well," said Perceval at last, seeing the persuasive nature of his visitor's warning. "I raise the matter and request further reports from the counties in dispute."

Sidmouth nodded in satisfaction.

"I trust Lady Sidmouth is well? And your boys?"

The old man continued to nod.

"Well," concluded Perceval, "if that is all I must attend ..."

"There is one other matter," interrupted the Deputy Ranger. "I have been requested by General Gascoyne ..."

"That man!" the Prime Minister exclaimed. "Do not mention his name in my presence."

"He is a good Tory, Perceval."

"He is in the pay of the slavers."

"He represents his electors."

Perceval sighed. "What of him?"

"There is a merchant in Liverpool, an unsuccessful one by the name of Bellingham, who was detained in Russia for several years and has a grievance against the government. In private he speaks against ministers, offering oblique threats and the like."

"Then he will not be the only one, my lord. But what of this? Should we hang him as well?"

"Gascoyne considers the man may have a case but no-one here will listen."

"Then the general allies himself to another lost cause as usual. It happens this man has attended on my offices and I have been advised of his claim. And you know better than most Sidmouth," Perceval continued, throwing the Deputy Ranger's words back at him, "that we cannot entertain such nonsense. His case rests against the Russian Emperor. The King's ambassadors are not servants of every commercial interest that may pass through the borders of the country to which they are accredited. My only advice to Mr Bellingham is to seek new counsel."

London, Twelfth Night 1812.

IT was their housemaid Sarah who discovered the bean in the cakes Jane Mahomet had made, and both the head of the household and his wife thought this entirely appropriate. The children would be made to attend on their part-time nurse for the rest of the day and, it was hoped, this would be a suitable lesson in humility. In truth it would amount to no more than Sarah resting, her feet raised by a small footstool, in the upstairs sitting room for an hour or so while William, Amelia and Henry brought tea and cake and sat with her in respectful silence. After that hour Sarah would put away her needlepoint and return to work in the kitchen, yet still in very good humour at being chosen. And for once her presence in the kitchen was much appreciated by her mistress, as custom in the coffee house was far busier than usual given the feast day.

It was early evening, and the number of patrons was lessening, when Mahomet was surprised to welcome a gaunt-looking gentleman to the coffee house.

"Mr Bellingham sir, what an unexpected but most welcome honour. Please be seated and I will attend on you presently."

Mahomet was indeed pleased to see the man who occupied his thoughts so regularly and, it seemed, in good heart. Bellingham nodded to his host and settled himself at a small corner table, sinking back into the large wicker chair. It was some minutes before Mahomet could attend on his table.

"The coffee house is well frequented today Mr Mahomet," remarked his guest.

The Indian bowed. "It is Twelfth Night sir, as I wish it were every day. Still, we must make merry when we can. Now, what can I tempt you with? My wife has created a very fine beef-steak pie, or perhaps you will favour one of our curried dishes?"

Bellingham was in a far more amenable mood than when he last called at the coffee house, and decided on the curried chicken accompanied by a draught of ale. Then, settling back, he took in his surroundings. There were a number of gentlemen in groups of three and four seated in relaxed conversation, with some partaking of the coffee house's hookahs. Mr Mahomet was moving between the tables and then disappearing behind a wicker screen, presumably to the kitchen as he re-emerged with salvers and cloched plates of food, as well as trays of coffee cups, tea pots and vessels for holding stronger drink. The coffee house was commendably busy, and Bellingham was comforted that Mr Mahomet was displaying industry and commerce. He had taken to the man when they first met, with the Indian showing a great kindness and sympathy – not something to which Bellingham was used. After several more minutes Mahomet appeared with Bellingham's order.

"I am sorry for the delay sir, but as you can see we are busy. Yet I think there may be an opportunity for me to join you once you have eaten, if you would permit."

Bellingham replied that there would be nothing better than to have

Mahomet's company and the host, bowing, disappeared once more to attend on his other guests. Yet it was nearly an hour later when he finally returned to Bellingham's table and, bowing once more, sat down.

"So Mr Bellingham," he began, "I am greatly pleased to see you again, and I think in much better humour than when last we met."

Bellingham nodded. "I arrived from Liverpool some days ago and will now stay in London until my matter is concluded. I have taken lodgings in New Millman Street, near to the Foundling Hospital at Coram Fields. Today I decided to walk to the other end of Oxford Street and remembered your past kindness."

Mahomet smiled. "And you have prospects sir, for the matter you last discussed?"

The Liverpool merchant shrugged. "Nothing is determined, Mr Mahomet. I have heard no more from the government or Mr Perceval. And General Gascoyne, the Member for Liverpool, is as deceptive as ever. But yes, I am hopeful of a resolution."

"How so sir?"

"Because I now have the support of my fellow merchants. I do not think to flatter myself, Mr Mahomet, if I say I am very well known in Liverpool, and could get the signatures of the whole town in support of my petition. And I value the opinion of one young gentleman in particular. Some weeks ago I was introduced by General Gascoyne to a man whose father traded with slavers working out of the Old Dock in Liverpool. As with many merchants in the Americas, he has suffered excessively by Parliament restricting his family trade, and has given me invaluable advice in pursuit of my cause."

"Well this is good news sir," cautioned Mahomet, "although you must know that I have no patience for men who trade in others, and am wholly in agreement with the campaigns of Mr Wilberforce and the like."

Bellingham looked surprised. "I cannot comment on the trade sir. As you know, while such debate was raging here I was suffering in one of the Tsar's gaols thanks to the British ambassador Lord Gower. Still ... the gentleman I met in Liverpool who is now advising me says this ministry of

Mr Perceval's is the most venal and corrupt yet devised and that I should seek my remedy through the courts. I have therefore submitted a petition to the police magistrates at Bow Street, in the expectation they will use their powers to solicit these ministers to let what is right and proper to be done."

Mention of the magistrates at Bow Street sent a cold shiver down the spine of Mahomet, and brought to mind yet again the death of Sir George Harding and the five hundred pound gesture he was ordered to pay. Nor was he certain of the advice Bellingham had been given.

"Are you sure, sir, that the magistrates have power to so order the government? In my experience it is the King's ministers who instruct the courts."

But Bellingham was adamant. "Yet they are the King's judges, Mr Mahomet, and have great powers. You may recall that I had recourse to the courts when so grievously held in Archangel. If a Russian judge can stand against the Tsar's governor in that city, then think how much greater the power of judges must be in this country."

Mahomet, who had such close experience of the Bow Street magistrates, thought his friend's confidence misplaced.

"And your new supporter? He is confident in such an action?"

"Most decidedly," nodded Bellingham.

"In which case I wish you every fortune, and you are most welcome here during your stay." Mahomet paused. "Though sadly the coffee house is rarely so popular as you see it today."

Bellingham looked at Mahomet. "You business is suffering?"

Reluctantly Mahomet nodded. While he had, just, been able to pay the rent, this had been at the expense of other debtors and the balancing act was becoming ever trickier. Slowly he described to Bellingham his problems and the fear that he would have to close the coffee house. Perhaps it was the stranger's own problems that allowed Mahomet to confess so much, from the size of his debts to a confused recounting of the poisoning of Sir Josiah Harding and the duel and death of Sir George. It seems to pour from him in a continuous flow. At the end he felt a sense of relief that at last someone else knew of his troubles.

"Well this is a great sadness, Mr Mahomet," replied Bellingham at last. "And you say this Walker arrived with a letter of recommendation from your former kitchen porter. So what does he have to say for himself?"

"Who? Samuel? Why, I have not asked him. He is far away on the High Seas defending the Realm ... At least, I think he is."

Bellingham dropped his voice to a whisper. "But you do not just go and recommend a stranger from the street. Surely the boy knows something of the man who poisoned the curry?"

Mahomet stared at Bellingham open eyed. Why had he not thought to contact Samuel before? He just assumed the boy had set sail and could not be contacted, yet Bellingham advised that the Admiralty would know what ship he was on and where he was. Letters were sent to captains and the like, so it may be possible to contact him, Bellingham continued.

"I consider you to be a man of great vision Mr Mahomet. You must not allow the coffee house to close for want of business. If only the affluent gentlemen of this city could be brought here, I am sure they would return time and again. No Mr Mahomet, do not despair." Then Bellingham had an idea. "I will invest in the coffee house, sir, as soon as my claim is settled with the government. And it will be settled, Mr Mahomet, I am sure of it. Would you consider me as a worthy partner?"

Mahomet was taken aback. "Why Mr Bellingham, I did not recount my woes to attract your money ..."

"I know you did not, Mr Mahomet. It is I who shows conceit in asking to be brought in as a partner ... but my offer still stands. Do you think you could consider it? I know of no other gentleman to whom I would wish to attach my suit. By joining our experiences of the world, Mr Mahomet, we can make quite a mark. What do you say?"

Mahomet was now embarrassed. "I will most certainly take your proposal under advisement, Mr Bellingham. It is a most generous and gracious offer."

Bellingham was now running ahead with plans. "I will move my family to lodgings close-by, sir, and Mrs Bellingham will be able to help in the kitchens. She had to manage in St Peterburgh for nigh on a year, alone and with our babe at her breast. She is a most able woman and I am sure Mrs

Mahomet will find her agreeable. Why this is a most advantageous meeting, Mr Mahomet! As soon as my case is settled I will have the means to lead your business onward. Most advantageous!"

After a few more minutes of polite conversation, Mahomet excused himself to attend on others and by the time he returned to the table Bellingham had departed, leaving sufficient coins to cover his meal and a bit more besides. Mahomet smiled. What to make of Mr Bellingham, the coffee house owner thought, as he began clearing the dining room prior to closing for the evening. He was so sincere in his contention that the courts would be able to help him and then he would help the Hindostanee Coffee House. People often went to court for justice, Mahomet knew, even though all they were ever served with was a portion of the law. Still, he had shown the foresight to ask why Mahomet had not contacted Samuel and establish why he had recommended Walker, a matter he would now act on. And even though he feared Mr Bellingham had raised his expectations too high he wished him well and, who knows, might just become his new business partner.

Some time later Mahomet had closed the main door to the coffee house and was beginning to extinguish the lamps when there came a loud knocking which made him jump. He quickly walked over to the door. Who could this be? Probably a guest who had left something behind, he thought, but recalling the first visit of William Rufus, he decided to call through the door rather than open it.

"Yes! Can I help you?"

"Is that Mr Mahomet?" came the reply.

"Yes."

"Sir, I have some papers for you."

Curious, Mahomet slowly opened the door but not before reaching for a walking stick with a silvered head he kept behind it since the visit of Mr Rufus. A man in a tall hat looking suitably official confronted him.

"Mr Mahomet sir?" he asked again and the Indian reluctantly nodded with a sense of great foreboding.

"Good."

And with that he took from his outside pocket papers tied together with a red tape and sealed. These he handed over.

"This is a summons sir, for you to report to Westminster's Great Hall in the case of *Harding -v- Mahomet*."

Chapter 17

London, Winter 1812.

THE Honourable Basil Cochrane had returned from his prolonged sojourn to North Britain, the term used in polite London society to refer to Scotland since the Jacobite Rebellion some seventy years earlier. Indeed since Bonnie Prince Charlie steps had been taken to remove the Scots identity entirely, including the 1746 Dress Act that for thirty-six years banned the wearing of tartan except for the Highland regiments of the British army. Yet of far more effect in diminishing Scotland had been the Year of Sheep – 1792, when Highlanders who had been cleared from their lands had decided they could no longer survive by fishing in the coastal villages to which they had been moved. They longed to return to their sheep, so headed in their thousands to the Carolinas and Nova Scotia of the Americas, thus achieving by themselves the depletion of the Highlands that the London government had worked so long to achieve.

In Scotland Cochrane had been the houseguest of his elder brother Archibald, the 9th Earl of Dundonald, who had succeeded their father thirty years previously. Yet while he inherited the title, there was little money. So Archibald had used the family estate as collateral to develop his invention of a coal tar, which he hoped would be used by the Royal Navy to seal the hulls of its ships and make them stay much longer in the water. Needless to say he did not anticipate the objection of the powerful naval shipyards, which relied as much on repairs for their income as the building of new ships. So the Navy was steered away from Archibald's coal tar, and his patent expired without him making any money. His younger brother Basil, however, was a Nabob of fabulous wealth and so a welcome visitor to the family home. Moreover Basil was unmarried, and had nominated his nephew Thomas, Archibald's eldest son, as his heir.

And it was this Thomas Cochrane who delayed Basil's return to London. After a glittering naval career as captain of *HMS Speedy*, *HMS Pallas* and

HMS Imperieuse, Thomas was made a Companion of the Most Honourable Military Order of the Bath. He then turned his hand to politics, and as the Member for Westminster allied himself to radicals such as Sir Francis Burdett. In 1810 Burdett was charged with libelling the House of Commons, and an arrest warrant was issued. Cochrane helped barricade his friend in a house in Piccadilly, and also gathered a mob in its defence. But when Burdett realised that Thomas was about to use similar military tactics to those he deployed in the Royal Navy, and which could lead to numerous deaths among the arresting officers, he decided to hand himself in. Cochrane, however, remained a firm favourite with the London mob, if not with his fellow MPs.

Yet it was not Thomas' political antics that caused the Honourable Basil Cochrane to delay, but news that his nephew intended to marry one Katherine Barnes – sweet Kitty – a girl twenty years Thomas' junior. She was an orphan with no family background and, more importantly, no money. Basil Cochrane was horrified that the next Countess Dundonald would not bring with her an income to repair the damage caused by his brother's speculation, and in a heated argument with his nephew over Christmas had warned that unless Katherine was put to one side, Basil would disinherit him.

Nor was the situation with his nephew Basil Cochrane's only concern while he was in Scotland. News reached him of the death of Sir George Harding, son of his Brother in the Ancients the late Sir Josiah. It seemed the younger Harding had gone and got himself killed in a duel, and Cochrane was sorely vexed. That was until a letter, by King's Messenger, reached him from the Deputy Ranger of Richmond Park. Lord Sidmouth advised in no uncertain terms that it was Sir George who had been responsible for his father's death, and while the duel had been unfortunate it brought to a close their investigation into the matter, distasteful as it was.

And so the affairs of the Harding family were firmly placed to one side, that was until his return to Portman Square in mid January when he was advised that Sake Dean Mahomet had been requesting an urgent audience for some time. The Indian had been summoned and now sat before

Cochrane in the elegant first-floor library relating a remarkable story of defamation, duels and death.

"This is most disconcerting," is all Cochrane could say as Mahomet finished. "I heard of Harding's death in the duel but not for one moment could I have conceived that anyone associated to myself could have been involved."

"It is more than that, sir." Mahomet lamented. "William Harding has now petitioned the Court of Chancery for the payment of the five hundred pounds the magistrate ordered. If I cannot pay, he asks the court to appoint a bankruptcy commissioner to take control of my assets and discharge my debts. I am to be ruined."

Cochrane was decidedly uncomfortable. "But what can I do Mahomet. You said yourself that you signed that paper at Bow Street recognising your liability ... a most inauspicious thing to do, might I add."

"I was advised it was a gesture, a conclusion of the matter and that it was something no gentleman would ever call on. To do otherwise might have implicated the others and Jane."

"Then William Harding is certainly no gentleman. But again I ask you, what can I do? Did you not accept the challenge and present yourself at the duel? And did not George Harding die?"

"Not by my hand!"

"So you say."

There was silence for some moments as Cochrane stared out of a large sash window into the square below, while Mahomet looked down to the expansive Turkish rug on the floor that was probably worth far more than the entirety of the coffee house.

"Rufus!" Mahomet said at last, "William Rufus! Why did you instruct him sir? He is the cause of all my ills."

Cochrane was lost for words. He had been uncomfortable with the redheaded man when introduced to him by Lord Sidmouth. Yet he could not tell Mahomet that he was a government spy or the like, nor the real reason why he had been commissioned. The Nabob was unhappy at withholding these facts, but reasoned to himself it was most necessary.

"I do not know of whom you speak Mahomet," he lied.

The coffee house owner was taken aback. "But he said he came from you sir, and disclosed much knowledge of the poisoning. Do you not know him?"

Cochrane reluctantly shook his head.

"Then who is he?"

Cochrane continued to shake his head. "I do not know. Where can we find this man?" he asked, throwing the emphasis back to his former servant.

"I do not know, sir, that is why I came to you. Rufus said he was acting on your behalf."

"Then he lied." Cochrane now squirmed in his chair. "I am deeply sorry Mahomet, but unless you can bring this Rufus forth nothing can be proven beyond the bare facts."

"But I provided him with details of our search for Walker and he was present at the duel, as my Jane will attest. If nothing else, it was he who spoke the words to William Harding at the cricket match and for which I was blamed."

"But you failed to counter that impression at the time. Why did you not write to me before the duel? Perhaps I could have interceded on your behalf. I knew Josiah Harding well and might have prevailed upon the sons. I am not without influence and this matter could have been settled amicably."

"Then perhaps you could speak to the court on my behalf," Mahomet pleaded, now wringing his hands, "and explain my peculiar circumstances."

Cochrane sighed and shook his head. "It would do no good, Mahomet, as I am not a party to the proceedings. I can act only as a character witness, which I am more than happy to do. Can you not settle with Harding prior to the hearing?"

"I have tried, sir, but without success. The man will not receive me or reply to my letters, and seems determined for his day in court. And I do not have five hundred pounds or any likelihood of ever achieving such an amount. The coffee house continues to struggle and my total assets I value at less than one hundred pounds plus the goodwill in the coffee house. Nor will I ask anyone to help, as I can never repay such a sum. I am ruined."

Cochrane tutted in sympathy but was anxious to pass on the problem to another. "You need advice, Mahomet, and quickly. When is your hearing?"

"It has not yet been listed and is unlikely to be heard until after Easter."

"So you have time. Have you consulted a lawyer … I know someone who might help."

"And how would I pay sir?"

Now Cochrane saw a way of ameliorating the shame of those lies. "No need to worry about that Mahomet, I will settle with him. Do you wish counsel? I know a man, Jauncy Vane, who is eminent in the field of commercial law. A good man and a King's Counsel. He would be only too happy to speak for you if I ask. Will you not at least let me do this?"

The Indian was crestfallen. He had not known what to expect from the Honourable Basil Cochrane, but had felt sure there would have been some solution that would have resolved the matter. Now he was to consult with a barrister about his appearance in court and possible bankruptcy.

"Very well, sir, if you advise. But I ask that no mention be made of this, especially to Manjai or the servants. I have told no-one, not even my wife."

THE first indication Decimus Doyle received of Mrs Siddons' return to London was a brief item in the newspaper detailing the latest performances of *Macbeth* at the Covent Garden theatre. He immediately wrote a letter imploring his former *amour* to grant him an audience, and delivered it by hand. To his immense surprise she replied by return and suggested he call on her the following morning.

When he arrived at her home off the Strand he waited a few moments on the doorstep, anxious of his reception, before firmly rapping the knocker. Mrs Siddons' footman, who until recently was accustomed to answering the door to Doyle, led him to a small ground-floor reception room and requested he take a seat. This Doyle did, but as soon as the door closed he jumped up and started pacing the room. Because of the limited space he ended up walking round and round the chair on which he had been seated. He stopped only when he heard footsteps on the marble floor outside and, in truth, his pacing had made him slightly nauseous. The door opened and in strode Sarah Siddons, who immediately took in the pensive state of her visitor.

"For Heaven's sake Decimus sit or you will make us both quite ill," she said as the door closed behind her. her tone was sharp but her heart nearly stopped on seeing him again. The couple now sat opposite each other to the centre of the room, Doyle in the chair he had been circling and Mrs Siddons on a small two seat sofa, over which she spread her dress to deter unwelcome guests.

"Thank you for seeing me Sarah," Doyle began. "You look ... decidedly handsome."

And indeed she did. The rest afforded by an extended stay with her Kemble relatives in Shropshire had rejuvenated her; that and her decision to end the relationship with Doyle which, she readily confessed to herself, was a great relief. She loved him dearly, but could not continue with the demands it imposed on her.

"Thank you Decimus, though I fear I can not say the same of you. You have been unwell?"

Doyle smiled. "No my love, not unwell, just unhappy."

She chided herself: she had invited that comment.

"Come Decimus. Do not look so sad. What is it you want of me ... that I can grant," she added quickly.

He leaned forward in his chair. "An exposition of that letter might be a start ..."

She openly sighed and shook her head. "What is there to explain? I thought my words were most delicate – I may have used the Bard too freely to express my feelings, but is that not why he wrote? Do not be angry with me Decimus. My actions were to the advantage of us both."

"Advantage!"

"Yes, I think so. Oh Decimus, you know I would not consciously wound you, yet I feared for you if I did not conclude our association when I did. You must understand that I acted only in your best interest. There simply was no future in our continuing in the manner to which we had become accustomed."

Doyle smiled. "You acted in my best interest?"

"Of course."

"Then what if I say it is in that same best interest to begin afresh ... renew our acquaintance without the baggage of what went before."

This conversation, Sarah Siddons decided, was not going to run smoothly, so she would have to change tack and be more forceful.

"Love, Decimus, is of a time. Once we have put it to one side then we cannot take it up again."

"But I have not put it to one side, my love. If anything, since your absence I feel it more intensely than ever. Surely I am not just a part to be forgotten when the play finishes?"

Sadly for Doyle that was exactly what he was, though Sarah Siddons was not about to confess it.

"Come Decimus, do not think me so shallow. Yet we can all be swept up in the moment. Ours was glorious."

"And fleeting!"

"It was too intense, and in your head if not your heart you know this."

"So as your brother said, I was a passing fancy!"

"Do not attend on his words," she snapped. "He knows little of love except for that of money. His response to you was driven by spite and jealousy."

"He is jealous of me?"

"He regards me as his performing monkey, to do with as he pleases. My consideration for you had altered his control of me, and he feared for his purse. That is why he is so hostile."

"So you still keep feelings for me."

She knew she would have to step carefully. "Of course, Decimus. I care for you greatly."

"But do not love me?"

She paused before speaking, but continued to avoid his direct gaze. "Young people use that word so freely, but what do they mean? What do any of us mean? The Bard ..."

"Please, no more Shakespeare," he interrupted. "Just in your own words."

The intensity of their speech had created a heat in the small room, or that is what she felt. She reached for the fan attached to the side of her dress and began to waft a faint breeze onto her face. She was grateful for the leaded make-up masking her flushing cheeks. He is so innocent, she thought, but that which attracted her now made matters far more difficult. She had never felt such pangs of conscience with other lovers.

"Decimus, if I was thirty, no twenty years younger I would consider your affections to be most desirous. What woman would not? You are the most handsome and considerate of gentlemen it has been my good fortune to meet. But I am not of that age, and this year I am determined to retire from the stage. You gave me my last passing glimpse of true love, but it was just that – passing, and now it has gone. I know you do not wish me to call on the Bard but you have mentioned seeing a particular play in Dublin. We have reversed roles and I am Puck to your Titania, if you can understand my meaning, and I created a magick only for your eyes. And we have ended up in as equally a confusing condition as in the *Dream*."

Doyle recalled the play and thought he understood her reasoning. "If you are saying, Sarah, that I have been enchanted by you then I am in agreement. But you cannot break the spell by walking away. I still hold your enchantment in my heart."

"You hold the love of love in your heart, Decimus, and not for me. We have not known each other long enough to create ties that bind forever. These can only be forged with time, and that is a commodity I do not hold in excess. Remember, we first met at the funeral of one of my past lovers. Now let the thought of me go and return to your real life. You are an excellent man Decimus and will make an exceedingly fine doctor. And in due course you will make an exceptional husband."

She had been more confiding with him than with any other man she had known intimately, and was now uncomfortable with the conversation. She looked pleadingly at him and restated her words: "Let me go." Then she closed her eyes. Whether or not it was just another performance, it had the effect of silencing Doyle. Finally she heard him ask: "And what now?" and she re-opened her eyes and smiled.

"I think it wise to let hearts heal. I will not forget you Decimus, nor will I dismiss you. In time I hope we will remain strong friends, but a friendship borne of empathy, not emotion. Do you not agree to this?"

Doyle looked down to the floor. "I have no choice."

"No," she confirmed.

After his departure Sarah Siddons sat alone in the small reception room. What a foolish, selfish woman she had been, she chided, to allow matters to progress so far. She had only wanted to be loved. And as she sat tears began to flow, tears which were soon accompanied by heart-wrenching sobs as she lamented for a lost love and the passing of that part of her life as she had known it.

CHARLOTTE Harding was also shedding tears over Decimus Doyle as she sat on top of a number of cases waiting for the servants to come and take the last of her belongings from the house. Ever since that dreadful letter had arrived from him early in the New Year she had taken to her room, and from which she was now being driven by her brother as the day for the sale of the estate drew close. She could still not understand how Decimus could have been so harsh in writing those words? He had lied to her, given her the most sincere wishes and affection, only to cut down her hopes so cruelly with the barbaric letter she still held tight in her hands, though the ink had long since smudged and half the words were unreadable.

She stifled a sob as servants entered the room and began to carry away more cases, only to let the tears flow again once they had left. She looked again at the crumpled paper in her hand. It has driven her to fly across the city to Doyle's residence in Soho, where his dreadful housekeeper had at first barred her entry. Still, on being faced with a tearful young woman on the steps of Dr Bunton's house in a busy London street, Mrs Mac had ushered Charlotte Harding inside.

"Decimus!" she cried as she saw the object of her affection standing to the centre of Dr Bunton's admirable library. "Please take it back! Take it back!" she continued, waving the letter towards him. He did not move.

"Please Miss Harding ... Lottie ... do not act so. Please, calm yourself."

"But how could you say such things," she sobbed, unaware that the housekeeper Mrs Mac was still standing behind her in the room.

Doyle sighed in pity and anguish. He had not anticipated such a scene. He looked to Mrs Mac. "Please can you see if Dr Bunton can provide a calming infusion for the young lady Mrs Mac. And please hurry back!" he implored. The housekeeper departed and Doyle managed to steer a trembling Charlotte Harding to a sofa, though he did not sit but stood before her.

"I said things as delicately as I could, Lottie, but for your own sake it had to be said. While I am happy to be a friend of both yourself and your brother, you must not mis-interpret my intentions. We can never be anything more than acquaintances. As I said in my letter, my heart belongs firmly to another."

Charlotte Harding squealed but Doyle resisted any attempt to comfort her. It had taken him some time to decide to write the letter but, once committed to it, he was determined to release himself from the burden of Miss Harding's "friendship". As she sobbed he tried to excuse both his and her actions.

"My dear Lottie, you have suffered so greatly during the past few months. Those you held dear have been taken from you but I can be no substitute for a father or brother. I fear you are not acting in a reasoned manner. I have never shown anything but the kindest of courtesies yet you have seen in these something much more. You continue to write to me every day even when I placed some distance between us. So I felt it necessary to explain in the way I did."

"But I love you Decimus!" Charlotte Harding cried, looking up at him through tearful eyes.

"That is not an appropriate thing for a young lady of your standing to say, Lottie, it really is not. How can you say this when we have hardly been together socially. You are the daughter of a noble house, Lottie, and should take care how you express your feelings. You simply cannot be so forward with gentlemen."

This slight chastisement brought about more wailing from the distraught young woman. Doyle was struggling to command the situation, given his own trials and tribulations with Mrs Siddons, and his words sounded somewhat hollow to his ears. To his great relief Mrs Mac returned to the library carrying a glass of hot liquid made from mint, called by the French the plant of happiness. Mrs Mac kept her own supply, though not usually intended for calming the lovelorn. She held the glass as she forced Charlotte Harding to sip from it, and this gave Doyle time to consider more carefully his next words.

"I understand from your brother that you are to move from Paddington shortly. It is a pity war ravages the continent so or I would have impressed upon him that you both make a tour of Italy or the like. But you must associate with other ladies of your own rank, Lottie, and I will write to William saying so. A ladies' school for manners perhaps, or a companion of experience in Society. Once you are distracted by the company of others your feelings for me will change, I promise you."

The mint infusion was having an effect, together with a stern look from Mrs Mac, and Charlotte Harding's breathing became more regular.

"But I do not want to go away, Decimus. I want to be by your side. Who is this other lady? Let us duel like George. She will not find me as weak as he was!"

Doyle was exasperated. "Enough of this nonsense, Charlotte. Enough I say. I told you a confidence to help you understand my reasoning, not to incite you. If your feelings for me are as you say then you will stop now or risk the chance of affecting our friendship for good!" He paused, catching himself before he said something he would regret. "Listen to me, Lottie. We cannot always have what we wish ... I know that only too well. And you are very young, and what I mean by that is you are young enough to recover well from this ... disappointment. Now, let us part as friends and Mrs Mac will escort you to your carriage. After a time it maybe possible for us to meet again, but not for the foreseeable future."

The housekeeper helped Charlotte Harding up from the sofa, keeping tight hold of her like a warder with her prisoner, and as the young lady went to speak again Mrs Mac interrupted.

"Come now my dear, there is nothing more to be said. Come along and leave Mr Doyle to his business. I will see you out."

Charlotte Harding gave Doyle one last despairing look as she was firmly escorted from he room but his eyes were already looking at nothing in particular on the library desk. As the door closed behind them Doyle sank into an accommodating chair and gave an involuntary cry of relief and guilt. Had Sarah been so harsh with him, he wondered?

SIR Jauncy Vane KC sat for some time considering the papers before him and then looked up at his latest client. A tall, thin man of middle years with a large hooked nose, Vane looked the caricature of a vulture-like lawyer about to pick at his prey. The small Indian, on the other hand, was enveloped in the large leather wingback that Vane's clerk provided for clients at the chambers in Lincoln's Inn. The features of Mahomet's face were frozen in time as he watched one of the country's greatest legal minds attend to his matter.

"Well Mr Mahomet, this is a fine to-do and no mistake," the legal knight muttered at last, "and you have been the victim of a very great injustice. How matters were allowed to progress in such a way is beyond comprehension. Of course, when you first held suspicions about Sir Josiah Harding's death you should have sought out the authorities."

"I was concerned for my coffee house ..."

"From the accounts you have here presented I doubt it could have made matters any worse. Your establishment has been losing several pounds a week for the past year, it seems. Your financial position, sir, is very weak."

Mahomet had no need of a highly paid lawyer to tell him that.

"And what of the paper I signed Sir Jauncy, at the Bow Street court? Can Harding enforce it?"

For the first time the King's Counsel smiled, albeit grimly. "A most indelicate instrument I must say, valuing a man's life in such a way. I have never come across it before, though I have heard rumour of death bonds and the like at Lloyd's Coffee House. But to have it embodied in an order of the court is most disturbing. I doubt the magistrate has any authority to issue such an order, and we could argue such at your hearing before the Chancery Court. But judges are minded not to gainsay their brother judges, and the man was, after all, killed ..."

"But not by my hand sir."

"As you say, but where is your evidence Mr Mahomet? Harding will contend you fired the shot that killed his brother, and unless you can present this ... William Rufus before the court with a confession then we must accept your liability. Well Mr Mahomet, do you know where this Rufus is?"

Mahomet shook his head. "He disappeared and Cochrane denies any knowledge of him. I now wonder if he actually existed, though of course my colleague Mr Doyle was with me at the cricket match and my wife accompanied him to the duel. What wickedness was he working to damage me so, Sir Jauncy? I had never set eyes on the man before he appeared late one night at my coffee house and look what he has wreaked!"

Mahomet dropped his head in despair, but it was all in a day's work for Sir Jauncy. "Come sir, it is not all bleak. You have me here to help."

"But if I am bankrupted, my family and myself will be incarcerated in the Marshalsea! The horror and the shame. My wife will no doubt leave me and take the children back to her father in Ireland. I will be left destitute, without prospect or ..."

"Stop sir!" barked the King's Counsel. "I will not have my clients wallowing in such pity and remorse. You are where you are, Mr Mahomet, and we must now take steps to remedy and ameliorate your lot."

From his pocket the lawyer took a small gold snuffbox and offered it to Mahomet who shook his head. Taking a sizeable pinch and placing on top of his clenched hand, the snuff was enveloped by the hooked nose and followed by a tumultuous sneeze into a large white linen handkerchief.

"There is nothing," he said at the conclusion of procedure, "like a clearing of the head. Now Mr Mahomet, your bankruptcy."

The Indian looked at him shocked. "Is there nothing I can do?"

The lawyer sighed. "I doubt it very much, sir. As I say, we can attempt to disprove your liability to Harding but I would not wish to raise any hope.

And after receiving your papers I sent my junior to speak to the plaintiff to see if he could be accommodated. He bears a great ill feeling towards you sir. His father died in your coffee house and, so far as he is concerned, you spoke a great slander and then killed his brother ..."

"I did no such thing Sir Jauncy and William Harding knows this!"

Sir Jauncy held up his hand. "I am stating his position sir, not the truth. If the truth could be proved then you would be seeking redress, not the other way round. As it stands you must either pay the five hundred pounds or he will apply to have you declared bankrupt. But again I say do not fret Mr Mahomet, this might not be the evil of which you so despair."

"Bankruptcy?!" Mahomet exclaimed, more in frustration than fear.

"Please sir, let me explain. Since the 1706 *Act of Anne*, made in the days of our last Stuart monarch, the discharge of debt is a normal outcome in bankruptcy proceedings, giving an honest but failed debtor such as yourself a fresh start and protection from further proceedings and imprisonment. There is no question of you and your family ending up in the Marshalsea or any other debtor's prison. You have my word on this. Moreover, for you it might be a blessing in disguise. By writing off your past failings, and by this I mean your coffee house, you can start anew to work and invest without being pre-empted by your creditors, in this case Sir William Harding. It would draw to a final close this very bloody business."

But Mahomet was aghast. "But I will have to close my coffee house, sir. I will have failed."

The lawyer looked hard at his client; he was used to presenting bad news in the most favourable light. "You business has been failing for some time, Mr Mahomet. No doubt it is a very worthy and honourable venture, but you cannot forever continue in this manner. Take the chance offered by this proposed bankruptcy and look on it as a renewal. I have taken the liberty of speaking with Cochrane and he has offered to undertake a number of things. Firstly to provide employment for yourself and a home for your family. He has also agreed to my putting his name forward to the court as the commissioner charged with liquidating your estate. This must be agreed with the office of the Chancellor of the Exchequer, and while usually it would mean tedious submissions to clerks at the Treasury building off Whitehall, Cochrane has personal acquaintance with the Chancellor himself – the Prime Minister Mr Perceval. Cochrane will obtain his assent. And finally, as your bankruptcy commissioner Cochrane will do all he can to achieve a sale of your failing coffee house. It might not be to your liking, Mr Mahomet, but in your position you must be most relieved to have a supporter to the degree of Basil Cochrane."

Mahomet sat back in the large wingback chair. It seemed his future had been decided for him. He was to be declared bankrupt and return to working for the Honourable Basil Cochrane. His coffee house was to be taken from him and he was to be diminished as a man through no fault of his own. If he had not been sitting in the chambers of Sir Jauncy Vane KC he knew he would have wailed with grief.

THE Large White Chamber in the Palace of Westminster was crowded with peers as the finest manhood of British nobility jostled with each other for position. The debate on the Bill that would make machine breaking punishable by death was in full session, and was now being countered by the young radical Lord Byron.

"Is there not enough blood upon your penal code?!" Byron demanded, "that more must be poured forth to ascend to heaven and testify against you? How will you carry this Bill into effect? Can you commit a whole county to their own prisons? Will you erect a gibbet in every field and hang up men like scarecrows? Or will you proceed – as you must to bring this measure into effect – by decimation; place the country under martial law, depopulate and lay waste all around you and restore Sherwood Forest as an acceptable gift to the Crown in its former condition as a Royal Chase ... and an asylum for outlaws?"

Across the Chamber, squashed onto a bench next to his friend Lord Liverpool, Sidmouth sighed and turned his head to his noble friend's ear.

"If I had my way I would have the man run out of the country," he hissed. Liverpool smiled but did not answer.

"His words encourage sedition across the land," the Deputy Ranger of

Richmond Park continued. "Curse the man and everything he stands for. Why was he allowed to speak?"

"Patience my lord," Liverpool replied. "It is good to let opposing forces have their say, so long as it is within the confines of the House. And you cannot deny the oratory."

The Chamber erupted at something Byron had said.

"When a proposal is made to emancipate or relieve, you hesitate, you deliberate for years, you temporise and tamper with the minds of men; but a death-Bill must be passed off-hand, without a thought of the consequences. Sure I am, from what I heave heard and from what I have seen, that to pass the Bill under all the existing circumstances, without inquiry, without deliberation, would only be to add injustice to irritation, and barbarity to neglect."

"Bahh!" hissed Lord Sidmouth and he rose from his seat, bowed to the Lord Chancellor and left the Chamber to the right of the Throne. He had heard enough of this nonsense; the Bill would be passed with a handsome majority and those disturbing the King's Peace would be taught a sharp lesson. He had prevailed upon Perceval and the Commons had already voted for the Bill. Yet Sidmouth remained disturbed. "Martial law", Byron had claimed, and his lordship wished he had been correct. But the army was stretched across the continents, fighting the French from the Caribbean to India, and Wellington's campaign in Spain continued to grind on. If there were a large scale rioting in the northern towns, the government would be pushed to contain it. He recalled his father's tales of the panic during the Jacobite rising all those years ago, with people fleeing London for the countryside, and he knew order could not be taken for granted. Even though he was not officially in government, Sidmouth considered his position as Deputy Ranger, held by politicians of the stature of Walpole before him, to be a watching brief for his master the King. All the more important, therefore, that he deployed whatever means he could.

Outside the Chamber he looked for the telltale sign of his Avenger: red hair. He spotted William Rufus standing below a portrait of John Churchill, Duke of Marlborough, and signalled for him to follow. Some minutes later both men were caballed in a small room off a corridor leading towards the Great Hall.

"That fool Byron is running off his prose," cursed the Deputy Ranger, "but he should keep to his poetry as it will do him no good. Parliament will speak as one on this, even if we did have to give it a little push."

Rufus smiled and nodded, happy his master confided in him so readily.

"Now you must journey north again, and make sure they arrest the trouble makers. But be careful. I know Perceval has already sent men to act as provocateurs, and I would not wish you stumbling over them. You have already mentioned some possible ring-leaders, so concentrate on them."

"Do you know the names of Mr Perceval's men, my lord?"

"No! He does not keep me in his confidence. The man really is contemptible. In my time as Prime Minister the country was in the greatest danger, but I managed to build and pay for a barrier of defensive towers along the south coast and the Thames estuary. And this was before Nelson prevailed at Trafalgar. We even had word Napoleon was exploring ways of digging beneath the Channel. Just think of it, a tunnel from France to here. Outrageous! It would be like tunnelling under our moat. Now the Prime Minister, who seems more content in his lesser brief of Chancellor of the Exchequer, is obsessed with the value of paper money and the price of wheat. These tasks are for bankers and farmers, not politicians. No, the country will only progress once Spencer Perceval is made to step down."

During Sidmouth's lament an idea of some deception occurred to Rufus which might bring forward his master's wish, but his train of thought was diverted by his lordship's continued instruction.

"Make sure you keep me fully informed. I warned Perceval there would be more trouble and now we have it. The latest reports of machine breaking in Leeds and Lancashire are most serious. A warehouse containing power looms has been burned down in Manchester, so you have little time to lose. It is my sincerest wish to see the end of this trouble, and in so doing we might also rid ourselves of Mr Perceval's government."

William Rufus nodded sagely.

Chapter 18

To make Shrewsbury cakes.
TAKE two pounds of flour, a pound of sugar finely searched, mix them together (take out a quarter of pound to roll them in) take four eggs beat, four spoonfuls of cream, and two spoonfuls of rose-water, beat them well together, and mix them with the flour into a paste, roll them into thin cakes, and bake them in a quick oven.
The Art of Cookery Made Plain and Easy

London, Easter 1812.

SAKE Dean Mahomet inspected the biscuits his wife had made for Easter. Lent was behind them, and he was looking forward to a family celebration that was to be their last at the Hindostanee Coffee House. He had yet to advise anyone apart from the Honourable Basil Cochrane and Sir Jauncy Vane KC that this would be the case. His wife suspected something was amiss when he announced they would close the coffee house on Easter Sunday so the family could appropriately mark the Resurrection of Christ. Yet rather than debate the correctness of his decision, Jane had embraced it wholeheartedly, even encouraging their housemaid Sarah and daughter Amelia to make Easter bonnets to wear to the service at the Portman Chapel. It was agreed that, if the weather were fine, after church they would make their way across to Hyde Park for a bracing walk before returning mid-afternoon for their Easter meal. So now, while he waited in the kitchen for the rest of the family to gather, he delicately broke off a corner from one of the Shrewsbury cakes for his own private tasting. The biscuit melted in his mouth. Jane had excelled herself once more.

During the service Jane Mahomet noticed her husband was unusually attentive to the sermon, which was on the appropriate theme of renewal. As they walked over to the park, with the children running ahead and Sarah following with young Horatio, Jane put her arm through her husband's and asked for his opinion on rebirth. As she did so she subconsciously stroked her belly with her other hand. She was five months pregnant and the bump was beginning to show.

"Of course the Hindus and the Sikhs believe in reincarnation," he began, "which I suppose is a rebirth, but the form you take in the next life depends on how you behave in this. What do they say? Every action has a reaction – karma. It is a pity more men in this world do not attend to the consequence of their actions."

"What do you think, husband. Can one be re-born?" Jane prompted.

Mahomet stopped walking and brought them to a halt. "Christians do not believe in such a concept, as you well know."

His wife smiled. "I was not asking the chapel congregation husband, I was asking you."

He returned her smile and they started walking again. "You are testing me. No, I do not believe we return again, whether as a man or a mouse ..." he paused. "But I do believe within our life we can be renewed, as the minister said. I believe this has happened to me several times. I was renewed when I entered the army camp in Patna, and again when I decided to accompany the late and honoured Mr Baker to Ireland."

"And again when you met me!" teased Jane.

"Exactly! Both our lives were renewed at our marriage ceremony. And when we left Ireland ... and when each of our children was born ... and when we opened the coffee house ..." This last statement was accompanied by a pause which was longer than the others. "And when we leave," he said finally.

Jane Mahomet looked to her husband but did not say anything.

"Let us head for the seating overlooking the Serpentine river," he continued, "and we can speak more while the children are at play."

They had planned to make for the road within the park that had originally been given the French name *Rue de Roi* (for King's Road) and had now been corrupted to Rotten Row by Londoners. Jane had been eager to see the fashionable at play as they sauntered along, some on horseback or in carriages, strutting in their finery. At Easter there was a particularly good display of such nonsense. But instead they turned aside and found an empty small bench overlooking the water. Sarah was instructed to take Horatio and join the children playing on the grass behind them, so long as it was not too damp.

When they were settled Jane turned to her husband.

"When we leave the coffee house, Mr Mahomet?"

Her husband nodded and told her of the writ from Sir William Harding and his meetings with the Honourable Basil Cochrane and Sir Jauncy Vane KC. Since his first meeting with Vane some weeks ago, most of the details of the proposed bankruptcy had been agreed. He told her of his settling their outstanding accounts with the exception of the five hundred pounds claimed by Harding and the outstanding rent. The latter would be settled as part of any sale of the business. He expected a fierce reaction from his wife – perhaps that was why he told her in such a public place – and was surprised by her silent reaction. She sat there for some minutes after he finished speaking.

"Please say something, my pearl, if only that you are ashamed of me."

Jane Mahomet reached over and squeezed her husband's arm. "I could never be ashamed of you Mr Mahomet," she said very quietly. "But I am shocked by your news. You say we are to move back to Portman Square?'

Mahomet nodded. "Our old cottage in the mews behind the house. It will be a lot smaller than you are used to in George Street, but it is a roof over our heads ... and a position. Cochrane wishes me to administer his bath house."

"And there will be no prison?"

"Not according to Sir Jauncy. We plan that Sir William will be the only debtor. If Cochrane is appointed my commissioner, as is hoped, then my only asset will be the coffee house. He has already told me he will turn a blind eye to our personal chattels, though we should remove them to Portman Square before the hearing. Sir Jauncy will ask the court to "deliver" me into Cochrane's control until the bankruptcy is discharged, which could be some time. I fear Harding might demand I be sent to the Marshalsea or Newgate, but Vane is adamant the court will not do so and, as he appears before it very frequently, I ... we ... must trust him. No, for me the real sentence is the overwhelming feeling of despair at my own failure."

Now Jane Mahomet found her voice again. "Nonsense husband, you have been the innocent party in all this. If anyone should be sent to Newgate it is Harding ... or that Rufus man, or both!"

The children, playing many yards away, heard their mother's raised voice and thought she was calling to them. Yet when they saw their parents in earnest discussion they became confused and concerned. Sarah, who was sitting nearby watching Horatio walk around her, instructed them to stay where they were until properly called.

Meanwhile Mahomet had moved to calm his wife. "Jane, my pearl, your anger is understandable but it will do no good, not now. Events have conspired against us. And if we are truthful with ourselves, the coffee house has not succeeded. If it had been profitable then I would have fought ..."

"It was fighting that brought us to this grief, husband!" she interrupted.

He caught his breath. "What you say is correct Jane. If Sir Josiah had not died on that fateful day then George Harding would have been alive as well and I would not about to be brought before the Chancery Court. But the coffee house would have still been failing."

They both sat in silence for some minutes looking out over the water. On the far side they could see a great number of people parading and in the distance could hear the sound of music; a military band perhaps.

"You are right, husband. We were not made to be prosperous merchants. It is our lot to be servants to a master such as Mr Cochrane, and in many ways it is a great relief knowing this."

Now it was for Mahomet to be angered. "You speak in confusion, Jane. We ... I have mis-judged the success of the coffee house though in time it will succeed. George Harding has robbed us of that time and that is his right, it seems. Earlier you spoke of re-birth and Sir Jauncy Vane says that this ... bankruptcy ... is meant as a fresh start for me, as he called it. This is how I must look on it. It will take time for Cochrane to sell the coffee house if he can, settle with the landlord and hand over the balance to Harding, but then I will start again. I married a gentleman's daughter and I promise you

Jane this is not an ending but a beginning. Once this is over then the time might come to accept your father's money, if he is still willing."

"Then you must write to him and explain everything. And I mean everything, husband. The whole story. Papa will understand. He will see that you are the injured party in this." She did not add that she had always considered her father's money to be her dowry gift and would write separately expressing this view. Her father would support them: she knew this as surely as Sir Jauncy Vane KC knew the Chancery Court. "But what if the coffee house does not satisfy Harding's claim?" she added anxiously.

"Then the court will rule him settled. Once Cochrane submits his commissioner's accounts to the court and they are approved they will discharge me."

"But what if they do not approve them, husband, what if they say you must pay Harding every penny?"

"That will not happen. Cochrane is a gentleman of great repute in the city, especially in matters of finance, and according to Sir Jauncy the court will look most favourably on his appointment. I will be protected from any further action from Harding."

The children had now stopped playing and were seated on the grass next to Sarah looking towards their parents.

"Do you recall my mentioning Mr Bellingham, my pearl?"

"The man from Liverpool who was arrested?"

"Yes, that is him. Our tales now seem so very much alike. I can understand the anger that burns within him at the injustice he has suffered. I could easily be like him. At chapel today when the minister spoke I thought of words I read in the Bible. Let all bitterness and anger be put away from you and be forgiving of each other, like God through Christ has forgiven you. The words of St Paul, I think, in one of his letters. It is a pity Mr Bellingham does not reach towards the Bible a bit more, as it is a cooling salve for the soul. He offered to be my business partner but it has all come too late, I'm afraid."

He breathed in and looked around him, and noticed for the first time the children sitting like puppies awaiting their call.

"The family is hungry, I think," he said, nodding his head towards their offspring and Jane turned around and smiled at them.

"Come family," he called. "Come William, Amelia and Henry. Sarah, bring Horatio. Mama had prepared a very fine dinner to celebrate the Lord's Day of renewal, have you not my pearl? Why, I have even tried one of the Shrewsbury cakes, and very tasty it was."

"Mr Mahomet," whispered his now smiling wife as she stood and watched the children come running towards them, "I may sometimes question your actions but I will never question my love for you."

MAHOMET was right; rage and anger was tearing at John Bellingham's soul. It had been three months since he arrived from Liverpool yet still no one had listened to him and his grievances. He had called on public office after public office but they all referred him elsewhere: the Foreign Office said it was a matter for the Treasury, the Treasury a matter for Parliament and Parliament sent him back to the Foreign Office. Yet at the centre of this web was the spider – the Prime Minister Spencer Perceval. It was this man, Bellingham now believed, who was denying him justice.

To stop himself from exploding with frustration he would walk the streets of London incessantly. So it was that on Easter Sunday his walking led him to the west of the capital and Portman Square. On realising where he was, he recalled the gentle Indian who had been considerate to him, and so sought the refuge of the Hindostanee Coffee House. It was late evening and the doors of the establishment were firmly shut, as they had been all day. Unperturbed, Bellingham rapped loudly to gain entrance, and seemed surprised when an upstairs sash window opened and a dark head appeared.

"Yes?" Mahomet called. "I am afraid we are closed."

"I want to enter," came the reply.

Recognising the voice, Mahomet said: "Mr Bellingham, is that you? Wait a moment and I will come down."

Mahomet opened the door to the coffee house and Bellingham entered without acknowledging his host.

"Come Mr Bellingham, we will go and sit in the kitchen which is still warmed by the range. I will make us some Turkish coffee and you can tell me your news."

Sitting his guest at the large oak table and setting down the oil lamp in his hand, Mahomet busied himself with the coffee, taking down a copper pot called a cezve which he filled with water and then added finely powered roast coffee beans and sugar. Placing the cezve on the range and turning back to his guest, he was shocked to witness his visitor's condition. It looked as if Mr Bellingham had not attended to himself for some time. His clothing was dishevelled, his skin grimy and his hair unkempt.

Mahomet sat at the table opposite. "So Mr Bellingham, the coffee will take just a moment. I am most glad to see you, and mentioned you only today to my wife. I wondered if you had returned to Liverpool. How are you? I am afraid I have some bad news to relate regarding our proposed partnership."

Bellingham seemed so distracted that Mahomet wondered if he had heard anything he had said.

"I am sorely vexed sir, sorely vexed," came the reply.

"So I can tell Mr Bellingham. You should not wander the streets alone at night. London is not a safe place. Have you come from your lodging?"

"Walking is my only solace, sir. When I walk I am free. If I stay still for too long they might know where I am and arrest me."

"Arrest you? Who Mr Bellingham? Who will arrest you?"

"The Russians, of course. Then who will help me? Not our government, oh no. They would leave me to the wolves."

Mahomet was greatly disturbed by what he heard, but before he could say more noticed the coffee bubbling on the range so stood to attend to it. He poured the hot liquid into two coffee cups and returned to the table. Bellingham had kept his head bowed the entire time.

"Mr Bellingham sir," said Mahomet softly, "the Russians have no power here. This is England. They cannot arrest you on our streets."

Again Mahomet was not sure whether Bellingham heard his words.

"Drink your coffee sir. It is very good. I have a special supply from a friend who attends on Ramadani Efendi, who is the Ottoman ambassador and lives with my patron the Honourable Basil Cochrane in his house in Portman Sq ..."

"Do not speak to me of ambassadors," Bellingham interrupted, "what good are ambassadors! It is they who caused my distress. Let me tell you of ambassadors sir. Take Lord Gower now, the British ambassador in Russia." Bellingham virtually spat the word British from his lips and then proceeded to recount his tale of woe yet again to Mahomet, who thought it wise to let the man have his say. Mahomet heard little that he had not already been told, and after several minutes of disjointed talk Bellingham again lapsed into silence.

"Last time we met Mr Bellingham you had great hopes of asking the court in Bow Street to act on your behalf. Have they considered your case?"

Bellingham did not respond.

"Mr Bellingham sir? The Bow Street magistrates?"

For the first time since arriving on the doorstep Bellingham looked directly at Mahomet.

"They say it is for the Chancellor of the Exchequer, and his office has told me I can expect nothing."

"Ahhh," is all Mahomet could say.

"I have warned them sir, warned them all, that if all redress was refused me I would be obliged to do justice myself and take steps against those who are responsible for resisting my applications. They will not heed my warnings sir, they will not heed them."

Mahomet was confused. What other steps could Mr Bellingham take if the courts would not consider his case?

"Do you know who Mr Perceval is sir, do you know?"

Mahomet nodded. He certainly did know given that the Honourable Basil Cochrane had recently approached the Prime Minister in his other capacity as Chancellor of the Exchequer requesting his approval of a letter of appointment as commissioner in Mahomet's proposed bankruptcy.

"But you do not know what he is sir," Bellingham was continuing. "He is no less than an agent of the Tsar! What do you think about that?!"

Mahomet thought very little of it.

"Come sir, you are obviously distressed by your situation. Surely it would be better to return to your wife and child in Liverpool than walk the streets of London. You have a family at home, Mr Bellingham."

"You don't believe me, do you? No one believes me. But I know. There are powers at work trying to expose Mr Perceval, but they are constrained. They cannot act against him. The man is too powerful. He has taken all the great offices of state to himself. Only a common man, acting alone, can unmask him and bring him down. I know this, I have been told."

Mahomet was now worried that his friend was seriously deranged.

"How do you know, Mr Bellingham? How can you be so sure?"

Bellingham tapped his nose with a finger and looked around him in the empty kitchen to make sure they were not overheard. "A gentleman confided in me."

Mahomet tutted. "What gentleman? And how does he know of this scheme of Mr Perceval's?"

Bellingham simply nodded. "Of course he knows. He is close to the counsels of great men. His father dealt with the merchants of Liverpool. Perceval destroyed their business with his slave law, which he brought about on instruction from Paris and St Petersburgh. Well, what do you think of that sir? I am being ruined by a man who would ruin his own country."

Mahomet now recalled Bellingham being advised by someone in Liverpool who had been affected by the anti-slave trade law. Yet this person seemed to have created a great conspiracy in Bellingham's mind.

"What proof does this man have of such a motive? Surely he is biased against Mr Perceval? I would not heed such talk Mr Bellingham!"

But Bellingham's eyes now flashed with anger. "You say that sir, because of your birth and your approval of Perceval's slave law. But my friend knows. He has even come to see me here in London. He understands the great injustice I have suffered, and says I should not stand for it. Only I can relieve my distress. You say I cannot be arrested, but Perceval controls a web of spies and agents throughout the land. I could be snatched at any time and transported once more to that prison in Archangel. My friend knows this, and together we have worked on a plan."

"A plan?" asked Mahomet, now greatly concerned.

"Yes. By my actions I will put to an end for once and for all the schemes of Mr Perceval, and make a play for all good and honest Britons."

With that Bellingham sat back but, within moments, stood and made for the door. He must depart, he told his host, to make further arrangements, and without any common courtesy headed for the main door of the coffee house, throwing it open and heading away along George Street. Mahomet paused at the open door watching the man disappear. Even with all his own worries, he was distressed to see Mr Bellingham in such a condition. The man was deluded. Closing and bolting the door against the night, he returned to the kitchen where he found Jane Mahomet clearing the coffee cups.

"I heard a great noise so came down," she said.

Mahomet nodded. "We were visited by Mr Bellingham, the man who was locked up in Russia. I am greatly concerned for him, my pearl."

He then told her of the discussion.

"Do you think this gentleman adviser exists?" she asked. "It is strange but it reminds me of when William had an imaginary friend called Joey? Was there no name?"

Mahomet shook his head. His wife, as usual, was right. Bellingham's delusions were such that he might well imagine a friend who would give him the advice he wished for. He was fearful for Bellingham's personal safety, but what could he do? Then he remembered that Dr Bunton took an especial interest in diseases of the mind and decided to call on him the following day.

THE annual dinner of the Masters of the Hunterian Medical School had taken place on Easter Sunday, and for Dr Simon Bunton the Monday afterwards was very decidedly a day of rest. He had risen well after the noonday chimes of his hall clock and had partaken of a soothing broth prepared by his housekeeper Mrs Mac. Then, with a damp cloth for his forehead in one hand and a remedial glass of Portuguese wine in the other, he had retired to that day's issue of *The Times*, which he read from the chaise longue in his library. Any thought of attending to the affairs of the medical school would have to wait for another day. It was mid afternoon when he was awoken from his slumber by Mrs Mac knocking at the library door.

"I'm sorry to disturb, doctor, but Mr Mahomet is here and would ask for an audience."

Mahomet? He had not seen the man since a brief discussion regarding Doyle before Christmas. In the past month or so the young Irishman had buried himself in his work and had become a model student with all signs of romantic attachment dissipated, much to Bunton's satisfaction. Raising himself, he asked Mrs Mac to show in his visitor and to prepare some of his best China tea from the locked caddy in his bedroom. It had just arrived on a tea clipper and was the first pick of the season. Bunton's supplier had sold it to him at a very reasonable price. He did not ask how the supplier came by it, but expected it probably involved a mislaid piece of cargo at the East India Company dock.

After a mutually warm greeting, Mahomet came quickly to the purpose for his call, describing the late night visit of Mr Bellingham.

"I am no expert on the matter, Dr Bunton, but I think my friend is labouring under a very great delusion."

Bunton listened attentively, or as close to that state as he could given his own mental incapacity brought about by last night's dinner.

"This is most interesting, Mr Mahomet, most interesting. Some years ago there was a great debate between two doctors of the mind over the meaning of insanity. Dr Battie, who was the physician at St Luke's Hospital for Lunatics, said that madness was a "deluded imagination". He considered it to be either original at birth or was produced as a consequence of something else, some tragedy. He said that the lunatic must be observed so the doctor can be certain which treatments could be beneficial. Dr Munro, the senior physician at the Bethlem, disagreed with this and defended the so-called "shock" treatment of evacuation he practices at that hospital. He claims vomiting is by far the best way of treating lunacy, together with bleeding and purging."

"And where does Mr Bellingham fall?'

Bunton considered this. "If, as you say, he suffered a great trauma in Russia then this may have turned his mind."

"He called in the New Year and was very reasoned, and confident that his case against the government would go well. Why, he even suggested I write to my old kitchen porter Samuel and ask how he came to know of Walker."

"You spoke of your recent troubles?" asked Bunton, surprised that the Indian would speak so openly to a stranger.

"Yes, it was like a confession, I suppose. I even acted on his advice and wrote to the Admiralty, though I have heard nothing since, so perhaps I was correct in assuming that Samuel is beyond our reach. Still, in the New Year Mr Bellingham was quite sensible, but during this latest visit ... well, Dr Bunton, I would certainly say he is suffering from delusions which could be dangerous to him. It is not wise to speak about powerful men in such a manner. What can be done?"

Bunton paused before speaking. "Well, I would not recommend committing him to the Bedlam for a start!"

The Bethlem Royal Hospital had started life as the priory for the sisters of the Order of the Star of Bethlehem in 1247. A hundred years later it started admitting mentally ill patients, universally referred to at that the time as lunatics. These lunatics became patients in 1700s, and "curable" and "incurable" wards were opened. The hospital, situated in Moorfields outside of the city walls, was one of London's great attractions, with thousands of visitors every year paying one penny to look into the cells at the inmates and watch the "show of Bethlehem", which often included fights and sexual depravity.

"No," Bunton continued. "There is a man, by the name of William Tuke, who has set up a place in York called the Retreat. No chains, no manacles, no beatings, just the treating of inmates humanely. Tuke is a Quaker, and the Retreat is guided by his religion, but not oppressively so. And where they have violent residents, they try and limit the restraint. The doors are encased in leather, and the bars at the windows look like window frames. Tuke calls it moral treatment."

Mahomet was greatly encouraged. "Would Mr Tuke consider Mr

Bellingham, do you think?"

Bunton nodded. "He might. I could write to him. We have a bursary at the school for medical research. No doubt I could arrange for a small portion of this to be allocated for your Mr Bellingham's board and lodging at the Retreat, at least for a time. Your problem Mr Mahomet is getting Mr Bellingham to attend of his own free will, or to ask a court to order his detention. Some ten years ago the government brought in the Criminal Lunatics Act after James Hadfield tried to shoot the King during the national anthem at Drury Lane theatre. But like Hadfield, unless your man creates a public harm there is little any court could act on. Usually inmates at hospitals such as the Bedlam are placed by there by family, keen to keep them from spending the family fortune. Perhaps that is where Sir Josiah Harding should have placed his elder son before your recent happenings," he quipped.

"Please do not speak of Sir George Harding, nor his brother William," lamented the Indian.

Bunton was curious and questioned Mahomet further. In the end the whole story was revealed: Harding's case in the Court of Chancery, the support of the Honourable Basil Cochrane, the opinion of Sir Jauncy Vane KC, and the impending bankruptcy. Bunton was horrified.

"Bankruptcy? Bankruptcy? The cad! He should be horsewhipped. Oh Mr Mahomet, if I had known Harding would take such an action I would never have forced your hand with the magistrate in Bow Street. What have I done?! How can I make amends? I have a considerable sum put aside and could help you settle the debt with Harding. I ...."

"No Dr Bunton, no," interrupted Mahomet. "Please do not blame yourself. It was not with you that I duelled and you have acted in my best interests at all times. No, what if I had been charged with Sir George Harding's murder? What then? No doctor, you have been a good friend. And I cannot accept your money. I will not take that which I can never repay. No," he said emphatically, then paused a moment in thought. "What is the medical term Decimus once told me? Cathartic ... yes, it has been cathartic. Like treating one of your lunatics, the shock treatment has purged me and made me realise I could not have continued with the coffee house. I did not have the means to maintain it and London is not yet ready for an establishment purveying Indian tastes. Perhaps it never will be."

"Does Doyle know about the ... you know ..."

"Bankruptcy? It is not a disease doctor. No, I will not tell him until the matter is settled. I do not wish to involve the family any further than I need. The case has been listed to be heard in Westminster's Great Hall on 11th May."

"Then at least allow me to accompany you Mr Mahomet. You cannot face such a trial unsupported."

Chapter 19

London, Early May 1812.

SAKE Dean Mahomet stood to the centre of the dining room of the Hindostanee Coffee House. The room was shuttered, dark and silent. Over the past two days he had moved his family out of their rooms above and across to the small cottage in the mews behind the mansion of the Honourable Basil Cochrane. The children had looked on in surprise and wonder, considering it a great adventure. Then yesterday he and Jane had returned for one last time and sat together in the kitchen. Tears ran down both their cheeks, but less for what had happened than for what might have been.

Now, far more composed, he had returned to wait on Dr Simon Bunton to call and accompany him to Westminster and the Chancery Court. He walked over to one of the wall murals and gently stroked the cheek of the large Buddha statue painted within. He had opened the coffee house with such confidence that he now blushed at his naïveté. He had fooled himself with his vanity, he decided, expecting all London to beat a path to the door of the coffee house to try the unique tastes he purveyed. But they did not, and now that door was firmly locked and bolted and would not re-open until, or if, Cochrane could find a buyer.

A sharp rap on the kitchen door disturbed his maudlin mood. Dr Bunton was early but no matter. With a deep breath he puffed out his chest and strode towards his doom. He was more than surprised to find young Doyle waiting at the door rather than Dr Bunton.

"Decimus?" he queried as he opened the door.

"Sake Mahomet," came the brisk reply as the Irishman entered.

The Indian looked suitably confused.

"Bunton is unwell so late last night spoke to me about your troubles. I am sorely aggrieved Sake Mahomet, that you did not speak to me yourself. I have been awake all night considering it. It is all my fault. How could I have been so stupid to anger Charlotte Harding so!"

"Miss Harding?" asked as confused Mahomet.

"Of course. This is why her brother pursues you, because of my rejection of his sister. How spiteful can a man be? Mrs Siddons always said he had a malign character, but we were so preoccupied with his brother to see it. And now I have neglected my family in their need. How can you forgive me?"

The young man looked on the verge of tears so Mahomet pointed to the kitchen table and they both sat down.

"Decimus, please do not take on so. It is not your fault. How could it be? No, do not answer that. You must accept that you are an innocent party. Indeed, we are all innocent to some extent, though I am to blame for the failure of the coffee house."

"But in time, Sake Mahomet ..."

"Time is what I do not have, Decimus. Within the hour I must be at Westminster. Come, I am glad it is you here rather than Dr Bunton. I hope he is not too poorly?"

Doyle shook his head. "Not truly. He took an anatomy lecture yesterday and ended up at the White Hart. By the time he returned he realised he would be in no fit state to attend on you this morning, so woke me and confessed all. He apologises for breaking your confidence. I could not make head nor tail of it all. You are going to work for Cochrane once more and he is declaring you bankrupt?"

Mahomet smiled. "Not quite, Decimus," he replied and explained as quickly as he could the circumstances of the day. As he finished Doyle looked around and, for the first time, realised that Mahomet was alone.

"Are Jane and the family ...?"

"Jane is at the mews cottage settling herself and the family. Though for the moment we are one less. William took up his apprenticeship at the post office in Paddington last week and stays there during the week, returning for a visit every other Sunday. So we have a little more room ... until the baby arrives, that is. No, Cochrane has been truly kind to us, even allowing us to keep on Sarah as help for Jane. She has been given her own room in the servants quarters of the main house, so has ended up the best of all!" He paused. "Indeed, this is the best of outcomes, it really is."

"But if ..."

"No Decimus, let us not travel that road. I know you mean well, but matters have come too far. William Harding ... I fain to grant him the honour of his title ... will have his say and I will be made bankrupt. But Cochrane has offered me a chance to begin again, and I do not need worry if people take to the bath house or not. There is a steady, if small, custom especially among ladies of a certain age who use the baths as a social club, so Jane and I will turn away from curries and embrace oils and soaps. And water is most therapeutic, don't you think doctor?"

Doyle smiled at last on seeing Mahomet in a decided mood. "Most," he agreed. "Indeed I too have some news for your you. My time at the Hunterian is coming to a close, and I have decided to set up in partnership with a fellow student."

Mahomet was overjoyed and clapped his hands together. "This is good news, Decimus, and just what I wished to hear on this of all days. We are both for a new beginning."

"Though mine will be in Brighton, Sake Mahomet, and not here."

"Brighton?"

Doyle nodded. "I tire of London ... and please do not quote Dr Johnson to me like Bunton has done incessantly. My colleague wishes to take on his father's practice on the Grand Parade in Brighton but is unsure. He is not too bright, I'm afraid, and fears he might be found out. So I have agreed to go into partnership with him. Yet I am afraid that, like you, I will have a surfeit of water cures and elderly matrons."

Mahomet suspected there was more to Doyle's decision than he had confessed. "And the lady, Decimus, what of her?"

Doyle shrugged. "I have been invited to her final performance at Covent Garden next month and then she intends to go to the country. Shropshire, I think. But no, Sake Mahomet, I am not running away. Brighton is a tempting offer for a new doctor and is only six hours away by coach. I will come to town often, if only to compare notes with the shampooing surgeon of a special vapour bath I happen to know."

They both smiled and sat back and Doyle reached for his pocket watch – a gift from his father on his eighteenth birthday. "We must depart soon if we are to attend in good time. I have a hansom waiting to the front. Do you know where we should go?'

"I am to meet Sir Jauncy Vane and Cochrane at the horse stand in Old Palace Yard. From there we will be taken to the Great Hall then wait until the case is called."

Doyle nodded and waited for Mahomet to move. When he did not, Doyle looked at the older man.

"So, Sake Mahomet. Are you ready?"

Mahomet sighed. "Yes Decimus, I am ready. When I lock the door today I will not return here again. This part of my life will be over. So be it!" he slapped his thighs and stood. As they were leaving the coffee house for the last time a postman shouted to them from along George Street. He had a letter for Sake Mahomet from abroad. Mahomet took it and studied the hand.

"Why, it is from Samuel, our old kitchen porter, after all this time. Look, Decimus, it is marked *HMS Bellerophron*. He has replied to my enquiries after all these months, but it will have to wait. After all, the murderer received his just reward at the hands of William Rufus. Come Decimus, I am ready to be judged."

THE Palace of Westminster was an eclectic mix of buildings, and had been the seat of government and the law since the 12th century. While the Great Hall was full of lawyers and their litigants, the remainder of the palace was the preserve of politicians, and it was in this part that ten years previously many changes had been made. The House of Lords, which had grown in size by the addition of numerous Irish peers following the Act of Union between Britain and Ireland in 1801, moved into the Painted White Chamber. Not to be outdone, the House of Commons provided for itself with a new suite of rooms for the Speaker, which overlooked the formal Speaker's garden that ran from the palace down to the bank of the river Thames.

This garden was a haven of solitude from the general bustle of the palace, and a particular favourite of the Prime Minister when the weather was fine. Unfortunately for Mr Perceval, 1812 was quickly becoming an *Annus Inclemens*, both meteorologically and politically. Bad weather since early spring was threatening the year's wheat harvest just when the country, straining under constant war, needed it most. And politically, after the introduction of the Destruction of Stocking Frames Act, attention had moved onto Perceval's Orders in Council. These Orders restricted trade between neutral countries and French dominated Europe, which at the moment included anywhere from Cadiz in southern Spain to Stockholm in Sweden. Moreover the Royal Navy had been most effective in enforcing them, blockading French controlled ports and boarding mercantile ships attempting trading in them.

The United States shipping fleet was by far the largest affected by these Orders, and the American President Mr Madison was becoming particularly agitated. Many American protests had been registered with Perceval over the past five years, but he continued to see the Orders as the most effective way of restricting Napoleon's ambitions. Now the Whig opposition in Parliament, together with leading Tories, were calling on him to show restraint in dealing with the United States.

So it was that Perceval found himself in the Speaker's garden, his back to the wall of St Stephen's Chapel where the House of Commons sat, and before him two of those leading Tories; his War and Colonies Minister Lord Liverpool and his newly appointed Lord President of the Council Lord Sidmouth. The House of Commons was holding an inquiry into the Orders in Council, and debating proposals on whether they should be suspended in the case of shipping from the United States of America. That heated discussion had followed the Prime Minister out into the garden.

"I will concede that the Orders have been mostly effective," Lord Liverpool was advising Perceval, "as any merchant in Liverpool, Bristol or London will confirm. But they have had a far greater and deleterious effect on our intercourse with America. We ..." and here he nodded to the noble Sidmouth, "are of the opinion that the time has come to suspend the

Orders, at least where they concern the United States."

Lord Liverpool was unusual for one so relatively young, an exemplary politician who seemed at ease with men both of liberal and conservative persuasion. He looked to Sidmouth for support.

"I wholly agree with Liverpool, Perceval, and as Lord President it is my duty to advise on the appropriateness of such Orders. Since you invited me to take this office last month my ears have been ringing with complaints, especially from cotton merchants both in Lancashire and from the Virginias and Carolinas. We have already taken from them a ready and profitable supply of labour through your Anti-Slave Trade Act. Let us not drive them into poverty by restricting their trade on the High Seas."

"I have yet to meet an impecunious slaver, my lord," was Perceval's quick response, unhappy that once again Sidmouth had raised the issue.

"Come Spencer," soothed Liverpool, "his lordship is not re-opening wounds but simply stating a case. Of even more concern to me is the continued impressment by the Royal Navy of British-born sailors now claiming to be American when the navy discovers them on board American ships. This makes the Americans most aggrieved."

But Perceval shook his head. "You know as well as I that this so-called naturalisation process of the Americans is simply a cover for British sailors to avoid service. How many have we taken off American ships? Five thousand? Six? All experienced sailors who have seemingly discovered patriotism for another country when hard duty awaits them here at home. The Americans cannot shelter such immigrants."

"But it is a nation of immigrants, Spencer!" said an exasperated Liverpool.

Perceval continued to shake his head. "The Orders in Council are just, and the Americans should look to themselves. They cannot disassociate themselves from the war in Europe, no matter how much they would pretend to do so. President Madison's protestations are encouraged by his eye on our colonies north of his country. Upper and Lower Canada is where his ambitions lay, not in righting the grievances of his merchant class."

The Prime Minister's lengthy discourse silenced the peers for some moments, before Sidmouth again raised the question of most concern to him. "And what of our merchants, Perceval? Do they not matter?"

"Of course they matter my lord. I work tirelessly in their interest. And trade with our colonies has become most profitable. Yet if they cannot wear lace from the Lowlands or drink French wine, then so be it. And if their sons cannot travel to Italy for an education then they had better read more books and visit the whores of Covent Garden. Gentlemen, the war will not last forever. At some time, sooner or later, Napoleon will stumble and make too great a gamble for his own glory. Until that time we must persevere, and America will be made to accept this."

"But what if they do not?" murmured Liverpool. "What if they join with Napoleon against us? We have fought and lost one war with them …"

"Then we will have to take care we do not lose another. Once we have finally dealt with the French then perhaps the time will have come to consider our American policy once more. Are we not in agreement that we should have created an American Indian nation on the Continent, rather than handing western lands over to the newly formed United States?"

The two peers nodded. "This is a long standing object," agreed Liverpool. "Yet our man in Washington, Sir Augustus Foster, says in his latest dispatch that another American complaint against us are the raids by the Indian peoples into their western lands which they say we are encouraging."

"And are we?"

Liverpool smiled weakly. "Perhaps. The Governor of Upper Canada has promised the leader of the Indian Shawnees our support for a nation east of the Mississippi river, which would be a useful buffer. This Indian considers white people to be poisonous serpents. Yet so long as his anger is against the Americans, I think we must continue to supply him with munitions."

"Well, that should keep them suitably occupied," agreed Perceval, smiling at last. "Come my lords, I must return to the Chamber and strengthen the sinews of the waiverers."

THE Star and Garter public house was situated just to the west of the Palace of Westminster, and separated from the main building by a tight alleyway leading to the river and somewhat grandly called Parliament Place. The hostelry was a frequent haunt for many of those who worked next door and was known to oil the wheels of government with a fine mix of beers, wines and beef-steaks: a place where the great mingled licentiously with the not so good. Now, in a corner of the downstairs bar, sat a gaunt-looking man wearing a dark coloured coat. He was obviously waiting for someone, and his head constantly turned to observe the passage of trade frequenting the inn. After some time he spotted his quarry.

"Sir!" he called, waving his arm in the air. "Over here!"

The object of his call responded by nodding and, as unobtrusively as he could, made his way across the room.

"Mr Bellingham. So, here you are."

"Yes sir. As we agreed. And I am wearing the coat we spoke about. I instructed the tailor to make the inside pocket."

As he said this he gently tapped his left side and his visitor looked around cautiously to make sure they were not being observed. They were not.

"Good. You are determined then?"

Bellingham nodded. "As we planned, sir."

"Excellent. This is a far greater thing you do today than even you can imagine. With your action you will not only be righting your own wrong, but ensuring the country can move forward. You are an exceptional man."

This praise seemed to make Bellingham grow just that little bit taller.

"And how have you prepared yourself?"

Bellingham smiled. "I have attended several debates of the House from the galleries. Today the House is in full session debating some Orders in Council. I expect him to appear by late afternoon to speak against a motion which has been laid. I intend to confront him before he goes into the Chamber. There is a position next to the fireplace in the lobby from where you can observe the comings and goings of Members. I will wait there and serve on him my judgment."

"Good." The gentleman then looked to the tankard Bellingham was holding. "You are not imbibing too much, I hope?"

"Oh no sir. This is for show. I will nurse it until I am ready to cross."

The gentleman nodded. "And you cannot mention me to anyone."

"Of course not, sir. You must be free to continue with our plan. Of what value would my part be if you could not complete it? This is the least I can do for my poor wife and child. No sir, no-one will know of our association."

Again the gentleman nodded. "I will be watching, Mr Bellingham, at some distance. Have courage and may God be with you."

He held out his hand and Bellingham shook it warmly. "Thank you sir, and thank you for your sincere words. I know we are making a just stand against a criminal injustice."

THE Great Hall of the Palace of Westminster had been home to the King's courts since Henry II. At one time the king dispensed his justice from a bench placed on the dais to the top of the stone steps to the west end of the hall, and now the King's Bench sat to one side of this dais and the Chancery Court to the other. The hall had witnessed some of the greatest trials in history: from Guido Fawkes and his gunpowder plotters to that of King Charles I. Now it was about to pass judgement on Sake Dean Mahomet, and he sat next to Sir Jauncy Vane KC waiting for his case to be called and looking up at the great hammer-beam roof. It was fortunate perhaps that he did not know the roof had been commissioned by one of England's early kings William II – the original William Rufus.

The noise inside the Great Hall was a constant hubbub, and Mahomet wondered if the judges could hear properly the submissions being made to them, particularly as the Chancery and King's Bench courts were separated solely by low wooden balustrades. Justice was certainly being seen to be done, and from his position below the steps he watched bewigged lawyers standing in the pews before the judges making what he assumed to be important statements of fact and law. He could not hear them properly, and the constant droning of their words had a soporific effect. He had risen very early that morning and had only slept fitfully for days, so now he felt his eyes slowly beginning to close. Fortunately he heard his name called before they closed completely and jumped up with a start, only to be restrained gently by Sir Jauncy. The party of King's Counsel, patron, wife's cousin and defendant ascended the steps and passed through the balustrade into the court proper. But of the petitioner Sir William Harding there was no sign.

Mahomet was seated in a low chair before the judge's bench, which was raised above everything else in the court. On the bench and in a large leather chair sat a spritely man of similar age to Mahomet and dressed in a black robe with very fine golden trim and thread; John Scott, the 1st Earl of Eldon and Lord High Chancellor of Great Britain. Mahomet was to be judged by the country's highest legal authority. The court was soon advised by Harding's counsel that his client had been unavoidably delayed, and the Lord Chancellor was not best pleased but began reading through the papers submitted to him. Then, after some minutes, he began to speak to both Harding's lawyer and to Sir Jauncy, though keeping half an eye on the defendant before him. Finally Mahomet was instructed to stand and the Lord Chancellor began to speak.

"I find this matter most inequitable, that a man be bankrupted by an order of a lower court as the consequence of a gentleman's duel. That injuries at such affairs do take place is beyond question, but I have never before witnessed a sum of money being enforced as if it were Danegeld. Sir William Harding and his brother entered the field in full knowledge of the consequences of their actions, as did Mr Mahomet and his seconders. For my part surely the time has come to outlaw such nonsense, which makes a mockery of our penal code. While Mr Mahomet is unfortunate to find such an order of the magistrates against him, in another time and place he could be standing before the bar of the Old Bailey on a charge of murder.

"That said, it is with a heavy heart that I order the bankruptcy of Sake Dean Mahomet on these grounds and give my agreement to the arrangements as instructed by Sir Jauncy Vane. Mr Mahomet not having the means to discharge the order of the magistrates court, I direct that the Honourable Basil Cochrane be appointed commissioner in bankruptcy of the defendant's estate, to come back to the court in due course with arrangements for the discharge of his debts."

With that the Lord Chancellor stood and, nodding to the court, disappeared through a curtain to the rear of his chair. Mahomet sat back down in some relief and as the court dispersed he looked around to find Doyle in the crowd. As he did, he noticed a shock of red hair beneath the vast west window of the Great Hall and felt a chill run down his spine. He looked again. The red hair was of a man whose back was turned to the court and was speaking to the Honourable Basil Cochrane! Quickly Mahomet stood and walked over to Doyle, but before he could say anything Vane was upon him saying how well the hearing went and that he hoped Mahomet would be discharged within six months or so. As the King's Counsel spoke Mahomet kept his eyes firmly on the back of the redheaded man speaking to his patron. Assuming Mahomet's silence to be that of shock, Vane slowly edged away to speak with a fellow lawyer, leaving the Indian and Irishman alone.

"Decimus look," Mahomet whispered, grasping hold of Doyle's arm and turning him around. It did not take long for the young Irishman to appreciate the reason for this action.

"Is that Rufus?" he asked shocked.

"I think so. Speaking to Cochrane of all people. Come, I will have words with both men."

They passed out from the balustrade surrounding the Chancery Court and made towards Cochrane, only to now find him standing alone and the red-haired man disappearing from the Hall along the passage that led to St Stephen's Chapel and the House of Commons.

"Decimus, after him!" called Mahomet and they brushed past the Honourable Basil Cochrane, who looked on with some shock. They passed through a set of doors and, unbeknown to them, came into the lobby of the House of Commons. The red-haired man could now be seen exiting left towards the cloisters that led to the Speaker's rooms. But instead of following immediately, Mahomet halted. There in the lobby, standing next to a large medieval fireplace, and near to the door of St Stephen's Chapel and the House of Commons itself, stood Mr Bellingham.

"What is he doing here?"

"Who Sake Mahomet? Look, Rufus is making his escape!"

Mahomet was confused and felt he was taking part in some bad dream. Mr Bellingham seemed not to notice him as they stepped forward again, striding with such purpose that they were unchallenged by the porter standing at the doors through which the red-haired man had just gone. They found themselves in a Gothic cloister, to the centre of which was a brick building with a large chimney – the Speaker's kitchen. As they looked the red-haired man appeared from behind it on the other side of the cloister.

"Mr Rufus sir!" Mahomet called. "Mr Rufus. Stop! We would have a word."

To their surprise the red-haired man did stop, and turned to look at them. William Rufus seemed as surprised to seem them as they him.

"One moment Mr Rufus. We must speak with you most urgently."

Mahomet and Doyle hurried around the cloister to the far side, passing as they did so a small group of gentlemen. Neither Indian nor Irishman were aware they had just passed the King's Prime Minister returning from his sojourn in the Speaker's garden. They were now closing in on the object of their chase.

"Mr Mahomet," said Rufus in as sweet a voice as he could muster. "And the young doctor. I see you have just been made bankrupt sir."

"Yes," spat Mahomet, "and you are the cause of all my misfortune."

"I?" questioned the red-haired man innocently.

Now both Mahomet and Doyle had moved close to Rufus to make sure he did not bolt. Looking around, Doyle saw the gentlemen they had passed standing in deep conversation on the other side of the cloister. This was a very public place to hold an inquisition.

"Why did you kill Sir George Harding?" asked Mahomet in a hoarse whisper.

"Me sir?"

"Yes you sir! You were at the edge of the duelling field having brought my own wife as a witness. You shot George Harding, didn't you?"

"That is a grave allegation Mr Mahomet, but I forgive you. Perhaps you are wallowing in self pity brought about by your fiscal distress."

"Do not bandy words with me Rufus," continued Mahomet, now

stepping very close to the man. "Have the decency to tell me the truth," he hissed. "I know there is nothing that can be done about it now. You killed George Harding, and probably killed my servant Walker as well."

"The poisoner?"

"Yes Walker."

"He fell," replied Rufus instinctively. A slow realisation was taking place that the small Indian knew far too much for his own good.

"Ah! So you admit you saw Walker before his death!"

"I admit nothing, Mr Mahomet."

Across the cloister they could hear a heated discussion between the Prime Minister and his colleagues. The gentlemen were far too concerned with the great issues of State to notice the peculiar mix of red head, Indian and tall Irishman on the other side. Rufus stepped back from Mahomet but the smaller man followed and the agent ended up feeling the cold stone of the cloister at his back.

"Come Rufus, tell me the truth now. Why did you say you were from Cochrane, and how did you know about the murder of Sir Josiah Harding. And I ask yet again, why did you kill George Harding?"

William Rufus sighed to himself. The Palace of Westminster was far too public a place for anything untoward to happen, so he must distance himself from the nuisance that was the Indian. Some explanation therefore was in order, even if it held only a smidgeon of truth.

"I was instructed by Cochrane, sir, to investigate this matter."

"Cochrane denies any knowledge of you."

"Really? Then ask him again if you will."

"Who are you sir?"

"I ... believe it nor not Mr Mahomet, I am a force for good. I am one of those gentlemen who acts when others cannot, or when the state is in great danger. I serve the King in my own particular way."

Mahomet was unconvinced by Rufus' high opinion of himself but it was Doyle who made a connection.

"You are a government spy?"

Rufus smiled. "If you wish to call me so."

But Mahomet was accepting little of the claim. "How did the poisoning of Sir Josiah Harding affect the condition of the country? What great purpose did that achieve?"

Rufus paused and shrugged. "The public good is not always achieved by heroic acts, sir. Those who poisoned Harding could not be left to benefit from their purpose."

"Then George Harding did kill his father! But why not bring him to trial?"

For the first time Rufus was unsure of what best to say. "I know George Harding killed his father, sir, it was just the concluding evidence which eluded me."

"You could not prove it," interjected Doyle.

Rufus shrugged.

"Then why kill him?" persevered Mahomet.

"Because of you, sir."

Mahomet stepped back, shocked. "Me?" he asked incredulously.

"But of course, sir. Was it not you who opposed him in the duelling field. What if you had died? I owed it to you and your family to make sure Harding did not take a second shot."

"You shot George Harding to protect Sake Mahomet?" repeated Doyle.

Rufus nodded and smiled, now relaxing at the thought of confusing the agitated gentlemen. "So let that be a lesson to you, Mr Mahomet. No more duels."

The Prime Minister's party had now concluded their discussion and the gentlemen were headed for the door to the House of Commons lobby, leaving Mahomet, Doyle and Rufus alone in the cloister. Mahomet was horrified by what he had heard from Rufus. The young man was clearly dangerous.

"I will report this," he said grimly.

Rufus smiled. "To whom, sir? No one will believe your tale and if you cause too much trouble, I might be moved to act. What then for your wife and children?"

"Do not threaten me. I am not afraid of you."

"Then you should be Mr Mahomet," cautioned Rufus. "You should be."

Mahomet was taken aback by the effrontery of the man, but was stopped from making another reply by what happened next. The retort of a shot rang through the cloister and after a moment a shout went up from House of Commons lobby nearby: "Murder! Bar the doors!"

"Ah," remarked a smiling William Rufus, "that will be Mr Bellingham."

Chapter 20

To the Reader.
I shall say no more, only to hope my BOOK will answer the ends I
intend it for; which is to improve the servants, and save the ladies a
great deal of trouble.

The Art of Cookery Made Plain and Easy

London, Late May 1812.

FROM the comfort of the small sitting room in the mews house behind the
Honourable Basil Cochrane's Portman Square mansion where the family
had now taken residence, Sake Dean Mahomet reflected on all he had
witnessed during the last few days. First had been the dreadful moment
when, standing in the cloisters of the Palace of Westminster, the pistol shot
was heard and the ensuing commotion followed. Both he and Doyle had
quickly turned and headed for the barred door into the lobby of the House
of Commons, only for them both to stop suddenly in confusion. Mahomet
remembered Doyle turning to him and saying: "Who is Bellingham?" The
Indian had then realised that William Rufus mentioned the man by name
and so turned back, intent of questioning his red-haired nemesis only to
find that he had disappeared.

At a loss as to whether to move towards the lobby door or head back
along the cloister to find Rufus, both Mahomet and Doyle found
themselves detained by two officers of the Sergeant at Arms, demanding to
know their purpose. It took some minutes for them to explain to the
officers' satisfaction that they had wandered into the cloister from the Great
Hall where they had been in attendance at the Chancery Court. Only then
were they told that a man had shot the Prime Minister Mr Perceval at close
range as he went to enter the House of Commons. Mahomet instinctively
knew who the gunman was, but held back from mentioning it to the
Parliamentary constables. Slowly they were led through the palace towards

the eastern entrance of the Great Hall and away from the centre of the commotion. By the time they emerged into the open large crowds had gathered around the building and the news was not good. The Prime Minister had been shot and killed by an assassin, probably French or American, they were told. Again Mahomet did not disabuse anyone of this speculation, and slowly the two men headed up Whitehall towards Dr Simon Bunton's house in Soho.

They carried the news with them, and soon found themselves ensconced within Dr Bunton's library, Doyle taking of a large medicinal French brandy while Mahomet sipped on herbal tea prepared by Mrs Mac.

"And this was the man we spoke about only recently?" a shocked Bunton asked Mahomet incredulously.

The former coffee house owner and new bankrupt nodded.

Bunton sighed. "I recall saying to you that the authorities would need a cause to detain your Mr Bellingham but I never imagined this. Mr Perceval ... dead!"

"We do not know it was Bellingham," cautioned Doyle but Mahomet shook his head.

"You heard what Rufus said. But how on God's earth did he know?! I believe this to be another of his works."

Bunton was confused so Doyle recounted their confrontation with the self-confessed spy.

"This is ..." began Bunton, though for once he was lost for words.

"I should speak to the authorities and tell them of our conversation with Rufus," stated Mahomet blankly.

"One moment, sir!" interrupted Bunton. "I know I advised poorly regarding the settlement with Harding, but I most strongly urge you to do no such thing. Let well alone. The King's Prime Minister has just been murdered within the precincts of the House of Commons and you are proposing to tell them that you know the murderer and that you suspect a government spy of being behind it. Not only that, but you were just feet away at the time the murder took place. Mr Mahomet sir, please, I implore you not to say anything. I consider you both most fortunate to have been escorted away from the scene without being questioned. It would be a most grievous error to say anything."

An oppressive mood fell on the library and for some moments no one cared to speak.

"Dr Bunton is right, Sake Mahomet," said Doyle at last, "albeit I wish he were not so. We can say and do nothing. And do not forget the oblique threats Rufus made. You must have care for your family, especially following the court hearing earlier today."

Mahomet looked at Doyle and shook his head. Anger had consumed him. Anger at William Rufus. The man had all but admitted killing Walker and openly admitted to killing George Harding because he could not prove guilt. And he readily identified Bellingham when they had heard the shot! Were they all to be sport for William Rufus' amusement? Was there nothing they could do?

"Could we not help Bellingham to plead insanity?" he asked Bunton, who was taken aback by the question.

"What, and lock him up in the Bedlam with the others? But is he? ... Insane that is. He has family. What do they say?"

Mahomet shrugged. "I have not been introduced to his wife. Yet I thought him distracted to the point of madness the last time we spoke, if you recall. He had this friend whom Jane thought could be imaginary ... Of course! William Rufus. Rufus has been encouraging Bellingham to kill the Prime Minster. Damn it! He is the most monstrous of men!"

Both Doyle and Bunton were startled by Mahomet's outburst.

"But why would he do that Mr Mahomet?" asked Bunton.

Mahomet paused, then slowly sat back in his chair. "I do not know. Because he wished the Prime Minister removed, obviously. He is an American, after all, who are our sworn enemies." He paused in thought again before continuing. "No, I do not know why. Indeed, I know so very little about any of this. But I do know that if Rufus mentioned Bellingham by name then he was up to his trickery. Mr Bellingham was greatly chastised by his circumstances, and last time I spoke to him was convinced Mr Perceval was his tormentor, calling him an agent of the Russians and the like. Bellingham had a febrile mind which I am sure could be turned by someone like Rufus ..."

Mahomet stopped speaking as he fell into more thought, before finally slapping his hands on the chair arms and standing up.

"I must speak to him ... Mr Bellingham," he declared.

"No Mr Mahomet, you cannot!" cried Bunton, "you do not even know if he is still alive!"

But the Indian was adamant. "Then I will wait on the reports in the papers but I will endeavour to speak to him if I can. Sir Jauncy Vane might help. I will call on his chambers at Lincoln's Inn. I must know if Rufus was behind this and whether Bellingham can be declared insane to keep him from the gallows."

And Sir Jauncy Vane KC did help. News soon came out that Bellingham had been detained at Newgate prison and that a trial was being hastily arranged for the Old Bailey. The country was in shock, and struggling to understand why Bellingham had taken such action. In the early days following the murder suspicion was still rife that a foreign party was behind it, and news of Bellingham's time in Russia only re-inforced these views. It took some time for Vane to arrange access to the prisoner, and he issued strong words of caution to Mahomet.

"There seems to be developing a great sympathy for Mr Bellingham among the public. Too many people have suffered at the hands of unsympathetic politicians and officials, and you can count me among the aggrieved. The government fears of making the man a martyr and prefers it if he were committed under the Criminal Lunatics Act, but the jury will have to make a finding as such and the coldness of his actions causes me great doubt. You will have read, of course, that after shooting Mr Perceval at close range he sat down calmly on a stone bench in the lobby and waited to be arrested. The Attorney General will present the case for the prosecution and will call on some senior men from the House of Commons to bear witness. You will have a short time to speak to Bellingham on the day before his trial and this has cost me considerable goodwill, so I hope you can convince him to say that his mind was unclear. Good luck, Mr

Mahomet, though I fear you may need too much of it if you are to keep your friend from the rope."

Newgate Prison was constructed in the style called *architecture terrible*, a French invention to ensure a building adequately described its purpose through the stone. So the west view of the prison in Newgate Street was almost without windows, with heavy blocks of stone and carved chains designed to instill terror on those who passed by and even more on those who entered. As he had walked through the main gate of Newgate the day before the trial Mahomet had been taken unawares by the fetid smells and the pervading darkness. The walls were overbearing and dank as he was led towards the lodge of the turnkey who was in charge of Bellingham's cell. The prison was divided into three large quadrangles for male felons, female felons and debtors. But special prisoners such as John Bellingham were kept in small cells with little light, and it was into one of these that Mahomet now paid for access. He was instructed he would have exactly ten minutes and the door was closed firmly, leaving him in virtual darkness.

"Mr Bellingham?" he called out into the cell, "It is me, Mahomet. I have come to see you."

From out of the dark came a confident response. "Mr Mahomet? The coffee house keeper?"

"Yes sir.'

"Wait a few moments, Mr Mahomet, and your eyes will adjust to the darkness. Thank you for coming. No doubt my family knows but I have heard no word from them. Step forward, Mr Mahomet. There is a chair to your left. I am over here, on the bedding on the floor. It is no coffee house, I'm afraid."

Mahomet's eyes adjusted to the gloom quickly enough and he could make out Bellingham hunched on the floor to one side of the cell. He reached out for the rickety chair and sat down.

"So Mr Bellingham, this is a pretty pass and no mistake. How are they treating you?"

Bellingham coughed. "Well enough I suppose ... for a murderer. I have been in worse gaols."

Mahomet sighed. "Oh Mr Bellingham, why did you do it?"

"I warned them I would, Mr Mahomet, did I not?"

"But the Prime Minister ..."

"Recollect, sir, my situation. Mr Perceval obstinately refused to sanction my claims in Parliament, so I trust that this fatal catastrophe will be a warning to other ministers. I was impelled to a desperate alternative but while my arm was the instrument that shot Mr Perceval, it was a refusal of justice that was the sole cause. I expect His Majesty's ministers to reflect on what has happened."

"But are you not sorry, Mr Bellingham? Mr Perceval has a family and children like the rest of us. He is only a man."

For the first time Bellingham's voice faltered slightly. "No man laments this calamitous event more than I, Mr Mahomet. If I had met Lord Gower in Parliament then he would have received the pistol ball, not Mr Perceval."

"And the consequences sir? If the trial goes against you tomorrow you will surely hang. Your mind must have been clouded by some madness, Mr Bellingham, for you to do such a thing."

Now Bellingham spoke more stridently. "I am not mad, sir. I fully understand the consequences of my action. Yet if I were to suffer hanging five hundred times, I should prefer it to the injuries and indignities that I have experienced in Russia. And what is my crime to the crime of the government itself, Mr Mahomet? Mine is no more than a mite to a mountain! I had no intentional malice towards Mr Perceval, but if a minister sets himself up above the law, as he did, then he does so at his own personal risk. If the upper ranks of society are allowed to act with such impunity, what then becomes of our liberties? No Mr Mahomet, I trust my action will be a warning to the other ministers. I will entrust my life into the hands of the jury and I am sure they will see the just nature of my cause."

Mahomet realised there was no turning Mr Bellingham yet there was one more question he had to ask.

"The gentleman you said advised you, Mr Bellingham. Does he have a head of bright red hair?"

Mahomet thought he heard Bellingham breathe in sharply.

"You know him?" came the answer from the darkened cell.

Mahomet inwardly groaned. Indeed he did.

"His name is William Rufus sir, though again I doubt that is his real name, and he is a government agent. He has caused great distress and killed two gentlemen to my knowledge. You must name this man at your trial tomorrow as a co-conspirator, describe him to the court and make them arrest him."

"You are mistaken Mr Mahomet."

"I wish I were Mr Bellingham. Tell the court that you were encouraged, and were acting for this man. He gravely misled you Mr Bellingham with tales of Russian plots and the like. Beg for mercy and say he confused your mind by playing on your fears. I am told the government does not wish you hanged, Mr Bellingham."

There was a pause and in the distance Mahomet could hear the turnkey's footsteps as he approached.

"And what then, Mr Mahomet? You would rather have me die a long death in Bedlam, where the sane would come and laugh at me for their entertainment? That is more cruel even than a Russian gaol. No sir. I shot Mr Perceval and if I cannot convince the jury of the rightness of my case then I will have an honourable death."

At that moment the lock turned and the cell door opened with the turnkey shouting time.

"Mr Bellingham, please consider what I said," pressed Mahomet. "Do not let this man walk away to cause more harm."

Mahomet felt the turnkey's hand on his shoulder.

"Mr Bellingham?" he called, now in desperation.

From the back of the cell he heard the reply. "I do not know what you mean. Have a good life, Mr Mahomet, and I hope God is kinder to you than he has been to me."

John Bellingham was convicted of murder at the Old Bailey the following day and sentenced to hang. Mahomet winced as he recalled in his mind the early chill of that dawn, with gallows erected from a window high up in the wall of the prison and from which the grim business was conducted. Below the gallows in Newgate Street a crowd had gathered, eager to witness the execution of the latest *cause célèbre*, the Prime Minister's assassin! Among this crowd stood Sake Dean Mahomet and Decimus Doyle. There was much chatter and it quickly became apparent that, rather than the usual festive air at such occasions, people were understanding of the condemned man and were muttering sympathetic words. And they all watched in silence as the final judgement was delivered.

London, Early Summer 1812.

IT had been over a week since the hanging of John Bellingham and the business of London had returned to normal. The master of the Indian vapour baths off Portman Square was settling into his new role of playing a courteous and knowledgeable host to the attending ladies whose numbers, contrary to the patrons of the Hindostanee Coffee House, were beginning to increase on his arrival. They took particular notice of his advice on the care of skin and teeth, and he had created a small apothecary stall within the bathhouse where guests could purchase a range of unguents, salts and perfumes. They were less inclined towards the new bathhouse masseuse however, who had a sharp Irish tone and somewhat brusque manner, as if handling cold meat.

It was during a quiet moment at the bathhouse that Sake Dean Mahomet happened to reach within his morning coat and came across a small paper tucked inside a pocket. Pulling it out he realised it was the letter received from his former kitchen porter Samuel on the fateful day when both he and the Ministry of Spencer Perceval had been declared bankrupt. He had completely forgotten about it in the following days and now sat down on one of the bathhouse chairs to read.

HMS Bellerophon, Easter 1812
Dear Master
Much thanks for your letter. I got it when we docked at Plymouth.

It made me very guilty as I didn't excuse myself right. I know your Missus will be very angry with me. Please say how sorry I am.

You know I wanted to be at sea, but my dada said no to me signing up. But the gentleman at our coffee house helped. You know him as he said he would talk to you for me. He said Walker would stand for me, the man you were asking questions of. I hope all goes well with him.

We are leaving next week for a year in the south. Gibraltar then on to Naples if the French don't fight! Life on ship hard but as you can see I am learning my letters and studying for my seaman-ship examunatens. A friend is helping me write this.

Please say my regards to your lady wife and Sarah, and also my respects to William Harding Esq, who as you know did so much to help me.

Yours&Etc.

Sam.

Mahomet slumped back in his chair and re-read the last paragraph over and over. William Harding! William Harding had placed Samuel in the Royal Navy and Walker in his coffee house. How could this be? They had all been convinced – Mahomet, Doyle and even the despicable William Rufus – that George Harding was behind the poisoning of Sir Josiah. Mahomet's first reaction was to assume that Samuel had confused the two brothers, but this was dismissed by his wife when she was shown the letter some time later in the day.

"I said Samuel was too close to that man," she barked, as angry as her husband by the deceit. "Remember I would chastise him not to speak so regularly to the gentleman. I used to assume they were talking about cricket and the like, not planning to send our Sam off to sea."

"But don't you see my pearl," interrupted Mahomet, "this means it was William Harding who placed Walker here. It was William Harding who planned the death of Sir Josiah!"

The consequences of this new disclosure soon dawned on Jane Mahomet.

"Oh! Then leave well alone, husband. In no event should you challenge the man. One duel in a lifetime is more than enough for me, never mind you! You are warned!"

Nor was Decimus Doyle any more receptive when he read the letter the following day in Dr Bunton's library.

"I can hardly believe it, Sake Mahomet. Are you sure Sam has the correct name?"

Mahomet nodded. "Jane would tell Samuel not to be so familiar with William Harding. Sir Josiah would often bring him along as he wished him to join the East India Company. I can hardly ever remember seeing George at the coffee house before that fateful day. So there was simply no opportunity for George and Sam to become acquainted. I was such a fool not realising this before!"

Both sat in silence for some minutes absorbing the news.

"Mrs Siddons said Sir Josiah mistreated his sons, did she not?"

"Yes Sake Mahomet. I recall her suggesting that it was his cruelty towards the boys that led to some distance being created between the two."

"So William Harding had a motive for killing his father."

"I suppose so, but ..." Doyle's voice trailed off.

"But?"

Doyle shrugged his shoulders. "I do not know Sake Mahomet."

Mahomet nodded. "But I do, Decimus. I intend to speak with William Harding immediately. He may have not have had the courage to attend at my bankruptcy, but I will make him answer for why he placed Walker in my coffee house and poisoned his father."

Doyle was about to argue with the older man but saw the look of defiance on the Indian's face. "Then I will accompany you, Sake Mahomet. I too would like to know the reasons for all this trouble."

And so it was that Sake Dean Mahomet and Decimus Doyle journeyed to the new Harding residence in Dorset Square, north London. The elderly footman answering the door at first refused to accept their calling cards, but on hearing Sir William Harding's voice in an adjoining room they pushed by the retainer and opened the door. After some moments of protest from both Harding and his servant, they prevailed and were left alone. Mahomet quickly came to the point, showing Sir William the letter.

"This is proof, sir. Now we know that you removed my kitchen porter, replaced him with your own man and subsequently poisoned your father. Why should I not go to the authorities with this?"

Sir William Harding remained seated, looking at the letter but hardly reading it.

"You must answer Sake Mahomet, Harding, or we will make you do so in public," Doyle continued. "Come now man, give us your reasoning. Did you plan the death of your father?"

"Yes," croaked William Harding at last. "Yes, I killed him, or rather Walker did so on my behalf. Have you seen him?"

"Who?" asked Mahomet.

"Walker. He disappeared. At first I was worried he might blackmail me, but then I heard no more."

"He's dead," answered Doyle dismissively.

"Murdered more like," added Mahomet, making sure they did not lose the confession now. "A government spy caught up with him. You see, Harding, that we are not without associates. The same man who killed Walker shot and killed your brother."

Sir William was confused. " But you ...?"

"The shot from my pistol did not kill your brother. The spy was observing the duel while hidden to the side and killed Sir George because he thought ... we all thought ... your brother was the one who instructed Walker. If that man were now to find out that it was you ..."

Doyle looked at Mahomet shocked. He was threatening the man.

"But I would now prefer that what was done be left done, even though it is against all justice," Mahomet continued. "That is if you can prove to me that there was a reason to all this madness. We know your father beat you. Was this the reason?"

A faint smile appeared on Sir William Harding's face. "His riding crop and fists? No sir, it was a far more delicate matter than that."

Mahomet was surprised. "Then what, sir?"

Harding swallowed hard. "I cannot say."

"You will say!" replied a now angry former coffee house owner, "or I will point out to a certain government agent the error of his ways. You have deprived me of my livelihood, sir, so you will not deprive me a good reason for that happening. Now, out with it!"

Harding looked to the floor, as if embarrassed at what he was about to say. "It was Lottie. I did it for her."

"Miss Harding!" and "Lottie!" Mahomet and Doyle cried in unison.

"Sssh, please gentlemen. She is upstairs, and I would not wish her to know of your presence Doyle ... Papa was very ... familiar with Lottie, especially as she grew into a young woman. People would comment on it."

Sir William Harding became very agitated and stood, pacing the room and not looking at either man. "Lottie needed her father's love," he continued. "Yet she turned from being anxious for papa's affections to being fearful of them."

Finally Harding stopped pacing and looked at Mahomet. "Lottie is not of this world in so many ways, Mr Mahomet, and I feared my father would take advantage of her."

Mahomet was unsure of what Harding was saying. "Are you telling me sir, that because your father displayed uncharacteristic affection for your sister you decided to do away with him?"

Harding looked shocked. "You do not understand me, sir. It was far more than that ... you cannot understand ... she was fearful of him, I say. I tried to encourage her to speak about it but ... damn it, I had to protect her gentlemen. I love her dearly, you see. Tell me you would not have done the same. But what could I do? I could not expose him. The shame of this ... well, it is simply unspeakable. And I knew papa only too well." At this remark Harding began rubbing his left arm and began pacing around the room. Doyle stood in his way to stop him.

But Mahomet was having none of his self-pitying patter. "If you feared for your father's actions then you should have confronted him, or removed both yourself and your sister from his influence. Instead you concocted a most elaborate plot to murder him and let others take the blame. You are a coward, sir, of the very first rank! Not only that but you pursued me and my family through the courts."

"But I could do no other, sir, if I were to justify George's death!"

"Poppycock!" exclaimed Mahomet, and Doyle reached out and touched the Indian's arm in an effort to calm him. "I did not think I would ever say this, sir, but your brother was twice the man of you."

Harding at first look shocked but then smiled. "It was George who gave me the idea to dispose of papa."

"Your brother?"

"He has ... had ... a small library of books, one of which concerned poisons. I asked him in jest what was the most effective, and he gave me the idea of monkshood. Said it was a killer but had a very bitter taste so anyone taking it would spit it out rather than swallow it. It would need to be masked by strong flavours. I tore the pages from the book relating to it and found an apothecary who would supply it. Then papa started taking me to your coffee house sir, so I might acquire a taste for Oriental food. The plan just dawned on me. Papa always ate the same curried dish, which I tried once but it was far too strong and hot. Yet there was a chance it would mask the monkshood. I became acquainted with your kitchen porter and, through contacts, secured a place for him in the Navy. In return he gratefully recommended Walker, whom I knew as a grave robber from a time he escorted my cricket team to Soho and the like. He hardly gave me the chance to work out the plan, so eager was he to make money. I did not expect papa to die so quickly. Then it was all over, and George took the baronetcy and sold the estate, and neither Lottie nor I was any safer than before."

"So you engineered the duel," continued Mahomet, as the chain of events became clear to him. "Did you tell George what was said at the cricket match?"

Harding nodded. "I could hardly believe it! Here was a man accusing my brother of poisoning my father. At first I was fearful, then saw how it could play to my ... to our advantage, I mean, Lottie's and mine."

"I always wondered how our conversation was overheard by your brother," hissed Mahomet. "Then you should be advised sir that the man who made the allegation against your brother in the tent is the same government spy of whom I have already spoken. He would not be best pleased that he shot the wrong brother."

"But I tried to help, Mr Mahomet, I truly did. I even had one of the pistols rifled to give you a better shot."

"Ahhhh!" exclaimed Doyle.

"But I would not have killed your brother, Harding, in any circumstance. Did you not understand that?"

The room fell silent as all three men continued to look at each other.

"So, what now sir?" asked Harding meekly. "Will you tell this man of his error and leave my sister to fend for her self alone?"

Mahomet looked hard at the man. "To hell with you sir, and your sister. You must live with these crimes but I will not make you pay, for now. Indeed I cannot, if only for my own family's sake. I do not know whether your suspicions about your father were true, but even if they were it was not for you to pass judgment on them. There are many cruelties and injustices in this country, but the desire for the rule of law is not one of them. I recently witnessed the hanging of a man against whom a great miscarriage of justice had been done, but like you he acted as his own judge and jury. That will not do. Come Decimus, let us leave this shadow of a man to his conscience, if he has one. Good day sir."

London, Late June 1812.

THE new Home Secretary looked down from the window of his office in Somerset House onto the river Thames and the preparatory work that was being undertaken for a new bridge. John Rennie, an architect more used to digging canals, had proposed nine equal arches spanning the river and carrying a perfectly flat roadway above. Surveyors were now working mid stream, gauging the depth of the river and the alignment from bank to bank. And so London progresses, thought the Home Secretary, on a never-ending march into the future. He was disturbed from his thoughts by a knocking on his door, and moments later his private secretary, the Rev. Williams, entered.

"My pardon my lord, but you must make for Carlton House presently if you are to be in good time for the Cabinet with the Lord Liverpool and the Prince Regent. And Mr Rufus attends on you."

Lord Sidmouth nodded. "Very good Williams. Rufus can accompany us in the coach. Have you a copy of yesterday's *Political Register*? I wish to read Castlereagh's speech to the Lords announcing the suspension of the Orders in Council. That should please the Americans, no doubt."

Williams bowed and left the room, and some time later joined his master and William Rufus in the coach headed down the Strand towards the London residence of the Prince Regent. They did not go far, however, before traffic was brought to a standstill by a commotion in the street. Rufus was dispatched to establish what was happening and returned a few minutes later.

"There is a large crowd, my lord, outside the home of Mrs Siddons. She performed on stage for the last time yesterday and is now taking her adieu of London. We could be some time. No doubt they will disperse soon enough once her carriage has left."

"Actresses!" snorted Sidmouth. "Well, we may as well wait. Short cuts make for long delays but see if you can find some Runners to create a path through the crowd for the traffic."

With Rufus sent away again Williams reached for his attaché case and took out some papers.

"While we are alone, my lord, I thought you would wish to see these. Copies of dispatches from Lord Castlereagh's agents in Paris. The Grande Armée is on the move, it seems."

The Home Secretary began reading the papers he had been given.

"So, Russia is to suffer French steel then. The French Corporal really has no limits to his ambition, but this is good news. The Tsar bought himself too little time in treating with the French. He was warned."

Lord Sidmouth sat back in the coach. "How ironic," he said.

"My lord?"

"Poor Perceval. He said Napoleon would over-reach himself and now perhaps he will. And no doubt we will be allies again with the Tsar. And that stupid man Bellingham. He might have achieved some of the justice he was wanting had he waited. Some men are fools, Williams."

"Yes my lord."

"We will watch and wait. Napoleon may think he rules all Europe but it is likely to be the other way round. Russia is a very distant land and it takes weeks for news to come from it. Just like the United States. If anything goes untoward with his campaign, the French Corporal will find himself stranded, like Cornwallis with our army in the Thirteen Colonies all those years ago. And we know how that ended. This could be it Williams, Napoleon's final strategy."

"It would be most fortuitous, my lord. This war has gone on too long."

The Home Secretary snorted again. "There will always be conflict Williams, if not on the Continent then here at home. The Deputy Constable of Manchester has just written to me advising that he arrested thirty-eight men at a public house. He's charged them with administering oaths to weavers pledging to destroy looms. This sedition is like a canker, but we will cut it out. If the twenty-three men just hanged in Lancashire thanks to the work of our Mr Rufus are not enough, then there will be more. And there is plenty of room on the ships to New South Wales. I have been charged with holding the line at home while our generals take to the field in Spain, and I will not shirk from the task."

Lord Sidmouth looked out of the carriage window and saw William Rufus directing two constables towards the crowd gathered outside Mrs Siddons' residence.

"I will suggest to Castlereagh that we send Rufus to the United States, I think. He can return for a while to his family estate in the Virginias and can keep watch on those Republican upstarts. It is still our desire to create an American Indian nation in the west of that continent. I am most pleased with his work and consider him a very great asset to us, and we can now provide a government sinecure to retain his services for the good of the country. But I think we might be able to consider his absence for a time. The

Regent was wise to appoint Lord Liverpool in Perceval's stead and now he has seen fit to appoint me Home Secretary I am confident we will prevail against the seditionists."

The Rev Williams looked to his master. "You are no longer concerned, my lord, by the young man's ... impetuousness?"

The Home Secretary sighed. "I cannot say I am wholly satisfied with his demeanour – he is still far too smug for my liking – but I cannot argue with his results. He handled that Cochrane business most ably, and his reports from the North helped me to convince our late Prime Minister to introduce new legislation. No, I would rather have a William Rufus working for our aims than a Lord Byron seeking to undermine the very fabric of society."

The carriage jolted and began to move slowly forward.

"And look!" declared the Home Secretary with a thin smile, "he can even make the traffic move in the centre of London. Is there no end to his skills?"

THE small Indian and tall Irishman sat together on a bench in the formal gardens to the centre of Portman Square. It was still a couple of weeks until St Swithin's Day but the weather was out to make a mockery of the fable and rain for forty days and nights beforehand. Still, there had now been a break in the continuous cloud cover, so Sake Dean Mahomet suggested to his wife's young cousin, when he called at their small mews cottage, that they take the air. They ended up on the seat which had been newly installed by the kind condescension of one of the square's residents, though the wood still felt slightly damp and Doyle was grateful he was wearing a dark pair of pantaloons.

"So your time at the Hunterian has finally concluded, Decimus, and you are to leave us for the pleasures of Brighton."

The young man nodded. "I will wait until cousin Jane gives birth Sake Mahomet, and then head south."

Mahomet sighed. Jane was already slightly over her expected date and the midwife had called several times. As yet, though, there was still no sign of her accouchement.

"It cannot now be long, Decimus. She experienced great spasms last night but in the end put it down to indigestion. But we are not concerned. Horatio was late, as was William."

Mention of the Mahomets' eldest led to Doyle asking how he was fairing at the Paddington post office.

"He has taken to it very well," smiled Mahomet, "and I had a most complimentary letter from the postmaster last week. I am glad I settled William's apprenticeship prior to my bankruptcy."

Doyle smiled. "I still remember him calling at Bunton's last year saying his mother had poisoned a patron at the coffee house!"

Mahomet groaned. "Do not remind me Decimus. We have experienced quite a year I must say. Murder, the duel, my bankruptcy and the assassination of the Prime Minister." He paused. "Oh, poor Mr Bellingham. I still have nightmares of his swinging from the rope outside Newgate."

"But he shot Mr Perceval, Sake Mahomet!"

"Yes, I know Decimus. But I do not think he meant to. I mean, he shot the man but really he was attacking the office. In his twisted mind he thought that he was teaching the King's ministers a lesson and that no jury would convict him."

"And he was encouraged by a bad man."

"Yes ... William Rufus." Mahomet paused and shook his head. "Now there is a man who should be hanged outside Newgate for murder. I am sorry that this man has escaped all punishment. Who employs such a man, do you think? Well I know the answer to that, Cochrane for a start. Rufus' arrogance knows no bounds, yet so often in this matter he has been wrong. Remember, he took the life of George Harding without any proof and then the man was innocent after all."

He paused again. "And I am most anxious, Decimus. I do not forget his threat made just before Mr Bellingham killed the Prime Minister. I feel very uncomfortable knowing the man is at large in the city and I fret for my family's safety and for yours. We both know too much about him. I questioned Cochrane again about Rufus and, while he still continues the fiction and denies knowledge of him, I saw fear in his eyes. While I take bitter satisfaction from the fact we know he accused and condemned the wrong brother, yet I sincerely hope we never come across William Rufus again. Now, as the weather is fine let us speak no more about him."

Mahomet sat back on the bench and then, remembering the damp wood, leaned slightly forward again. Yet Doyle was not quite finished with speaking about Rufus.

"I thought I saw him very recently, Sake Mahomet. William Rufus, that is."

"Really? Where?" replied Mahomet anxiously.

"He seemed to be instructing constables in the Strand who were shepherding a large crowd which had gathered."

"Oh? Do you think he works at Bow Street then?"

"I do not know. But the constables were giving him due attention."

"Hmmm," said Mahomet and fell into silence, before adding: "And what was the crowd about?"

He turned to see his wife's cousin blush. "Mrs Siddons, Sake Mahomet."

"Ahhhh."

"I heard well-wishers were gathering outside her house so ventured to look."

"Really."

"Yes. There was a considerable crowd and it was blocking half the Strand it seemed. They were waiting for Sarah to depart."

"And did you see her."

Doyle nodded. "From a distance and I doubt she recognised me in the crowd. She was wearing the necklace the Prince Regent had presented to her at Covent Garden after her last performance."

"The dreaded jewels!"

"Yes. She briefly waved before getting into her coach and driving off."

The two men again fell into silence before Mahomet said: "And so it ends", and Doyle slowly nodded in agreement.

"And so to new beginnings, Sake Mahomet," continued Doyle at last.

"Yes Decimus, and on that point I have some news. Cochrane may have found a buyer for the coffee house. Oh, the money on offer will only partly discharge the debt to that cad William Harding, but the prospective purchaser does wish to continue the name of the Hindostanee Coffee House, and the sale will discharge my bankruptcy."

Doyle turned to his companion. "But this is good news, Sake Mahomet."

"Yes. If the purchase is settled then I will consider it some justification in my opening the place in the first instance. Such an affirmation provides me with a little solace I think."

"Would you ever consider opening another?"

Mahomet paused for some time thinking on this. "A coffee house? Perhaps not, and I do not think Jane would be amenable to such an idea. The events of the past few months have left too deep a scar on her. But I fully intend to set up in business again, once my bankruptcy is discharged."

"Really, Sake Mahomet. As what?"

"I have been thinking. You mentioned, did you not Decimus, that water cures are very *à la mode* in towns such as Brighton?"

Doyle nodded. "Drinking and dipping, as they say. It is very profitable business, especially as the gentry cannot travel to the Continent because of Bonaparte. Yet while spa water can be quite beneficial, I think drinking sea water is questionable – though bathing in it is most therapeutic."

"Yes," enthused Mahomet, "as would an Indian vapour bath."

Doyle looked at him quizzically.

"Cochrane's baths may not be too popular here in the west end of London, but in a resort such as Brighton or Bath they could become quite a favoured treatment."

"And does Mr Cochrane agree?"

"Pffff! I have not mentioned it to him. I am still angered by his plainly false denial of any knowledge of William Rufus. I feel betrayed. No, my intention is to set up anew in one of those towns."

"Then make it Brighton, Sake Mahomet," smiled Doyle. "After all, you will already have family there."

Mahomet returned the smile. "Agreed, Decimus."

From across the square they heard the call of "Papa! Papa!" and turned to see young Henry Mahomet running across the cobbles towards them, narrowly missing a dogcart on the way. They both stood, with Mahomet thinking he understood the urgency of the call.

"Henry! What is it? Your mother?"

"Mama?" questioned the boy, and his confusion was passed to his father.

"If it is not your mother then why have you come running across like a dervish?"

"I am sorry papa, but Manjai says I should bring you the news. He heard it from Mr Cochrane himself."

"What news?"

""It's war papa, we are at war."

This, Mahomet decided, was not news. "Of course we are at war. We are always at war …. Wait, they have not invaded have they? The French?"

"Invaded?" asked the confused child. "No papa. It is not the French. We are at war with the United States of America!"

Mahomet sighed. Always more war, he lamented to himself. Still, he hoped this meant the government – and its agents – would be concentrating on other matters to unduly concern themselves with his family. He would put them some distance from William Rufus at his first opportunity by joining his wife's cousin in Brighton. So resolved, Sake Dean Mahomet and Dr Decimus Doyle followed young Henry Mahomet back across Portman Square towards the small mews cottage and home.

Acknowledgements

WHILE the narrative of this book is fictional, many of the characters and events are not. Indeed it would be difficult to invent lives of greater interest than those I mention, even in passing. Take Thomas Cochrane, for example, whose antics delayed the Honourable Basil's return to London. In real life after this book finishes he elopes with his dearest Kitty and is disinherited by Basil, is imprisoned for his part in the Great Stock Exchange Fraud of 1814, and on his release is invited by the Chileans to command their navy in the war of independence against the Spanish. There is still an Avenida Lord Cochrane in Santiago.

It is a great pity that, apart from a plaque in George Street, there is no similar acknowledgement for the life of Sake Dean Mahomet, as his tale becomes the more remarkable in every telling. He is widely acknowledged to have been the first Indian to have written and been published in English, and is the first man to have established a curry house in London and, ergo, anywhere beyond the Orient. Nor did he have any social advantages; while he presented himself as an Indian prince, this could not have been further from the truth. Rather he was a fatherless waif who found himself in an East India Company army camp and ended up as Shampooing Surgeon to the Prince Regent (even if this was his own self-aggrandisement). I hope this book is the first step in remedying this lack of recognition.

I have kept with the spelling of "Mahomet" used by himself in his first book and that of "Hindostanee" he used in his advert for *The Times*. My thanks in particular go to Prof. Michael Fisher and his study of Mahomet's published work *The Travels of Dean Mahomet* (Fisher, University of California Press, 1997), and also to those thousands of contributors to Wikipedia who unknowingly but altruistically allowed me to piggyback on all their hard work.

Colin Bannon, Brighton, Autumn 2013

The story continues ...

... read the first chapter here

Chapter 1

Dawn on the English Channel near Brighton, Early July 1817.

THE water came over the side of the boat with some force, soaking the boy and knocking him to the deck at the same time. He gasped for breath and reached out for support to a guy rope running down from the small mast.

"It's not good," shouted the old man behind him. "It's too rough. There 'aint no point trying to fish in this swell."

The boy hauled himself to his feet.

"Bring in the net, lad, and let's 'ead back to the beach."

The old man turned the tiller and the boat lurched sharply right into the oncoming waves. The boy fell onto the deck once more.

"On yer feet lad!" the old man yelled. "Bring in that net before we lose it!"

The boy looked back sharply at the old man but didn't say a word. He crawled forward along the deck of the boat towards the net line and, taking a firm grip, started to pull.

"It's 'eavy, master!" he called. "I thought you said there won't be no fish."

"Pull 'ard boy!" came the reply.

"I am pulling! It just won't budge!"

The old man grimaced, lashed the tiller and made his way forward.

"I knew it was wrong to come out w'out yer father," he chided to the boy. "You can't send a lad to do a man's work."

He scrambled behind the youth and together they began to pull in the net.

"You're right boy," the old man wheezed, "it is 'eavy!"

A thin smile of justification appeared on the young man's face as together, mariners ancient and modern, they brought the net alongside the lurching boat and, finally, landed it on the deck.

"That'll do," said the old man. "Let's 'ead back to the beach."

The boat was a hoggie or hog-boat, common in Brighton because it had a very wide beam to cope with the Channel's rough seas, and a flattish bottom so it could be hauled up easily onto the shingle beach.

As they landed the lad jumped down quickly, with the old man struggling to follow. Both grabbed a side of the boat and began to haul. It was as the boat cleared the water that the old man saw a bundle stuck beneath the bow.

"No wonder it's 'arder than I thought, we've got somethin' stuck!" he called, indicating that the boy should go and pull it away.

As the lad did so, he noticed a thin white hand sticking out from a heavy piece of cloth.

THE reflection of the man in the silvered glass seemed to be full of doubt. He was facing a decision of some consequence yet couldn't make up his mind. He was sure that his instinct was right, but the question still remained ... was the current tying of his snow-white linen cravat in the Osbaldeston style, where he'd started with the cravat behind his neck and brought it round into a large knot, acceptable with his dark green waistcoat? He had already tried all the styles he knew – the Napoleon, Mathematical, Oriental and the Irish – and used up four cravats in the last half hour, for which profligacy he would be duly chastised by his wife, no doubt. He really couldn't face tying yet another! So be it ... this was going to have to do.

He ran his hands down his black morning coat, pulling at the lapels. He tugged at the bottom of the waistcoat and smoothed down the cream pantaloons. He still had the boots – Wellingtons, of course, though they had seen better days – to wrestle with, but he seemed to be almost there, and it had taken him less than half an hour to dress. Quite an achievement.

The impression you presented to others, he knew from long experience, was the means to making a fortune, though during his fifty or so years on this earth the attainment of wealth had been frustratingly elusive. And if he were truly honest with himself he would acknowledge that quality, stylish clothing helped him fit in – to be accepted – by those around him. Moreover, his clothing was also a reflection of his changing fortunes; since they had settled in Brighton three years ago his latest business venture had been the most encouraging to date. He looked again into the glass and considered the complete picture. "Not bad Mahomet, if I say so myself," he thought. His head was still full of typically Indian dark wavy hair, if somewhat thinning at the brow and accompanied by fashionable sideburns. His teeth were in fair shape thanks to his Indian tooth powder and, though only just touching five foot in height, he still stood out in the crowd. Of course, his dark skin helped in a land full of pale people.

This musing was interrupted by a knock on the door, which opened a few seconds later. His wife Jane entered the bedroom.

"I am sorry to disturb your toilet, husband," she said caustically in her sharp Irish tone, followed by a raising of the eyebrows when she caught sight of the discarded cravats, "but we have a visitor downstairs."

Jane Mahomet was a quite few inches taller than her husband, and over twenty years younger. She had soft, delicate features which belied the fact she had borne and brought up six children, the most recent two years ago when in her thirty-fifth year. Baby Rosanna had come as a surprise to the Mahomets, who nevertheless embraced parenthood once more as a divine blessing. In fact, in the very early years of their marriage Jane had difficulty in conceiving. That was until she was encouraged by her husband to try powders made from the crushed berries of the chaste tree, a well known infertility remedy both in Asia and the eastern Mediterranean. So the arrival of baby Rosanna was testament to the long lasting efficacy of the remedy, and on hearing the news Mahomet even suggested they sell of chaste berry powders on her recommendation, something that Jane quickly quashed. She had no intention of letting every Tom, Dick and Harry into the secrets of her domestic arrangements, thank you very much.

"Visitor? I am not expecting anyone, am I?" Mahomet asked his wife.

"It's a Captain Hunter from the cavalry barracks. He makes his apologies for arriving unannounced and so early, but begs a moment of your time."

Curiosity took hold. "A captain? Well, I must see him. Help me on with these boots, my love, and I will attend to our honoured visitor while you attend to the children."

Some minutes later a well turned out head of household entered his small sitting room. "Captain Hunter?"

"Your servant sir," said the soldier, coming to attention. "Have I the pleasure of addressing Mr Mahomet?" he asked, knowing quite well he had.

Mahomet took in the uniform of the young soldier before him. As was the fashion for Hussars officers in the 10th, the Prince of Wales Own, the tunic was dark blue with a vivid yellow velvet collar and cuffs. Down the front were elaborate panels of white embroidered Russian lace. The tunic made quite a statement, and took Mahomet back to an earlier age, where he was a jemander of the 30th Infantry Regiment in the Second European Brigade of the East India Company, parading proudly before his grenadiers in the Residency at Cawnpore.

He introduced himself. "Sake Dean Mahomet at your service," he said, making a small bow then holding out his hand, which the captain grasped firmly. Mahomet called himself "Sake", or Sheikh, as he claimed his family were of Arab descent and accompanied the great Mughul emperors when they first invaded India.

"I'm sorry to call on you unannounced sir, but the colonel thought it best that I came here straight away, seeing the surgeon-major is in London."

"Have you some emergency at the barracks captain?"

"Not among the men, Mr Mahomet, no," said the captain, who then paused and seemed to think hard of what to say next.

"Then ...?" started Mahomet.

"It is delicate, sir," interrupted Hunter. "We had an arrival this morning ... a body ... a young woman."

"A woman's body? At the barracks?" Mahomet was taken aback.

"She was found on the beach, sir, very early this morning. She had been trapped beneath a boat as they hauled it onto the shingle. An old man and boy discovered her. The men thought it best to bring her up to the barracks ... law and order and all that. We've set up a temporary morgue next to the surgeon's office."

"Very sensible," Mahomet remarked, " but what has it to do with me? She is unlikely to want an invigorating vapour bath, I think."

"No sir ... in fact she's in a bit of a mess. But you may know our surgeon-major acts as the ad-hoc coroner for Brighton and ..."

Mahomet finished the sentence: "... and he is in London, yes, you said. Can you not pack the body in ice till your surgeon-major returns from London?" he advised.

"We've already got her on ice, sir, much to the irritation of the mess steward as we have depleted the barracks ice house, but we don't know when the surgeon-major is likely to return ... it is, ermm, delicate. He is on what we are calling indefinite leave."

"Indefinite?" queried Mahomet.

"Yes sir, I'm afraid so. All I can really say is that it comes down to the surgeon-major's shaking hands and the colonel's toothache. Everyone thought it best if there were some distance kept between the two until something settles: either the surgeon-major's shakes or the colonel's tooth.

"The colonel speaks very highly of your skills sir," Hunter continued, "and as you know frequents your bath house. He has great confidence in you, sir, and is hoping you would be available to have a look at the body .... after all, while we are awash with experts in Brighton there are few proper doctors!" Both men smiled at Hunter's pun on Brighton's reputation for water cures. "We understand you were a surgeon in the Indian army, as well as being the Prince's shampooing surgeon. We would like to keep all this ... discreet," he concluded.

Mahomet wondered whether this appeal was an attempt at flattery or a sign of despair. Mention of the baths made him realise he would soon have to open for business. "This is a nuisance," he said, voicing his thoughts then, looking at the captain, feeling embarrassed for doing so. "While I was trained as a surgeon in India, captain, and attended to the soldiers in my care, it has been many years since I dissected a body and, as your colonel will know, have turned my skills to water treatments." He paused in thought. "Yet it seems I am obliged to help, for Colonel Reynolds sake. Very well, I suggest you go on ahead and advise him I will be there in the next hour or so."

After the captain departed Jane Mahomet came into the room.

"It seems, my pearl, that I have to go to Preston barracks to examine a woman's body."

"You husband? How curious," replied his wife in her most unflappable tone?

"I will need some help, so think I will call on Decimus along the way. You will have to open the baths alone this morning, my pearl."

"Then it is indeed fortunate we have no gentlemen clients of importance today, or we would have had to cancel them," she chastised, irritated that her husband was once again distracted from the business of making money. Jane then paused, already thinking she was going to regret the next remark; "And could I suggest a change of clothing? It could be quite ... messy."

"Very wise my dear," nodded Mahomet sagaciously, and he made his way back to the bedroom, wife in tow.

In took him half an hour to choose on an alternative outfit, prepare for the task ahead and leave the double fronted house in Black Lion Street which he called home with Jane and six of their children: Amelia, Henry, Horatio, Frederick, Arthur and young Rosanna. All the children had olive coloured or darkened skin and dark hair except Rosanna, whose skin was alabaster white and hair was becoming redder than a soldier's tunic. While he loved all his children dearly, including his eldest William who now lived in London, his youngest was special as she was unique within the family, just as his family was unique within the country.

Mahomet turned in the opposite direction to his usual morning walk down to the beach and his Battery House baths. He zig-zagged through the narrow streets of Brighton, making his way towards the Steyne, the landmark enclosure of fields in the middle of the town. It was covered, as usual, with fishing nets which he carefully negotiated as he crossed. The gulls were evidently mating, and the noise of their screeching as they vied for partners was, at times, deafening. They soared and swooped over the nets and the nearby fish market, on the lookout for scraps and inattentive fishwives.

He and Mrs Mahomet arrived in Brighton three years previously from London, leaving behind them William who had taken a position as postman with His Majesty's Mail and did not wish to move yet again. Mahomet's contacts from the East India Company had always served him well, and for most of their time in London he worked for a former Nabob, or provincial governor, the Honourable Basil Cochrane, who was the sixth son of the Earl of Dundonald. Thanks to this patronage, the Mahomets had lived with the Nabob in the largest house in the very fashionable Portman Square, along with the Ottoman Ambassador to the Court of St. James and a small mosque. Cochrane's great wealth, amassed from a contract to victual the Royal Navy stationed in the Eastern oceans and successfully defended against charges of embezzlement, allowed him to indulge in several projects, including an Indian vapour cure. The altruistic Cochrane was determined to improve the health of London's lower classes by establishing a vapour bath for their therapy at his Portman Square house. Sadly this was not very popular among the working poor, who balked at paying money to clean themselves. Yet Mahomet had been encouraged by his patron's endeavours, and took his opportunity to introduce something similar when he arrived in Brighton, "the First Watering Place in the British Dominions" as the town commissioners claimed.

Crossing the Steyne he arrived at the house in which his wife's cousin, Decimus Doyle, lodged. Mahomet had arrived in Ireland from India in the 1780s, and within a few years had eloped with the very young Jane Daly. Jane's family were a part of Cork's Anglo-Irish Ascendancy, and her elopement to Dublin with a native Indian army surgeon was the talk of the town. Yet through charm, a quick marriage and the judicious use some of the considerable funds he had brought with him from India, Mahomet became accepted in Irish society – as much as any foreigner could be, that is. The Irish did not distinguish between a Frenchman and an Indian, both being foreign, but ranked them far ahead of any Englishman. It was also maliciously gossiped that Jane's father saw the sense in accepting the elopement of a daughter for whom the sobriquet "plain" was apt, not to mention a sharp tongue that could frighten the horses.

One of Jane's uncles was a squire with considerable property in County Kildare, and his son Decimus attended the Hunterian Medical School in

Great Windmill Street during the Mahomets' time in London. When he concluded his studies, the young Dr Doyle had left for Brighton and was soon followed by his cousin and her exotic husband to the south coast, Doyle worked in partnership with another doctor from consulting rooms along the Grand Parade, one of the best addresses in town and directly opposite the Prince Regent's seaside palace of the Royal Pavilion.

He was greeted at the door by young Doyle's valet John, and requested a meeting with his master. Mahomet was shown into a consulting room on the first floor, with views looking out over the Steyne towards the Royal Pavilion – now forever clad in scaffolding as the builder Prince made yet more improvements. Since early spring work had begun on both the left and right wings of the building as the Prince's architect, John Nash, made good the latest part of his master's plan. No doubt critics of the Prince Regent in Parliament would use this work as yet another example of his wasteful spending, but Mahomet was pleased the Prince continued to maintain an interest in the town – for no other reason than he enjoyed the occasional patronage of the Prince and his royal brothers at his Indian vapour bath. It was before the windows enjoying this view that Dr Doyle found his in-law waiting a few minutes later.

"Sake Mahomet," said Doyle, using the man's formal title as he entered the room, "you are a most unexpected and most welcome guest, even at this early hour. My cousin Jane is well, I hope?"

Mahomet smiled. The young Irishman was considered quite a beau, combining an easy manner with a very attractive look. He reminded Mahomet of a dark haired version of his very first patron Godfrey Evan Baker, thirty years ago in India, and this was another reason why the Indian held the younger man in such high regard. "She is very fine, sir, and looks after me well, does she not. She sends her fondest regards."

Doyle nodded and gestured that they sit, but Mahomet shook his head.

"I have little time I am afraid Decimus, as I have been summoned to perform a post mortem on a body held at Preston barracks."

Doyle looked surprised. "You?"

Mahomet smiled sheepishly. "It would seem so. The colonel is a patient at the baths ... he suffers greatly from the gout ... and I fear mine was the first name he thought of. His surgeon-major is in London ... on indefinite leave."

Doyle paused then nodded. "I know the surgeon-major and am not surprised he has been sent away again. Has there been an accident? Someone fallen off a horse?"

Mahomet shook his head. "No. The body of a young woman was found on the beach early this morning. I was ... hoping ... you would accompany me. It has been so long since I undertook a physical examination, and you are still fresh from medical school."

The young doctor smiled. "Of course I will come. If nothing else, it is a chance to cut open a body ... something I have not done since my time at the Hunterian. I think we should take Hunter's *Essays and Observations*, just in case we come across something unusual."

As the tall, even lanky, young Irish doctor and his diminutive and older Indian relative left the Grand Parade house they turned to their right. At the northern end of the Steyne two dirt roads struck out. To the left was the main drag to London that was constantly busy with traffic of all sorts: coaches, carts, horses and ponies, together with large numbers of walkers. As the road went north it rose towards the South Downs, the line of hills that cut Brighton off from the rest of England. Mahomet could just make out the black and maroon livery of a mail coach as it bore down on the town.

The two men took the other road that led to the town of Lewes, some five miles away. Passing the cricket field to their left where the gentlemen of Sussex played in the summer, they arrived shortly afterwards at Preston barracks. A hodge podge of timber huts and brick buildings, the barracks had been established 25 years ago in response to revolution in France. By 1811 there were 10,000 men stationed in the town and, while numbers had dropped since, the cavalry barracks stabled 1,000 horses and remained an important establishment even after the French corporal had been packed off to St Helena. It also provided hospital facilities and a mortuary. The royal shampooing surgeon and his young assistant reported to the colonel's office.

"Mr Mahomet, so good of you to come," said Colonel Reynolds, grasping the older man's proffered hand as if claiming his prize and looking curiously at Doyle. "It is very sad, of course, but we have laid the woman out as best we could."

Mahomet reclaimed his hand and introduced Dr Doyle. The colonel, now in his late forties, had taken to wearing a short powdered wig to cover a quickly receding hairline. This, together with his small stature, large belly, ill-fitting uniform and ruddy complexion, made him look like a creature from a Hogarth print. Yet as the commandant of the Preston barracks he was a local grandee, and together with the magistrate and the two superintendents of the Watch and their constables and beadles, he was the embodiment of legal authority in the town. Except, that is, when the Prince Regent and his entourage were around.

"It's probably best that we see the body straight away colonel," Mahomet advised, "but before we do, can you tell us anything about the circumstances of the discovery?"

"Not much to tell," replied Reynolds. "She was brought in about six o'clock this morning, give or take, by half a dozen fishermen. From what I could make out, a boat went out just before first light this morning, cast a net but then, because the sea was too rough, decided to head back. As they hauled their boat back onto the beach they found the body stuck beneath the bow. There was nothing on her ... she'd been wrapped naked inside a heavy piece of cloth when she was discovered, and I doubt the fishermen had taken anything. In fact," he said, reaching towards his desk, "they found this still clenched in her hand."

The colonel handed over to Mahomet a small round silver medallion, perfectly plain except for an inscription on one side.

"Poor Fanny," he read. "What on earth does that mean?"

"Haven't the faintest idea," replied the colonel. "Her name perhaps?"

Mahomet paused in thought and absently passed the medallion to Doyle. There was a short silence as the three men considered the situation.

"I think we should see the body now," suggested Doyle, and Mahomet nodded.

This was in a small room at one end of the hospital building. Fortunately, the room had an external door onto the main path that ran through the barracks complex, so they didn't have to enter the hospital building to gain access. There were several men sitting on benches along the outside wall of the hospital, and Mahomet noticed they were wearing a mismatch of dirty uniforms. They looked like survivors of the last battle in which he had served thirty-five years previously, against the Raja of Ramnagour. Some of the men jumped to attention as the colonel approached but a couple stayed put, which surprised Mahomet until he saw they were missing limbs – legs or arms or both.

"Our flotsam and jetsam," whispered the colonel. "Some have been here since Waterloo two years ago ... the Iron Duke's damaged goods. I always mean to clear them out, but where would they go? We give them light duties around the place, so they still feel useful."

Mahomet noted the colonel's compassion, seeing another side to the man who usually sat in his vapour baths bemoaning the pain in his leg, and marked him down as a patrician type. At the door to the mortuary the colonel stopped.

"I'll leave you to it gentlemen," he said. "I've no desire to look on that unfortunate creature again. Poor Fanny indeed. The inscription on that medal was more prescient than she could ever have realised."

He bowed to Mahomet and Doyle and turned back the way he came, stopping to talk to some of the injured men along the way. A marble slab in the centre dominated the small room, on which had been placed a bed of ice and the naked woman, laid out face up but with her modesty covered by a muslin shroud. To one side of the room was a butcher's block, and here Doyle placed his surgical bag, and then sought out his copy of Hunter's *Essays and Observations* while Mahomet pulled back the shroud and looked down at the body.

"My God!" the Indian exclaimed, "what are we supposed to do with this?"

The body of the young woman was severely bloated and gave off a sharp salty odour. The fingers of her right hand, however, were partially clenched, and presumably this was where the fishermen had found the medallion. For the next hour Mahomet and Doyle made as full an inspection as they could, and while Mahomet felt disinclined to open up the body and mess up his clothes, they needed proof that death had been by drowning, so Doyle began to cut her open. Inside there was ample evidence of salt water. There was also a severe head wound and Doyle took a particular interest in the woman's sexual organs, much to Mahomet's distaste.

"From what I can surmise from my limited experience," said the young doctor, "she wasn't a spinster of the parish. In fact," he continued, reaching for the Hunter, "I'm pretty sure there are clear signs here of venereal disease."

John Hunter, whose elder brother William founded the medical school Doyle had attended in London, was an acclaimed expert on venereal disease and teeth. After a few minutes reading Doyle went back to the body. "Yes," he exclaimed, "there are lumps around the vaginal entrance which definitely signify gonorrhoea. Fanny here must have been in some discomfort before she died."

"Poor Fanny!" mused Mahomet, who was cleaning some of the instruments, and watching his relation examine the body. There was a sharp rap on the door. It was the colonel.

"Mr Mahomet, sir!" called Reynolds, "have you finished?"

As the military man made no move to enter the room Mahomet went to open the door, but before he did so carefully inspected his clothing and brushed away some imaginary particles of dust, which brought a wry smile to Doyle. On opening the door he was faced by Reynolds accompanied by Captain Hunter.

"Gentlemen," he addressed them, "we have quite finished. Would you like us to give our report here or back in your office, colonel?"

Looking around and seeing they were quite alone, the colonel indicated the former and both men stepped outside.

"From what we can make out from her teeth, hair and other visible organs, she had just reached maturity, so we would age her between 18 and 21 years old," Mahomet began. "We can also confirm that, with so much salt water in her lungs, she died after entering the sea and would say she had been there for a few hours. There was severe bruising to the left side of her head which leads us to surmise either a bad fall or a heavy instrument."

He paused, seeking confirmation from his young colleague, who nodded.

"It is likely that if we opened her head we would find that the skull had been cracked," added Doyle. "The open gash at her temple indicates she was bleeding before drowning."

"You mean she had been murdered?" asked the colonel.

"No sir, we are not saying that," cautioned Mahomet. "We are saying that either she had a bad fall or had been hit over the head prior to drowning. In all likelihood this would have made her severely concussed. She either lay unconscious on the beach when the tide came in or, more likely in our view, she entered the water with some help."

"No one has come forward to claim the body," Hunter stated.

Doyle looked at the colonel. "You should also know that she was not unfamiliar with sexual congress."

The colonel flushed. "What!? Do you mean she was married?"

"That we can't say," said Doyle.

"There is no evidence of a ring on her left hand," Mahomet explained, "but Dr Doyle says there is clear and evident signs of sexual disease. Given her age, we suspect she used her sexuality as an income."

"A prostitute!" the colonel exclaimed, his face by now the same colour as the bright red of his tunic. Mahomet made a mental note to offer Colonel Reynolds an additional herbal infusion at his next shampooing, possibly one proven to calm the spirit.

"We are not entirely sure, but we'd say so ... yes," confirmed Doyle, and Mahomet nodded.

"To summarise, what we have is a young woman, probably a prostitute, who had gonorrhoea," the young doctor continued. "Having received a serious blow to the head she was found naked apart from the cloth in which she was found, on the beach, having drowned. So she was still alive when she went into the water. The only evidence as to her identity is a medallion with the words "Poor Fanny" inscribed on it. Make of it what you will. For myself, I feel truly sorry for her."

"If she were a prostitute, that may explain why no one has come looking for her," surmised Captain Hunter. "If anyone had told the constables about a missing person, especially a young woman, we would have been informed immediately. As it is, these girls travel to and from London with the frequency of the changing of the guard."

The colonel coughed. "You have to realise, gentlemen, that such girls provide ... ahhh ... an essential need to many of the men here. It keeps down the tension."

"You have no need to explain, colonel," Mahomet delicately responded, "but if there are any of your men who frequent such girls, I advise you ask them to take a look at the body."

"Yes, a good idea," Reynolds agreed. "And I will ask my counterpart at the Guards barracks next to the Pavilion to do the same. Thank you, gentlemen, for your time. I will have to report this to the magistrate but, as we think she is a prostitute and as no one has reported her missing, I doubt he will do anything. More likely he will just hush it up. A suspicious death is not good news for the town, though I doubt now they'll be able to keep a report of her body being found from being printed in the *Herald*."

To be continued in The Jane Austen Murders.